essentials
greg laurie
2

foundational topics for Christians in today's world

essentials
greg laurie
2

Essentials 2

ISBN-13: 978-1-61291-563-0

Published by: Kerygma Publishing

Coordination: FM Management, Ltd.

Contact: mgf@fmmgt.net

Production: Mark Ferjulian

Contents

Part 1

knowing Him

chapter **1**

Who Is God? Part 1

K nowing God is the most important thing you can ever do.

In fact, you and I were created to do this very thing. We were uniquely wired as human beings to seek and to know the God who made us.

This isn't true of the animal kingdom. As far as I can see, my dog doesn't invest any time at all in contemplating the meaning of life. He doesn't think to himself, *There is an emptiness in my life right now. And it cannot be filled by chasing cats, eating roadkill, or drinking out of the toilet. There must be more to life than this.* If anything is on his mind at all, it is taking another nap or eating.

Animals don't think about the meaning of life because animals weren't created in the image of God, as you and I are. We did not evolve from lower life forms, as some would assert. God created us in His very image.[1]

The Bible says,

> He has planted eternity in the human heart,
> but even so, people cannot see the whole

scope of God's work from beginning to end. (Ecclesiastes 3:11, NLT)

What does that mean? This verse is simply saying that deep inside every man, woman, boy, and girl, there is a sense of "something more" in life, a sense that there is some meaning, purpose, or significance to existence. I believe many people today—especially young people—take their own lives because they haven't found that purpose. They feel hopeless and don't know what they're living for. They have no idea what their life is all about—or if it means anything at all.

C. S. Lewis made these statements years ago. Speaking of a relationship with our Creator, he wrote,

> All the things that have ever deeply possessed your soul have been but hints of it—tantalising glimpses, promises never quite fulfilled, echoes that died away just as they caught your ear.[2]
>
> If I find in myself a desire, which no experience in this world can satisfy, the most probable explanation is that I was made for another world. If none of my earthly pleasures satisfy it, that does not prove that the universe is a fraud. Probably earthly pleasures were never meant to satisfy it, but only to arouse it, to suggest the real thing.[3]

Lewis was saying there is nothing in this world that will fill the emptiness in your soul—no sexual experience, no drug high, no relationship, no amount of success, no quantity of money, no accumulation of possessions. And even if you did possess all of those things at this moment, there still would be something in the deepest part of you that realizes there is more to life than this. The real thing that Lewis was alluding to is the very thing for which we were created. It is that drive to know the God who made us.

John 17:3 says, "This is eternal life, that they may know You, the only true God, and Jesus Christ whom You have sent."

As the Lord said to the prophet Jeremiah, "Let not the wise boast of their wisdom or the strong boast of their strength or the rich boast of their riches, but let the one who boasts boast about this: that they have the understanding to know me, that I am the LORD, who exercises kindness, justice and righteousness on earth" (Jeremiah 9:23-24, NIV).

That is why we are here. No matter what anyone else might tell you, that is why we draw breath on this planet. We are here to know God.

Knowing Him

Before I can truly know God, however, I must first know *about* God. We call learning about God "theology." That word frightens some people. I have heard people say, "I'm not into theology; I just love Jesus." That sounds good, but in reality it is a dangerous statement.

Theology simply means "the study of God." You can say you don't want to "get into theology," but the problem is that you might end up committing yourself to a counterfeit Jesus. You might end up worshiping another god who isn't the true and living God at all. You might end up believing the wrong thing, and that would be an incredibly serious mistake—even an eternal mistake.

That would be like someone saying, "I'm going to climb behind the controls of a 747 and just fly that thing. After all, I know how to play video games." Are you crazy? You don't know what you're doing! You can't do something of that caliber without knowledge and training.

C. S. Lewis gave this warning years ago: "If you do not listen to Theology, that will not mean that you have no ideas about God. It will mean that you have a lot of wrong ones."[4]

Again, having wrong ideas about God is a serious matter. Before we can discern the difference between right and wrong, we have to know who God is. Morality is based on spirituality—and spirituality is based on a relationship with God. If we don't know God, we won't really have any idea about our purpose or what life is all about. And we won't know right from wrong.

Someone from our church went out with a video camera recently, asking people on the streets the question "What are right and wrong?" Here are some of the answers we received:

- "Well, you *feel* if you are doing the wrong or right thing."
- "A right thing is when you make someone smile or make someone happy. Wrong is probably when someone is mad at you."
- "Right means morals. You do good. It's something you learn when you're younger."
- "You can definitely feel the difference."
- "If anyone has a conscience, they know right and wrong."
- "I don't know. I think it's something you feel inside. You know by instinct what is right and wrong."

Did you notice the use of the word *feel* in some of these answers? But wait a second. If right and wrong are determined by what I feel, wouldn't that mean I am setting myself up as the judge? By saying that, I have essentially made myself the moral center of the universe. Instead of God telling me what right and wrong are, I am making that determination. But am I qualified?

No, I am not—and neither is any other human being.

We Need a Moral Compass

This is why we live in such a crazy culture today, with people doing such off-the-wall, senseless, and insane things. It's because they don't have a moral compass. And the reason they don't have a moral compass is because they don't have a relationship with God.

Have you ever thought to yourself words like these: "I just don't know what's going on in the world today. To hear people talk, it seems like wrong is right and right is wrong. White is black and black is white"? The words of the prophet Isaiah are just as relevant to our twenty-first century culture as they were when God originally gave them. He said in Isaiah 5:20, "What sorrow for those who say that evil is good and good is evil, that dark is light and light is dark, that bitter is sweet and sweet is bitter" (NLT).

This lack of absolutes in our culture is called moral relativism, and we see it on all sides today. We have all heard people make statements like these:

"Well, what is true for you is not necessarily true for me."

"One man's art is another person's pornography."

"There are no objective morals, just differing opinions."

"If it feels good, do it."

"Anything goes."

"No culture is better or worse than another."

It reminds me of a fragment from an old song: "There ain't no good guys, there ain't no bad guys. There's only you and me, and we just disagree."[5]

So many people today will say to you, "You can believe whatever truth you want, just as I can. But what's important is that you respect my truth, and I will respect yours. I don't want your truth to infringe on me, and therefore my truth will not infringe on you."

But that is completely absurd. It isn't even logical.

Peter Collier, a one-time sixties radical who has gone on record with some second thoughts about those turbulent years, wrote, "The stones we threw into the waters of our world in those days caused ripples that continue to lap on our shores today—for better and more often for worse."[6]

Sociologist Robert Nesbit wrote, "The ideologies which gained entry into the academy in the sixties claimed that the fundamental intellectual principles of Western culture were illegitimate and must be overthrown. With that destroyed, terms like truth, good, evil, and soul could be discarded."[7]

You might be asking, "Greg, what do events from the sixties have to do with me in the twenty-first century?"

The answer is quite a lot.

The hippies and radicals of the sixties are the ones who now shape public opinion in our culture today. That is why the very foundations of our culture have become so deeply eroded.

In Psalm 11 David asks, "When the foundations are being destroyed, what can the righteous do?" (verse 3, NIV). Earlier in the psalm he says, "In the LORD I take refuge. How then can you say to me: 'Flee like a bird to your mountain'" (verse 1, NIV).

The stability and security that we desire in life are found in knowing God—and then walking with Him and not anywhere else.

No Absolute Truth?

I read a statistic the other day that I found quite alarming. It pointed out that 67 percent of Americans believe there is no such thing as absolute truth.

Can you imagine that? That's almost seven out of ten Americans.

More shocking than that, 52 percent of those who called themselves born-again believers *agreed* with the statement that there is no absolute truth. How can you be a born-gain Christian and not believe in absolute truth?

If the Bible isn't absolute truth, what is?

Some would say that it's no big deal, and it really doesn't matter whether you believe in absolute truth. Of course it does! If we don't, the result is chaos.

What if you were to take the same principle that you apply toward God and apply it toward driving? I might say, "I don't really believe in absolute truth when it comes to driving. I believe the stoplights are there to entertain us. What if we did away with all of the stoplights? What if we ignored all of those little dotted lines in the street? After all, they're so irritating and *confining*, aren't they? Why shouldn't I be free to drive wherever I want to drive? Shouldn't I have room to exercise my individuality?"

You know as well as I do what the result of such a view would be: mayhem, chaos, and carnage. You would have blood in the streets—people crashed, crushed, and dying all over the place. We can all agree that, in our nation at least, we need absolute rules for driving that we will all live by.

Or imagine this. You board a plane for Honolulu, Hawaii, and as the plane lifts off the runway, the pilot says over the intercom, "Good evening, ladies and gentlemen. Welcome to flight 232 with service to Honolulu, Hawaii. Our cruising altitude will be 35,000 feet. By the way, folks, I don't believe in maps or aviation equipment. It seems so narrow and restrictive to me. That is someone else's truth, and not mine. I prefer to rely on my feelings. I like to let my conscience be my guide. I'm not really sure where we're going to land today."

How would you enjoy *that* flight?

Someone else could feel that stealing is wrong, while their neighbor doesn't see anything wrong with it at all. Maybe you think that murder is wrong. But *why* is it wrong? Is it just because it seems wrong to you? But not everyone feels that way!

That is why we need absolute truth, as we find in the Bible.

The First and Most Important Truth

Let's go back to the very beginning and start with this simple point. It is obvious, but still it needs to be stated: God exists, and He is the Creator of the universe and mankind.

There is no better place to start than the first verse of the Old Testament and of the entire Bible, Genesis 1:1. It says, "In the beginning God created the heavens and the earth."

It is worth noting that the Bible doesn't try to prove the

existence of God. It simply says, "In the beginning God . . ." You can't go back any further than that.

There are certain people who would like to eliminate that last word. They like the "In the beginning" part, but they don't like the notion of a personal Creator.

If you don't believe in the Creator, if you close your mind to that obvious reality, Scripture describes what begins to happen to you. And it isn't a pretty picture:

> What happened was this: People knew God perfectly well, but when they didn't treat him like God, refusing to worship him, they trivialized themselves into silliness and confusion so that there was neither sense nor direction left in their lives. They pretended to know it all, but were illiterate regarding life. They traded the glory of God who holds the whole world in his hands for cheap figurines you can buy at any roadside stand.
>
> So God said, in effect, "If that's what you want, that's what you get." It wasn't long before they were living in a pigpen, smeared with filth, filthy inside and out. (Romans 1:21-24, MSG)

Many are interested in a relationship with God—but on their own terms. In other words, they want to remake God in their own image. As one philosopher said, "God made man in His image, and man returned the favor."

Ever since man ruined the image of God, in whose image he has been created, man has been seeking to create gods in his own image. That is because we are incurably religious. At the same time, we want a deity that we can *control*. In other words, we're looking for a user-friendly God. We want faith lite, a do-it-yourself spirituality. That is what is being followed by many people today.

I heard about an unusual place of worship in Kyoto, Japan, known as the Temple of the Thousand Buddhas. On display inside this shrine are a thousand different likenesses of the Buddha, each a little different from the rest. The idea is that the devotee can walk in, find the statue that most closely resembles his or her idea of Buddha, and worship *that* one.

That is what we want to do. We want a divine buffet line, where we can pick out this or that quality we appreciate in a god, but leave out those we don't much care for. We want to find a god who basically agrees with us — a god who will go along with the lifestyle we have chosen to live.

You will hear people say things like, "I don't believe in a God of judgment. The god I follow would never do that. *My* god would never allow this or that to happen."

But will *that* god be able to save you on that final day? Will that god be able to take you by the hand and lead you into eternal life at the moment of your death? It's an important question that deserves a definitive answer.

I saw an episode of *The Simpsons* a while back in which the great theologian Homer Simpson had an interesting encounter with God. In this episode, titled "Homer the Heretic," Homer decided he wasn't going to church anymore. So he stayed home. But then God Himself came down, opened up the roof of Homer's house, and sat down to have a conversation with him. Homer said to God, "I'm not a bad guy. I work hard, and I love my kids. Why should I spend half of my Sunday hearing about how I'm going to hell?"

God replied, "Hmmm. You've got a point there. You know, sometimes even I would rather be watching football."

Later Homer concludes, "So I figure I should just try to live right and worship You in my own way."

And God agrees.

That is a pretty good summary of American religion today. People are saying, "I want my own brand of 'spirituality.' I want to worship God in my own way and on my own terms."

That is the way many of us have chosen to live.

In the Beginning . . .

The Bible says, "In the beginning God . . ." But if you eliminate God from that sentence, you have a big problem. What do you have left? In the beginning . . . *what?* In the beginning a mass of gases floating in space? But that isn't the beginning. Where did that mass of gases come from? Were they always there? How could that be? Where did space come from?

Eventually every child gets around to asking the question, "Where did God come from?" There is no easy answer to that question because God has always existed. He is *self-existent*. He has existed from the beginning because He has no beginning nor does He have an end.

When I say, "In the beginning God . . ." I recognize that the whole universe is not here by accident but by design.

The experts (so-called) would tell us that Earth came into being because of an accidental compression of gases and explosions that cooled off and formed planetary systems, resulting in a particular planet with special atmospheric conditions that just came into being—the planet we call Earth. It just happened that way.

Let me respond by asking, was it a coincidence that Earth is 93 million miles from the sun? If it were any closer, we would fry. If it were any farther, we would freeze. Was it by chance that the atmosphere on our planet is a combination of nitrogen and oxygen, a balance of 78 percent to 21 percent with 1 percent of variant gases?[8] Was it happenstance that Earth is covered with a blanket of ozone?

Of course not.

We know—deep down, everyone *knows*—there was a Creator behind all of this. *God* was behind it. It's the only possible explanation.

Take a close look at a shiny new 757 sitting on the airport tarmac sometime. What if I were to tell you that this magnificent aircraft was not built by a bunch of engineers, technicians, and workmen at Boeing? What if I were to insist that this gleaming, state-of-the-art airliner came into being because a tornado swept through a junkyard one day, and the result was this amazing jet that you see sitting before you?

That would be a definition of absurdity. You would laugh at such a thing. You wouldn't even begin to consider it.

Yet people will offer explanations even more ridiculous than that for the creation of the universe.

It would be as though I told you the ceiling of the Sistine Chapel that was so meticulously painted by the great artist Michelangelo wasn't the work of that man at all. What actually happened was that someone pulled a wagon of paint into the middle of the chapel and threw a stick of dynamite into it. It exploded, and what you see today is what simply splattered up on that ceiling—down to the last magnificent brushstroke.

That's crazy. Insane. It could never happen like that.

But if a 757 had to be conceived, planned, and built by intelligent designers, or if the Sistine Chapel had to have been so carefully composed and painted by a brilliant artist, how much more do we see evidence of design in the complexities of our universe? If you try to deny the existence of God "in the beginning," you have no basis from which to start. It leaves you entirely without a foundation— not to mention the fact that you have to suspend all reason to even consider such a concept.

Why Do People Claim to Be Atheists?

Personally, I think that it takes more faith to be an atheist than it takes to be a believer. I think that even atheists have their moments of doubt—though there aren't that many of them out there.

I believe that many people *say* they are atheists because they have rejected the standards of the Bible and don't want to live by them. They haven't arrived at their atheism by carefully searching the Bible and concluding that it is not true. They haven't rejected Jesus because they have examined everything He said and concluded that it isn't true or doesn't make sense.

Most people I talk to who say they don't believe in God have never even read the Bible. Wouldn't you think that it might be a good idea to read at least a few verses of the New Testament? After all, here is this man Jesus who claimed to be the only way to God. Shouldn't you check out His words for maybe ten minutes or so?

But no, many are not willing to do that.

They will try to be dismissive and say, "The Bible is full of contradictions."

I always like to reply to that, "Here is a Bible. Why don't you show me one?"

They might even be offended, however, if you even hold a Bible close to them. Have you ever noticed how some people don't like the Bible itself — not just what it says, but the actual object? When you pull out a Bible, it's as though people are saying, "Get that thing away from me. Do you have a permit to carry that?"

Maybe they are afraid that it's a Living Bible and it will attack them! In reality, they fear and loathe the Bible because they *know* that it represents absolute truth. They *know* that it shows something they need but don't have, and they don't want to hear about it.

Who Is God?

Thousands of years ago the ancient Egyptian ruler Pharaoh asked a question that is still being asked today: "Who is the LORD, that I should obey His voice?" (Exodus 5:2).

That's not an easy question to answer.

Why? Because we are trying to grasp the infinite with the finite. We are trying to understand the Almighty with our limited, puny brains. It has been said that if God were small enough for your mind, He wouldn't be big enough for your needs.

We try to wrap our minds around God, and we fall a million miles short. There are some things about God I will never understand until I get to heaven.

I always want to laugh when I hear people say, "I have a few questions I want to ask God. When I get to heaven, I'm going to walk right up to the throne with my list and get some answers."

Trust me, when you see God, you will forget all about that list of questions. If you say anything at all. you'll whisper, "Never mind, Lord."

The apostle Paul writes, "For now we see in a mirror, dimly, but then face to face. Now I know in part, but then I shall know just as I also am known" (1 Corinthians 13:12). The reality is, I can only grasp so much about the mysteries of life on this side of heaven. But when I get to the other side, it will (finally) all make sense.

You say, "Greg, that's a cop-out."

No, it is a simple acknowledgement that there always will be certain things about God and about spiritual realities that I won't be able to grasp with my finite mind.

As David expressed it in Psalm 145:3, "Great is the LORD, and greatly to be praised; and His greatness is unsearchable."

At the same time, with the help of His Holy Spirit, there are many things we can know and understand about God. After all, as I have said, knowing what God is like is foundational to knowing God Himself. It's just as Jesus prayed to His Father in the book of John, "Now this is eternal life: that they know you, the only true God, and Jesus Christ, whom you have sent" (17:3, NIV).

"My Determined Purpose . . ."

The apostle Paul said, "[For my determined purpose is] that I may know Him" (Philippians 3:10, AMP).

What is your "determined purpose" in life? What do you live for? Everyone lives for something—something that gets us excited, something that persuades us to pull our tired carcasses out of bed every morning and get ready for the day, something that we believe in.

Many reading this book would say, "Well, I live for Christ. I live for Jesus." Obviously, that is the "spiritual answer." But the bottom line isn't what you *say* you live for; it's what you actually *do*. If I could follow you around for a day (frightening thought, I know) I would know what you live for just by listening in on your conversations, taking note of what kind of music you listen to, watching what you do with your spare time, and checking out what websites you visit. By the end of the day, I would know who or what you are living for. I would see it more clearly in your actions than by the words you might use.

The fact is, *everyone who is a true follower of Jesus should say, "My determined purpose in life is to know Him."*

What Is God Like?

Once again, we sent our camera crew out into the streets here in Southern California, asking people, "What is God like? How would you describe Him?" Here are a few of the answers we got:

- "God is someone who helps us in all we do. He guides us when we need help."
- "I think He is the Creator of the universe and stuff."
- "If He is there, He is something so big and so powerful, it's just unimaginable."
- "He created everything on this earth."
- "I believe in the scientific part of it—like evolution. It's ridiculous to think that Adam and Eve were the beginning of the race when we have scientific evidence that we came from monkeys. Humans evolved from some type of monkey-type things."
- "I don't really associate any feelings with Him. Just that He exists. That's all."
- "I believe He is really caring. Forgiving. I believe He is a

mixture of all things except for angry things. You can always ask for forgiveness, but I don't necessarily think of Him being angry at you."
- "Almost like your Friend. Father. That type of thing. All of the above."
- "I cannot describe God because I have never seen God."
- "Omnipresent. All-knowing. All-telling. Creator of the universe."
- "Maybe He isn't a form, He is a spirit."
- "He is a force that people look to for guidance and strength in their lives."
- "That's a tough one. I think it is very personal for everyone. I think everyone has their own thoughts about what God is—whether it's a man or a woman."
- "I don't know. Sorry."

That last response may be the most honest answer we got all day.

You have the sense that people just make up things about God as they go along. But if people would only turn to the Word of God, they would find some wonderful portraits of who God is and what He is like. Think for instance, of all the knowledge that's contained in the first six verses of Psalm 139:

O LORD, You have searched me and known me.
You know my sitting down and my rising up;
You understand my thought afar off.
You comprehend my path and my lying down,
And are acquainted with all my ways.
For there is not a word on my tongue,
But behold, O LORD, You know it altogether.
You have hedged me behind and before,
And laid Your hand upon me.
Such knowledge is too wonderful for me;
It is high, I cannot attain it.

God Is All-Knowing

We see, for instance, that God is omniscient, or all-knowing.

God knows what is going on in His creation—right down to the tiniest, most microscopic corner of it. Some people envision God as sort of a disconnected deity with more important things to do than think about someone as insignificant as you or me. But that is simply not the truth. The Bible says in Psalm 147:4, "He determines the number of the stars and calls them each by name" (NIV).

I can't even remember the names of five people at a time, but God knows the name of every star in the heavens and every human being who has ever lived. Not only that, but He knows about the little details of your life. Jesus said, "Not one sparrow . . . can fall to the ground without your Father knowing it. And the very hairs of your head are all numbered. So don't worry! You are more valuable to him than many sparrows" (Matthew 10:29-31, TLB).

Can you imagine that? He keeps track of every little bird that falls to the ground because some kid got a new BB gun for Christmas. And all of those hairs that come out of your hairbrush have a number attached to them. God doesn't miss a single one.

What does this tell us about God? It tells us that this powerful, awesome God who created the universe is interested in you. That is something you never have to wonder about. It's true. The Bible says so.

In Psalm 56:8 the psalmist says of the Lord, "You keep track of all my sorrows. You have collected all my tears in your bottle. You have recorded each one in your book" (NLT).

Have you ever brushed away a tear when you thought no one was looking? Well, Someone *was* looking. God took note of that tear. In fact, He marked it down. Sometimes you might go into your room, shut the door, and have a good cry—or maybe you're all alone in your car, feeling sorry for yourself, and the tears come. Others might laugh at you or dismiss your tears, saying, "Why are you all worked up? You're just being emotional."

Not God. He cares about your tears and keeps them all in a special bottle. He keeps track of all your sorrows. Why does He do that? Because He loves you.

The book of Hebrews says of Jesus, "For we do not have a high priest who is unable to empathize with our weaknesses, but we have one who has been tempted in every way, just as we are—yet he did not sin" (4:15, NIV).

Jesus knows what you're going through. He truly does. When Jesus became a human being, He walked this earth just like you and I do, experiencing the very limitations that we face. He knew what it was like to be hungry, thirsty, lonely, and abandoned. Not only did all of His disciples abandon Him in His greatest hour of need when He went to the cross, but even God the Father had to momentarily turn His face away from Jesus as He bore all the sins of this world—past, present, and future. In that darkest of moments, Jesus cried out from the cross, "My God, My God, why have You forsaken Me?" (Matthew 27:46).

Never let yourself think that "God doesn't understand what it's like" to be a human being or that He can't really identify with what you're going through. He does understand, and He does identify. And He doesn't just know about it. He cares about it.

No Hiding Places from God

God sees and hears everything that happens everywhere. That can be good or bad news, depending on how you have chosen to live. If you are walking with the Lord and don't have anything to hide, that's great news. It's encouraging to be assured that He knows about your day and is thinking about you. God says in Scripture, "For I know the thoughts that I think toward you . . . thoughts of peace and not of evil, to give you a future and a hope" (Jeremiah 29:11).

It makes me happy to remember that God thinks about me. It would have been amazing enough if the Lord of the universe had said, "I know the thought that I once thought about you, Greg Laurie, twenty years ago." Just to think that this great God, at one point in His everlasting life, had given a single thought to me would make me happy. But that's not what this verse says. The Lord declares, "I know the thoughts *that I think* toward you." It's not just a singular thought about me; He is thinking about me on a continual basis. I am on His mind at this very instant. Incredible!

But what is He thinking? Is He disgusted with me? Discouraged by me? Is He frustrated that He ever got stuck with me? No! He has "thoughts of peace and not of evil" toward me, and He is thinking about how to give me "a future and a hope."

God is thinking about all He wants to do and accomplish in and through your life. It's true!

God is aware of everything. He sees everything you do and reads every thought you think. Nothing in your life is hidden from Him. The book of Proverbs says, "For your ways are in full view of the LORD, and he examines all your paths" (5:21, NIV). In the Gospels, Jesus said, "You must give an account on judgment day for every idle word you speak" (Matthew 12:36, NLT). Can you imagine that? God has taken note of every word you have ever said. He is listening to those phone conversations. He hears what you say to your friends, parents, or whomever.

Here's the thing about a God who is present everywhere and knows everything: You can do your best to shut Him out of your thoughts or your awareness, but that won't cause Him to go away. He's as close to you as ever. He knows you now as well as on the day when you were born.

You can run from those truths, but you cannot change them. You can't make up the rules of life as you go along. You can't cobble together a designer deity who fits in with your lifestyle.

God has told you how to know Him—right in the pages of the Bible. And the only way you can come into a real relationship with this all-powerful, all-knowing, everywhere-present God of the universe is through His Son, Jesus Christ.

2

Who Is God? Part 2

We live in a time when everybody claims to
be "spiritual."

That seems to be the latest trend among people
today. You turn on the television and see some
rock star or Hollywood celebrity who may be
known for a depraved lifestyle talking about their
"spirituality."

That's the new code word.

Why do twenty-first century people like this
word so much? Because it's like an empty shell
into which you can pour your own meaning. You
don't have to believe what somebody else says.
You can decide for yourself what it means to be
"spiritual."

Certainly belief in God in our country is at an
all-time high. I read a poll recently that said 91
percent of Americans believe in a god or a univer-
sal spirit.[1]

But what does it mean to be a "spiritual
person"? We went out with our video camera and
asked, "Are you a spiritual person?" Here are
some of the answers:

- "I don't see how anyone could really know who God is."
- "I am spiritual to a certain level. I mean, I go to church, and I worship Him, but I'm not really into death right now. I need some guidance."
- "I don't know. But I believe that God is all around us. Every time you feel alone, He is there to hold you."
- "Very. Look, I've got the Virgin Mary right here."
- "I'm not too strong with my faith. I do believe some things. I do believe in God, but I'm just not too strong on it."
- "Yeah . . . I think that there are different kinds of spirituality. You can go to church every Sunday and still not be a spiritual person."
- "Not in the meaning of organized religion, but spiritual in other means, yes."
- "I believe in a higher being, just not God. I believe in some type of higher force. If you look at a huge mountain, what created that? I don't know, but I don't think it was some white guy named 'God.'"

People are skittish about admitting they're "spiritual" because they don't want to be somehow linked to organized religion. They like the idea of some kind of spiritual dimension, but they don't want rules. They don't want boundaries. They want the freedom to define "spiritual" on their own terms.

Puerto Rican singing star Ricky Martin once complained that the "spiritual side" of his music is often overlooked. He told an interviewer, "My concerts are about joy, not feeling judged, and being in touch with your soul. I want to find peace and I want to project peace."

The article I read points out that a video for one of Martin's singles has him dancing on top of a glass box with a bunch of naked women inside. He says, "Let's live, let's get rid of taboo, and let's start breathing, please."[2]

Maybe this is part of the problem. We have gotten rid of all the taboos. We've rid ourselves of all the absolutes and rules.

And that is why our culture is in the place that it is in today. That is why we need to understand and follow absolute truth—because our culture has turned away from it. We need standards to live by, and to find those standards we need God. We do need boundaries in our lives, and God places them there for our own good—and for our happiness as well.

Singing in the Cage

Some years ago I saw a brightly colored little bird nestled in the grass of our backyard. It was obviously someone's pet and wasn't the kind of bird you would see in the wild.

I had a German shepherd at the time, and he was looking at that little bird with a hungry look on his face. I realized that this little, lost bird was about to become an appetizer.

Walking up to this bird, I crouched down and put out my index finger. He hopped right on. I walked into the kitchen with the bird on my finger and said, "Cathe, look at what I just found."

She was cooking something and looked up with a surprised expression. "Where did you get that?"

"It was in the backyard," I said. "It's obviously somebody's pet."

This was the most depressed bird I have ever seen. He was down . . . *really* down. But what could we do for him? My son Jonathan spoke up and said there was a little girl down the street who used to have a bird, and she had a birdcage.

"Go get it," I said.

He came back with the cage a few minutes later. I opened up the cage and set the little bird down by the door. Immediately he hopped inside and then hopped up on the little swing. Suddenly, the little bird was no longer depressed. He was happy, rocking back and forth on the swing. And he began to chirp and sing.

The little bird loved that cage.

Well, that can't be, can it? No bird could really like being in a cage.

This one did! He was happier in the cage than he was out in the wild. He felt secure and at rest.

Here's my point. Some people look at the Christian faith with our beliefs, standards, and absolutes and say, "You people live in a cage."

Really? It's all about how you look at things, isn't it? For some people, the guiding principles of Scripture might seem like a confining cage. For others, the structure brings great happiness and peace. It's like a floor under your feet and a roof over your head on a stormy night. For the little bird, the cage was protection from a hungry German Shepherd who could have swallowed him with one gulp.

You can look at the standards that God gives us as something to fence you in and make your life miserable, or you can look at them in the right way and realize they are barriers of protection to keep you safe from all the dangers that are out there in our culture.

"Do You Believe in God?"

We sent our camera crew out on the streets with the question, "Do you believe in God?" Here are some of the answers we received:

- "No. I've never been religious."
- "Yes, because I am very religious. I have seen all God's miraculous work in other people. I have strong faith that He exists."
- "I can't say yes."
- "Yes, I do. It's just what I was taught, and I kind of feel it."
- "I believe in God, but I don't really follow Him as closely as I should."
- "It's a tradition type of thing."
- "It's something that kind of explains the unexplainable."
- "No, not God."

- "Christians say that if you don't believe in God, then you're going to hell, right? That's what they have told me. But I don't think all the Buddhist people in the world are going to hell."
- "I'm a Buddhist. So I believe there is a God, but not the type of God the Christians believe in."
- "Everything comes from somewhere, and basically God is where I think it comes from."
- "I believe there is something out there. I don't know exactly what."
- "I believe in God, but I am not denominational. I don't believe in organized religion."
- "I am not completely sure He exists, but I take it on faith that He exists."
- "I don't believe in God just because I don't know. I think the world is pretty messed up as it is, so I don't see how someone who is good or whatever can supposedly have stuff like this happen."

In the previous chapter, we looked at some of the early verses in Psalm 139. David wrote,

> O LORD, you have examined my heart and know everything about me. You know when I sit down or stand up. You know my thoughts even when I'm far away. You see me when I travel and when I rest at home. You know everything I do. You know what I am going to say even before I say it, LORD (verses 1-4, NLT).

From these verses and many others we learn that God's knowledge is as eternal as He is. What God knows now He has always known and will always know.

We learn new things every day. I think of little toddlers who are processing incredible amounts of new information at any given moment. As you get older, maybe you learn less than you used to, but you are still learning.

But God doesn't learn. God just knows it already.

This brain God has given us is an amazing instrument. The human memory moves faster than the speed of light. Through memory I can be instantly transported to my distant past. Isn't it interesting how you can hear a song on the radio and all of a sudden find yourself in a flashback? You might remember exactly where you were when you first heard the song. Or it might be a certain smell. Whenever I smell Coppertone lotion, I am immediately transported back to when I was a little kid in the early sixties, listening to Jan and Dean sing "Surf City" down on Corona del Mar beach.

The memory stores all of this data, and God has given us this amazing capacity to remember things.

God, however, doesn't have to remember because He never forgets. He doesn't have to be reminded of something because the knowledge is always before Him.

My problem is that I learn something new—and then I forget the things I've already learned. I will memorize passages of Scripture, only to forget them. But then, of course, I will remember stupid songs from years ago that I didn't even want to learn in the first place. Why do I still know all the lyrics to the theme song of *The Flintstones*? I don't want to know them, but I do.

Aren't you glad God doesn't forget things like we do? Can you imagine if God had a lapse in memory?

"Good morning, Lord, how are You doing today?"

"And you are . . . ?"

I forget people all the time. I'm not proud of it, but I do. Someone will come up to me and say, "Greg, how are you doing? And why do you have that blank look on your face?"

It's because I have no idea—not a single clue—who they are.

Not only does God know everything and remember everything, but He sees the future just as clearly as He sees the present and as we would see the past.

In Isaiah 46:10, God says, "I make known the end from the beginning, from ancient times, what is still to come. I say, 'My purpose will stand, and I will do all that I please'" (NIV).

He knows the end from the beginning. I barely know the end at the end, because I forget what just happened!

I have a number of friends who are police officers, and they always face this challenge. There will be a traffic accident, and the officers will interview the witnesses. The problem is, each person will give a different account of the same thing, which they all saw at the same time.

God isn't that way. He can look at the future and speak of it with the same accuracy that He can speak of the past.

For God, yesterday is as today. Tomorrow is as yesterday. It is all the same to Him.

Did you know that the Bible is the only book that dares to predict the future? Do you know why that is? If other religious books tried to do it, they would fail. The reason God can speak of the future with such accuracy is because *He has already seen it.* He is omniscient. He knows all things.

God knows the future and is in control of the future. It is worth noting that two-thirds of the Bible is prophecy. Half of these prophecies have already been fulfilled. So if half of them have happened exactly as God said they would, do I have any reason to doubt that the remaining ones will happen exactly as God has said? God has told us how the world will end. God has told us where the world will fight its final battle, the Battle of Armageddon. The Bible has told us about so many things that are happening in the news, right before our very eyes.

Another thing to realize about God's omniscience is that He knows what I am going to ask for in prayer before I pray. In Isaiah 65:24 the Lord says, "I will answer them before they even call to me. While they are still talking about their needs, I will go ahead and answer their prayers!" (NLT).

Along these same lines, Jesus said, "Your Father knows the things you have need of before you ask Him" (Matthew 6:8).

When we pray, we are not informing God of anything. He already knows! I think sometimes people feel as though they have to fill God in on the details, as though He needed a fuller understanding. Trust me: God already has a full understanding. He knows all there is to be known about anything.

You don't have to enlighten God. Nor is the objective of prayer to move God your way. No, the objective of prayer is to move yourself *His* way. It is not to get your will up in heaven; it is to get God's will on earth.

Everywhere Present

Not only is God omniscient, but God is also omnipresent. Let's go back to Psalm 139 and drop down to verses 7-12:

Where can I go from Your Spirit?
Or where can I flee from Your presence?
If I ascend into heaven, You are there;
If I make my bed in hell, behold, You are there.
If I take the wings of the morning,
And dwell in the uttermost parts of the sea,
Even there Your hand shall lead me,
And Your right hand shall hold me.
If I say, "Surely the darkness shall fall on me,"
Even the night shall be light about me;
Indeed, the darkness shall not hide from You,
But the night shines as the day;
The darkness and the light are both alike to You.

Wherever you are, God is there. Wherever you go, God will be waiting for you. That thought could be either comforting or terrifying to you, depending on where you stand in your relationship with God. It is comforting if you love the Lord and seek to follow and obey Him. But it's not so comforting when you are living in sin or deliberately breaking His commandments.

When you entertain an evil thought, God knows about it.

When you commit a sin no one else sees, God sees.

What you mutter under your breath, God hears.

God even knows what you will do before you do it.

If, on the other hand, you are alone and frightened, it is comforting to know that the Lord is there. Through the centuries, God's people have drawn hope and peace from passages such as Isaiah 43:1-3:

I have called you by your name;
You are Mine.
When you pass through the waters, I will be with you;
And through the rivers, they shall not overflow you.
When you walk through the fire, you shall not be burned,
Nor shall the flame scorch you.
For I am the LORD your God,
The Holy One of Israel, your Savior.

God said, "I will never leave you nor forsake you" (Hebrews 13:5). That is a promise to every Christian. If you have placed your trust in Jesus Christ as your Savior and Lord, that means you are never alone in life. Jesus said, "And be sure of this: I am with you always, even to the end of the age" (Matthew 28:20, NLT).

Sometimes people imagine that God lives in the church building, as though it were His street address. You can see it by the way people approach church. They'll be laughing and talking until they walk in the door. Then it's, "Sshhh! We're in church now. Keep quiet. Take your seat. Don't talk too loud. You might bother God."

Yes, He is in church. But He is also in your car . . . and in your home . . . and in your living room, where you're flipping through the channels . . . and on that airplane, when you're heading out of town . . . and in your office, where you're checking out the Internet.

God is there, wherever you are and wherever you go.

God is omniscient, and God is present everywhere. He is listening to every prayer that you pray, He never dozes off, and His attention never wanders. The Bible says, "Behold, He who keeps Israel shall neither slumber nor sleep" (Psalm 121:4).

God Is All-Powerful

Finally, God can do all things because He is omnipotent, or all-powerful. There are no limitations to the power of God.

We all have heard people try to cloud that issue by saying, "Well, if God can do anything, does that mean He can tell a lie? Does that mean He can create a rock so heavy that He can't lift it?"

The short answer to all such questions is no.

God can't sin, because that is against His nature.

God can't deny Himself.

God can't do something that is inconsistent with His divine nature.

To say that God is omnipotent means He is infinite in His power. His power can never be depleted, drained, or exhausted.

I always travel with a lot of gadgets. Usually that includes my computer. For years now, I have been on a quest to find a computer with a long battery life. When you fly to a place like Australia—a nonstop flight of fourteen hours—you need a computer that will last for a while. It seems like I am always running out of battery power and looking for places to plug in. Sometimes I will take extra batteries. One time when I was on an airplane putting something in the overhead bin, one of those heavy extra batteries fell out of my case and bounced off the head of a bald guy. It was not a happy moment for him or me. I took my seat as quickly as I could!

God's power, however, can never be depleted or drained.

He had no less power after He created the universe than He did before He started.

Job 42:2 says, "I know that you can do all things; no purpose of yours can be thwarted" (NIV). In Genesis 18:14 God says, "Is anything too hard for the LORD?"

And the answer, by the way, is no.

Nothing, nothing, nothing is too difficult for Him.

That is why it is ridiculous to despair or give up hope when we find ourselves enmeshed in a difficult situation. Maybe you have a severe illness, or the doctor has told you your case is terminal. Maybe you've been fired from your job, and you can't find work. Suddenly you're in a traumatic, stressful situation and you think there's no way out for you. You say, "I've done everything I can think of to do, and I've called all my friends, but nobody can help me. I guess all I can do now is pray."

What an insult to an all-powerful God!

There is nothing too difficult for the Lord to accomplish.

If you have placed your faith in Christ, it is always too soon to despair.

Other Features of His Character

In these last two chapters, we have spoken of His omniscience (He knows everything), His omnipresence (He is present everywhere), and His omnipotence (He is all-powerful). We call these *attributes* of God. They are features of His nature, or His character. But there are many more than three!

God is truth.

This is very important. This means that He and He alone is the true God. His knowledge and words are true; His Word is the final standard of truth.

That is why we have so many problems in our culture. Nobody can figure out what "spirituality" is, because nobody can figure out who God is. As a result, there is no consensus on right and wrong. How can we agree on right and wrong if we can't even agree on who God is?

That is why you have to start with God, believe that He

exists, believe that His Word is truth, and then believe what He says about life.

In Jeremiah 10:10 the prophet says of God, "But the LORD is the true God; He is the living God and the everlasting King." This means that God, and God alone, is the final court of arbitration. Jesus said, "I am the way, the truth, and the life" (John 14:6).

In the person-on-the-street interviews about God that I have included in the last two chapters, how many of the people did you hear saying, "I *think* this . . ." or "I *feel* this . . ."? Did you notice they had no basis for their opinion? They just went with their feelings. They built their concept of truth on what seemed right to them at the time.

That's a dangerous way to do business.

The fact is, the universe does not revolve around you or me.

If *God* says something is true, then it is *true* whether I agree with it or not. He is the final authority because we human beings are flawed in our ability to discern true from false and right from wrong.

In the book of Isaiah, God gives us this amazing analogy:

You turn things upside down,
    as if the potter were thought to be like the clay!
Shall what is formed say to the one who formed it,
    "You did not make me"?
Can the pot say to the potter,
    "You know nothing"? (29:16, NIV)

It is the picture of a potter working on his clay. Then all of a sudden, the clay on the wheel starts talking back to him, saying, "What are you doing? I don't like the way you're shaping me."

It's just as ridiculous for us to say to our Creator, "God, I don't agree with You. I think that You're wrong on this."

You don't *agree* with the almighty, all-knowing God who created the universe?

So what?

God is the one who determines what truth is. His knowledge is perfect and without flaw. He is the final standard of truth.

Do you remember being a child and hearing your parents say no to something you asked them to do?

You said, "But why?"

And they answered, "Because I said so."

Kids might hate it, but it's a parental right to say that.

There are times when children need to obey without necessarily receiving a ten-minute explanation.

In a much broader sense, we may say to the Lord, "God, I just don't understand this. Why would You allow this to happen? I'm not sure I agree with Your decision here."

And God replies, "You're going to have to trust Me on this."

He has reasons for what He does or doesn't do, and He doesn't have to explain Himself. God is the one who determines what absolute truth is, and that is the bottom line.

God is holy.

The prophet Isaiah had the unique privilege of getting a glimpse of the glory of God. He described the moment like this:

> It was in the year King Uzziah died that I saw the Lord. He was sitting on a lofty throne, and the train of his robe filled the Temple. Attending him were mighty seraphim, each having six wings. With two wings they covered their faces, with two they covered their feet, and with two they flew. They were calling out to each other, "Holy, holy, holy is the LORD of Heaven's Armies! The whole earth is filled with his glory!" (Isaiah 6:1-3, NLT)

Isn't it interesting that the angels did not cry, "Eternal, eternal, eternal"? They could have. Or they might have shouted, "Faithful, faithful, faithful" or "Mighty, mighty, mighty." God is certainly all of these things and more. But what the angels sang was "Holy, holy, holy."

We need to know that God is holy.

In Psalm 24 the Bible says, "Who may ascend into the hill of the LORD? Or who may stand in His holy place? He who has clean hands and a pure heart, who has not lifted up his soul to an idol, nor sworn deceitfully" (verses 3-4).

Because God is holy, that means He hates sin. The Bible says in Proverbs 15:9, "The LORD detests the way of the wicked, but he loves those who pursue godliness" (NLT).

God, who is holy, hates it when we sin. The Bible even says of God, "Your eyes are too pure to look on evil; you cannot tolerate wrongdoing" (Habakkuk 1:13, NIV).

That is why the death of Jesus Christ was necessary. As you recall, Jesus was nailed to that cross two thousand years ago. At one moment there was darkness in the middle of the day, and Christ cried out the words, "*Eli, Eli, lama sabachthani,*" which means, "My God, My God, why have You forsaken Me?" (Matthew 27:46). Many say that is the moment when God the Father, who is holy, turned away His pure eyes as all of the sins of the world—past, present, and future—every sin that you and I have ever committed or will commit—were poured upon Jesus, the Son. In that moment, Jesus *became* sin for us, so that we might have a relationship with God.[3]

God is righteous.

Not only is God true and holy, God is also righteous. Holiness describes His character, His essential nature, while righteousness and justice describe how He impacts this world. The Bible says that "the LORD is righteous, he loves justice."[4]

Some people don't like this; they don't agree with the justice of God. In the Old Testament book of Job, Job was having a difficult time with some of the things that God was doing in his life. After chapters of the afflicted man's protests and complaints, God posed a series of questions to Job.

In chapter 40, the Lord says to Job, "Do you still want to argue with the Almighty? You are God's critic, but do you have the answers? . . . Will you discredit my justice and condemn me just to prove you are right?" (verses 2,8, NLT).

Then God answers Job—not by explaining Himself, but by simply stating some of the truths about His own majesty, power, and righteousness.

He basically says to Job, "Let Me ask you a few questions . . ."

> Do you have an arm like God's,
>> and can your voice thunder like his?
> Then adorn yourself with glory and splendor,
>> and clothe yourself in honor and majesty. . .
> Have you ever given orders to the morning,
>> or shown the dawn its place? . . .
> Have you journeyed to the springs of the sea
>> or walked in the recesses of the deep? . .
> Do you send the lightning bolts on their way?
> Do they report to you, "Here we are"? (Job 40:9-10;
>> 38:12,16,35, NIV)

God was saying to Job, "Who are you to tell Me what is right or just? Who are you to tell Me what I can or can't do or should or shouldn't do?"

God is righteous, and He doesn't have to defend Himself before anyone in heaven or earth.

God is good.

The word *good* could be understood to mean that God is the final standard of good and that all God is and does is worthy of approval.

God is good whether I believe it or not, whether I acknowledge it or not. Again, He is the final court of arbitration. Jesus said, "No one is good—except God alone."[5] The psalms frequently refer to the goodness of God. Psalm 34:8 says, "Oh, taste and see that the LORD is good."

If God is good and therefore the ultimate standard of good,

then we have a definition of the meaning of good that will really help us with our personal ethics and morality. What is good? *Good is what good approves.*

There is no higher standard of goodness than God's own character.

God is love.

Scripture doesn't just say that God *has* love or even that God is loving; it says that He Himself is love.

Nowadays we have a Hollywood version of love that, upon closer examination, looks a lot more like lust. "I love you (lust after you), so go to bed with me." Real love, however, is marrying that person and staying with him or her for the rest of your life.

Often we use the word *love* without any real understanding of the meaning of the word. In the English language we have one word for love. We use it for everything from "I love God" to "I love life" to "I love ice cream" to "I love surfing" to "I love my dog" to "I love my girlfriend."

It's the same word.

But I hope you don't love your girlfriend in the same way you love your dog. I also hope that you don't love your girlfriend in the same way that you love tacos. We use the same word to mean many different things.

In the original Greek language of the New Testament, however, they had many different words for love. They had a word that spoke of friendship, another that spoke of sexual intimacy, and another that was used to describe the love of God. That last one is the word *agape*. That is the word used to describe God's love toward us.

Our love for one another can be very fickle. *I love you if you do something for me. I love you because you love me. I love you because you are beautiful. I love you because you make me feel good when I am around you.*

The problem with that sort of love is that it's totally based on what someone does for us. *If there comes a day when I am no longer attracted to you, however, I will dump you. If there comes a time when you no longer give me a good feeling, then I no longer want to be around you.*

That is not the kind of love God has. Isn't that great to know? God would say, "I love you when you are in church. I love you when are walking with Me and trying to please Me, and I love you when you have sinned, failed, and have fallen out of fellowship with Me." The Bible shows us that God loves us no matter what we do.

That is not to say that God *approves* of what we do. That is not to say that God isn't offended by what we do. It's simply saying that no matter what you do or where you go, He will never stop loving you.

God is just.

This attribute is closely related to His holiness and righteousness. Because of this, God expresses His wrath and anger.

That bothers some people. They don't want God to be wrathful or angry. As we saw in our person-on-the-street interviews, some people will say, "I believe in a God of love, but not in a God of judgment." What they are really saying is, "I don't want a God who gives rules. I don't want a God of absolutes, because I want to have my own version of spirituality and do what I want to do and live in the way I want to live. I want to have the hope of heaven when I die and live like hell in the meantime. I want to have freedom to break all of God's commandments and have all of the fun this world has to offer, but still know that God loves me."

Though it is true that God loves you, it is also true that God is just. Because He is just, there is a penalty for breaking the law.

Some of us say that we don't like the concept of justice— until we are the victim of a crime. Someone steals from you. Someone assaults you. Someone defrauds you. You give a report to the police, and you want that person apprehended! If someone cuts you off on the freeway and the highway patrol goes after them, you say to yourself, "Yes! There is still justice in the world." And that's good, isn't it? There needs to be justice in the world.

Guess what? *God* is just.

This means that if you have broken His commandments and seem to be getting away with it, you will still stand in a final court someday — and it won't matter who your defense attorney is. You won't escape the consequences of your actions. Unless you have Jesus Christ to defend you, you will face God's justice and His just punishment.

It is true that God loves you and that God is good. It is also true that God is just. And because He is just, He will judge sin. The Bible says, "The soul who sins shall die," and "the wages of sin is death."[6] God clearly tells us that if we sin against Him and break His commandments, we *will* pay a penalty.

Someone might say, "But this doesn't make sense. How can God be good and loving and then go and hate something (like sin)? That doesn't seem right."

You might think of it like this. If you are a parent, you love your children with all your heart. As a result of that love, and closely connected to it, you also hate anything that would harm them. What if you looked in your backyard, saw your toddler playing quietly, and then noticed that your child was being stalked by a large wolf? What would you do, if you knew that wolf was about to attack your child?

Would you say, "Don't bother the wolf. The wolf is our friend"?

No. You would say, "Kill that wolf! Stop him right now!"

It is possible to love and hate at the same time. It is possible to have love and also a perfect hatred for that which is wicked and depraved. God hates what would harm you.

Someone asks, "How could a God of love send someone to hell?"

That question bothers a lot of people. They see this big, loving God, just brimming over with good feelings for us, and somehow the concept of an eternal hell doesn't fit in.

The truth is, God never created hell for people. He didn't say,

"I will create heaven for all the good people and hell for all the bad people. Therefore, if you do a lot of good works, and if I'm in a good mood and grading on the curve, you will probably make it to heaven. If, however, you live a bad life and your bad deeds outweigh your good deeds, then you will go to hell."

Most people have a view of heaven and hell that is completely wrong and unbiblical. God created heaven, which is His dwelling place, and He wants you to join Him there when you die. Hell, according to Jesus, was created for the devil and his angels.[7] God doesn't want any man or woman, uniquely created in His image, to go to this horrible place where people will be eternally separated from Him.

Every one of us, however, has broken God's commandments. Some of us have broken *all* of the commandments many times over. As the New Testament affirms, "For all have sinned and fall short of the glory of God" (Romans 3:23).

We can't measure up to God's holy standards.

None of us can.

Unless God had found a way to rescue us, we all would be doomed. We could never make it to heaven on our own merits. As it says in Ephesians, we all were "without hope and without God in the world" (Ephesians 2:12, NIV).

But that same good and loving God provided a way that would enable sinful men and women to be reconciled to Him so that we could have everlasting life and be received into heaven when we die.

Jesus, the Son of God, paid the price for our sins that we could never pay—not in a trillion years. In so doing, the love of God and the justice of God came together on that terrible, wonderful day when Jesus gave His life for us on a Roman cross.

In the prophetic words of the psalmist, "Unfailing love and truth have met together. Righteousness and peace have kissed!" (Psalm 85:10, NLT).

3

What God Is Like

Man is incurably religious. Down through the ages, most people have believed in the existence of God or gods. It may be that most human beings have given more attention to this idea of a supreme being or beings than all other concerns—food, clothing, housing, work, pleasure—put together.

The Greeks and Romans had their gods like Jupiter, Mars, Mercury, and Venus. When the apostle Paul passed through Athens on his way to Corinth, he had a little time on his hands and took a walk through town. When he saw that the fabled city was filled with images and idols erected to various deities, it filled him with distress. It's easy to understand why. Paul had been a champion of the one true God from childhood. And Athens in that day probably had more temples, shrines, and altars than Los Angeles has McDonald's.

But as common as this belief in something or someone might be, the nature of who God is and what He is like is a mystery to most people. The first-century Athenians hedged their bets by erecting an altar "to an unknown god." In other words, "If there is a god out there that we've missed or overlooked in the religious life of our city, we want to make sure we're covered, even though we have no idea who that particular deity might be."

In Acts 17, Paul seized on that altar to a mystery and set out to declare to them the good news about this unknown God. With that idea as his on-ramp, he preached to them about the true and living God, who sent His Son to redeem the world.

Making God Known

God is still unknown to many people today. They don't know His name, they don't understand His nature, and they can't comprehend His holiness, power, and love.

And that's why God gave us the Bible. From one cover to the other, it was written to tell us what He is like. In fact, that was one of the principal objectives of Jesus when He walked on this planet.

John tells us that "no one has ever seen God, but the one and only Son, who is himself God and is in closest relationship with the Father,, has made him known" (John 1:18, NIV).

Jesus said, "No one has seen the Father except the one who is from God; only he has seen the Father" (John 6:46, NIV).

To help people grasp a God they didn't really know or understand, Jesus told stories that illustrated His Father's nature and heart of compassion. In the story of the prodigal son, for example, Jesus told of a father who longed for fellowship with his ungrateful, runaway son and ran to meet him when the boy came straggling back home. It's a story that has touched people all over the world for thousands of years.

"The Lord Bless You. . . ."

Some would suggest that the God of the Old Testament is different from the God of the New Testament. Nothing could be further from the truth. From one end of the Bible to the other, we see a God who loves, cares, and remains vitally interested in the course our lives should take.

Way back in the book of Numbers, the fourth book of the Bible, we come to a passage that reveals God's heart for His people and gives us yet one more clue of what He is like:

> The LORD spoke to Moses, saying: "Speak to Aaron and his sons, saying, 'This is the way you shall bless the children of Israel. Say to them:
>
> "The LORD bless you and keep you;
> The LORD make His face shine upon you,
> And be gracious to you;
> The LORD lift up His countenance upon you,
> And give you peace.'"
>
> "They shall put My name on the children of Israel, and I will bless them." (6:22-27)

The book of Numbers is a record of the wanderings of the Israelites in the wilderness. It tells us of the trials they faced and the mistakes they made on their way to the Promised Land. It chronicles their rebellion, stubbornness, ingratitude, and complaining—and the ramifications of their disobedience. But it also shows God's incredible longsuffering and patience with them.

We, too, live in a wilderness and are passing through to another place. We also face our trials and make our mistakes. In addition to that, we face threats each and every day. Since 9/11, we all look over our shoulders a bit more. With the government uncovering more and more terrorism attempts—and evil plots so hateful and destructive that it boggles the mind—it can be a bit frightening sometimes.

Then there are all the normal concerns of our lives: our livelihoods, our health, our marriages, our children, our futures.

These concerns only increase as we get older. The fact is, we are a fallen people living in a fallen world in need of a little help—actually, a lot of help.

So God instructed the priests to pronounce a special blessing on His people, a people wandering in the wilderness. He wanted that blessing spoken again and again. The Lord was saying, "I want this ingrained in their brains, etched in their hearts. I want them to know this blessing by memory and be able to recite it at a moment's notice."

Why? Because it reminds us of who God is and what He is like and how He sees you and me.

There are six truths that shine out from these verses, six things that show us who God is and what He is like.

Truth Number One: God Loves to Bless You

The LORD bless you. (Numbers 6:24)

Christians like to toss around the words *bless* and *blessing*. We say it quite a lot, and most of the time we mean it.

We also abuse the term. Sometimes we use the word to let people know the conversation is over and that it's time for them to leave. We stand up from our desk, or if we've met someone out in public and get tired of talking to them, we'll say, "Bless you!" Which, being translated, means, "Good-bye. Go away!"

Bless, however, is truly a spiritual term. The world may try to hijack it, but they really have no idea what it means. In fact, true blessing is something only a child of God can experience.

Jesus both began and concluded His earthly ministry with blessing people. After His resurrection, when He met the two downhearted disciples on the road to Emmaus, He blessed them. When children came to Him, He took them in His arms and blessed them. Just before He ascended into heaven, Jesus lifted His hands and blessed His followers. Jesus loved to bless people. In a portion of the Sermon on the Mount we call the Beatitudes, He tied together a whole string of blessings:

Then He opened His mouth and taught them, saying:

"Blessed are the poor in spirit,
    For theirs is the kingdom of heaven." (Matthew 5:2-3)

Our word for "blessed" comes from the Greek word *makarios*. This was the Mediterranean island of Cyprus. Because of its geographical location, balmy climate, and fertile soil, the Greeks believed that anyone who lived on this island had it made in the shade. As far as they were concerned, everything anyone needed for happiness and fulfillment could be found right there on that sunny island. There was no need to import anything, because if you lived in Cyprus, you had it all.

In other words, *makarios* was a metaphor for real blessedness or happiness. From this we learn two important things about God and blessings.

First, God want us to be blessed and happy. He truly does. In the opening chapter of Genesis we read, "So God created man in His own image; in the image of God He created him; male and female He created them" (Genesis 1:27). And the very next words are: "Then God blessed them" (verse 28). So just know that the Lord loves to bless you.

Second, blessedness, or true happiness, is independent from circumstances. The point Jesus was making is the blessedness, the happiness that God has for you, is independent of what may be happening in your life at the moment.

So here in Numbers, the Lord tells the priest to do this for His people—to stand before them and say, "The Lord bless you."

Some of us might feel as though this benediction ought to read, "The Lord curse you." That is because they have lived apart from God's blessings and feel like they are dealing with His curse on their lives. Is it true that God cursed certain people or

places? Yes, it is. But there was always a reason for that. His blessings could not fall on people who rejected His kindness and love.
For all practical purposes, they had chosen to be cursed instead.

God cursed Cain because of his constant disobedience (see
Genesis 9:25). God said there would be a curse on the person
who worshiped false gods (see Deuteronomy 27:15) and on the
person who lived immorally (see Deuteronomy 27:20). The list
goes on.

But there is one key passage in the book of Deuteronomy
that shows us we have a choice between God's blessing or curse:

> I call heaven and earth as witnesses today against you, that
> I have set before you life and death, blessing and cursing;
> therefore choose life, that both you and your descendants
> may live; that you may love the LORD your God, that you
> may obey His voice, and that you may cling to Him, for
> He is your life and the length of your days. (30:19-20)

For those of us who have chosen life, who have chosen to love
Him, cling to Him, and obey His voice, there is blessing—
blessing in abundance. Your Father loves to bless you! Jesus said,
"Fear not, little flock; for it is your Father's good pleasure to give
you the kingdom."[1]

As a father, it was my joy to bless (some would say spoil) my
sons. Looking back, I have to say that it never felt like a task or a
heavy burden for me to feed or clothe them. You never would
have heard me say, "What? More baby food? Do you have any
idea how much this is costing?" Or, "Are you kidding? I have to
pay for diapers for this kid again?"

It was a privilege and a joy to have my boys in the house, and
now I get to experience it all over again as a grandfather (and I
don't even have to mess with diapers!).

Truth Number Two: God Has Promised to Keep You

The LORD bless you and keep you. (Numbers 6:24)

God wants us to be constantly reassured that He will keep us and care for us. The Israelites needed to hear that as they moved from place to place in a desolate wilderness. And in the twenty-first century, in such an evil and uncertain world as this, we need this reassurance, too.

Sometimes we worry about our safety and security, not only for ourselves, but for our families. At other times we worry about our relationship with God and our personal salvation. Even mature believers have times of doubt. Elijah did. So did Moses, Gideon, Hezekiah, Thomas, and others.

But God promises to *keep* us. The psalmist wrote,

I will lift up my eyes to the hills—
From whence comes my help?
My help comes from the LORD,
Who made heaven and earth.

He will not allow your foot to be moved;
He who keeps you will not slumber.
Behold, He who keeps Israel
Shall neither slumber nor sleep.

The LORD is your keeper;
The LORD is your shade at your right hand.
The sun shall not strike you by day,
Nor the moon by night.

The LORD shall preserve you from all evil;
He shall preserve your soul.
The LORD shall preserve your going out and your coming in
From this time forth, and even forevermore. (Psalm 121:1-8)

The Hebrew word used for *keep* means "to keep, to watch, to guard, to hedge about."

Remember the story in Job when the angels came to present themselves before the Lord, with Satan among them? God started bragging on His beloved servant, and Satan challenged Him:

> Then the LORD said to Satan, "Have you considered My servant Job, that there is none like him on the earth, a blameless and upright man, one who fears God and shuns evil?"
>
> So Satan answered the LORD and said, "Does Job fear God for nothing? *Have You not made a hedge around him, around his household, and around all that he has on every side?* You have blessed the work of his hands, and his possessions have increased in the land." (Job 1:8-10, emphasis added)

Those things are true for you, too. God has put a hedge, or wall of protection, around your life. Satan cannot scale or penetrate this wall. And if he tries to go in the front door, he has to face the Great Shepherd! Jesus said, "I tell you the truth, I am the gate for the sheep. . . . Yes, I am the gate."[2]

Many passages remind us of the keeping power of God:

- "The Lord is faithful, who will establish you and guard you from the evil one." (2 Thessalonians 3:3)
- "Now to Him who is able to keep you from stumbling, and to present you faultless before the presence of His glory with exceeding joy." (Jude 1:24)
- "[You] are kept by the power of God through faith for salvation ready to be revealed in the last time." (1 Peter 1:5)
- "To those who have been called, who are loved in God the Father and kept for Jesus Christ." (Jude 1:1, NIV)

The original language uses what Bible scholars call the perfect tense. The nearest equivalent in English is "continually kept." It is a continuing result of a past action. Because He has decided to keep us, He will carry that commitment forward through all the days and years of our lives.

Whatever your difficulties may be, you need to know that you are preserved in Christ! The apostle John tells us that "Jesus knew that His hour had come that He should depart from this world to the Father, having loved His own who were in the world, He loved them to the end."[3]

You don't lose something that you love. You don't carelessly toss aside your favorite hat or sunglasses or the latest cell phone. You keep your eye on what you value. You know where it is. You don't go to Disneyland with your kids, only to leave them behind and completely forget them. (Although you may be tempted!)

God never forgets what He loves. In the book of Isaiah He says, "Can a mother forget her nursing child? Can she feel no love for the child she has borne? But even if that were possible, I would not forget you! See, I have written your name on the palms of my hands."[4]

He has invested heavily in finding you, saving you, and adopting you into His own family, and He will protect His investment! Were it not for the preserving grace of God, not a single one of us would make it. I don't care how strong you think you are, you would spiritually vapor-lock on the spot.

The Bible leaves no doubt: Jesus is always there, loving, preserving, and praying for those who belong to Him:

He is able to save completely those who come to God through him, because he always lives to intercede for them. (Hebrews 7:25, NIV)

Scripture makes it abundantly clear: You and I are preserved, protected, and continually kept by the power of God.

Someone inevitably will ask, "So, Greg, does that mean I can never really fall away from my faith?"

No. Actually you can fall away. In the book of Jude, we are warned and encouraged to "keep [ourselves] in the love of God."[5] Though God's love is unsought, undeserved, and unconditional, it is possible for you to turn away and fall out of harmony with that love. Here's the way the writer of Hebrews puts it:

> See to it, brothers and sisters, that none of you has a sinful, unbelieving heart that turns away from the living God. But encourage one another daily, as long as it is called "Today," so that none of you may be hardened by sin's deceitfulness. We have come to share in Christ, if indeed we hold our original conviction firmly to the very end. (3:12-14, NIV)

So what does Jude mean when he tells us to "keep [ourselves] in the love of God"? Simply put, it means this: *Keep yourself from all that is unlike Him.* Keep yourself from any influence that violates His love and brings sorrow to His heart. Keep yourself in a place where God can actively demonstrate His love toward you. That means staying away from certain people, places, and activities that make it easier for you to fall into temptation. Now that you've been delivered from the kingdom of Satan, you want to make sure you never place yourself in his clutches and back under his control.

When we pray (as Jesus taught us), "Do not lead us into temptation," we're asking the Father to help us so we won't deliberately place ourselves into volatile situations. Bottom line, if you truly *want* to be kept safe, preserved, and to enjoy God's hedge of protection around your life, it's there for you.

"Okay," you say, "I'm enclosed in the hedge. Does that mean God will keep me from trials, sorrows, and difficulties?"

No, not at all. If we think the road to heaven is all sunlight and daisies, we'll be thrown for a loop when hardships or tragedies come into our lives. We will incorrectly conclude that God has somehow failed in His promise to keep us.

The truth is, God has never promised to keep us from all the bumps, bruises, and heartaches of life in this world. However, even though He may not keep us from the hardships, He will keep us *through* the hardships. He will be with us. He will give us His grace. He will see us through. He promises,

> When you pass through the waters,
>   I will be with you;
> and when you pass through the rivers,
>   they will not sweep over you.
> When you walk through the fire,
>   you will not be burned;
>   the flames will not set you ablaze.
> For I am the LORD your God,
>   the Holy One of Israel, your Savior. (Isaiah 43:2-3, NIV)

The Lord didn't say, "*If* you pass through the waters . . . *if* you pass through the rivers . . . *if* you walk through the fire. . . ." He said that those things will be a part of our lives during our short stay on earth. I would guess that almost every person reading these words has seen his or her share of waters, rivers, and fire.

But what a difference to face those things knowing that God is watching over your every step and will keep you in His power and love! He is no less our keeper for allowing difficulty to come our way. And if we trust Him, He will walk with us, keeping us through that difficulty until we reach the other side of it.

When the Israelites came up against the dead end between Pharaoh's army and the Red Sea, they had already been walking in a miracle. With a mighty hand, God had delivered them from centuries of slavery and brought the whole nation out of captivity. When had such a thing ever happened in history?

So the sea stretched out before them, and they could hear the rumble of horses and chariots behind them as a vengeful Pharaoh and his army were in hot pursuit. Terrified, the

Israelites pointed the finger of blame at Moses, crying out, "Why did you bring us out here to die in the wilderness? Weren't there enough graves for us in Egypt? Why did you make us leave? Didn't we tell you to leave us alone while we were still in Egypt? Our Egyptian slavery was far better than dying out here in the wilderness!"

You know the rest of the story. God parted that Red Sea, and the Israelites passed through safely to the other side. Then those same parted waters crashed down on the Egyptian army, drowning them.

Why didn't God just lift up the whole nation and teleport them to the other side? Because then they (and we) wouldn't have learned a priceless lesson: While God may not keep us *from* the trial, He will show His power and love by keeping us *through* the trial.

The same is true with those three courageous Hebrew teens: Shadrach, Meshach, and Abed-Nego. They not only had to face the possibility of execution by fire in the king's blazing furnace, they actually had the experience of being tossed alive into those hungry flames.

I love what happened next. It has to be one of my favorite stories in the Bible:

> Then King Nebuchadnezzar was astonished; and he rose in haste and spoke, saying to his counselors, "Did we not cast three men bound into the midst of the fire?
>
> They answered and said to the king, "True, O king."
>
> "Look!" he answered, "I see four men loose, walking in the midst of the fire; and they are not hurt, and the form of the fourth is like the Son of God." (Daniel 3:24-25)

It wasn't just three individuals walking through the fire that day; there was a fourth, and that fourth was the Son of God. In the same way, He will keep us through our trials, no matter how fiery.

There are so many illustrations of this principle. Right away we could name Noah and the flood, Jonah and the great fish, and Daniel and the lions' den.

"Yes," you say, "but it isn't always a happy ending. John the Baptizer got beheaded. Herod killed James with a sword. Stephen was stoned to death. Where was the keeping power of God for them? Or what about when a godly man or woman is hurt or killed in a terrible accident or stricken with a massive heart attack? Has God failed to keep them?"

In even asking a question like that, we are assuming it is somehow our right to live long, easy, and relatively tranquil lives and then die peacefully in our sleep one day. But that is not what the Bible says. Jesus did not say, "In this world you will only have blue skies and sunshine." Rather He said, "In the world you will have tribulation; but be of good cheer" (John 16:33).

Whatever happens in our lives, our times are in His hands. Our life is a gift to us from God right now, and that breath you just took is a gift as well. Don't take that for granted. Even death doesn't mean that God has somehow failed in His promise to keep us. Barring the Rapture, there will come a time for each one of us to make that journey home to heaven.

And when that moment comes, *however* it comes, God will be right there, taking us by the hand and guiding us from one life to the next.

So far we've seen that God wants to bless you and that He will keep you. But there's a third truth to consider here.

Truth Number Three: God Smiles on You

The LORD make His face shine upon you. (Numbers 6:25)

God wants us to be reminded daily that when He looks on us . . . He smiles! That's what this text means.

That's not the picture many people have of the Lord. They

see Him as a frowning Father in heaven, looking down on us with arms folded and foot impatiently tapping, rarely if ever pleased by us. But that is not the picture God gives us of Himself.

God's face shines with pleasure toward us as His people. When He sees us, His face just lights up with joy! He isn't angry with us, and He isn't disappointed with us.

He is merciful and tender toward those who don't deserve it; he is slow to get angry and full of kindness and love. (Psalm 103:8, TLB)

He isn't a God who is by nature grumpy and unhappy with us until we do something nice to change His mood and His mind. He loves us, and the very thought of us, the very sight of us, puts a smile on His face.

When you read about the ancient religions, you encounter angry, fickle deities. There was no pleasing them. They always had a chip on their shoulders, and you had to walk on eggshells around them. You never knew what side of the bed they'd be getting up from morning by morning.

But through this blessing in the book of Numbers, the Lord was basically saying, "I want my people to know on a regular basis that I am not like that!"

Paul wrote, "What then shall we say to these things? If God is for us, who can be against us? He who did not spare His own Son, but delivered Him up for us all, how shall He not with Him also freely give us all things?"[6]

Not only does God's smiling, shining face look at you, but He *sings* over you as well! Consider this amazing passage:

The LORD your God in your midst,
The Mighty One, will save;
He will rejoice over you with gladness,
He will quiet you with His love,
He will rejoice over you with singing. (Zephaniah 3:17)

I wonder what God's voice sounds like. As the prophet Ezekiel was describing a vision of the glory of the Lord, he wrote that "His voice was like the sound of many waters" (Ezekiel 43:2).

I've always loved the ocean. The very sound of it calms me. God's voice is like the roar of rushing waters . . . or maybe the crash of the surf on a moonlit beach.

Truth Number Four: God Is Gracious to You

The LORD make His face shine upon you, and be gracious to you. (Numbers 6:25)

This is also something He wants us to be reminded of. It's important that we understand what grace is: God's unmerited favor.

Justice is getting what I deserve.

Mercy is not getting what I deserve.

Grace is getting what I don't deserve.

Let's say I loaned my Harley to a friend one weekend and he crashed and totaled it. Well, that friend of mine owes me a new bike! That's what justice demands. But let's say I decided to be merciful instead of demanding justice. In that case, I would ask for nothing in return; I would simply pardon him. But if I dealt with him in grace, I would take him out to dinner and afterward go to the Harley dealer and buy him a brand-new Harley of his own.

You say, "That sounds a little extravagant."

And yet it is *nothing* compared with what the Lord has done for you and me.

We deserve hell, and we get heaven.

We deserve punishment, and we get rewards.

We deserve wrath, and we get love.

We deserve exile, and we get adopted into God's own family.

The Lord is gracious to you! How we need His grace on a

daily, even moment-by-moment basis. Why? Because we sin each and every day, carrying out sins of omission and commission—things I've done that I shouldn't have done and things that I should have done but didn't. That is why in the Lord's Prayer, Jesus taught us to pray, "And forgive us our sins, as we have forgiven those who sin against us" (Matthew 6:12, NLT).

We know this prayer is a *daily* prayer because it includes, "Give us this day our daily bread" (verse 11). Just as surely as we need God's physical provisions every day, so we also need His forgiveness every day. We are essentially praying, "Lord, extend Your grace to me today."

This is how we are saved in the first place, by His grace:

> For by grace you have been saved through faith, and that not of yourselves; it is the gift of God, not of works, lest anyone should boast. (Ephesians 2:8-9)

His grace is also that which surrounds us and preserves us each day. When Paul felt he couldn't go on, praying and pleading for the removal of an agonizing burden in his life, God replied, "My grace is sufficient for you, for My strength is made perfect in weakness" (2 Corinthians 12:9).

At the beginning of this chapter, I mentioned the story of the prodigal son. I think it must be one of the most beautiful illustrations of God's graciousness in all of Scripture. If the father in Jesus' parable would have been just, he would have had the boy stoned to death. If he had been merely merciful, he would have taken him on as a hired hand, as the young man requested.

But the father's response went beyond justice and beyond mercy . . . all the way to grace. He ran to meet the dirty, emaciated young man and walked him back home again with a smile of pure joy on his face. So God blesses, keeps, smiles on, and is gracious to us. And if all of those things weren't enough, there's yet another truth here.

Truth Number Five: God Is Attentive to You

The LORD lift up His countenance upon you. (Numbers 6:26)

What does that mean, that He lifts up His countenance? It literally means that He lifts up His face to look at me, to see my situation, to have a keen interest and give full attention to what's going on in my life.

Incredible! God is saying, "I watch out for you each and every day, and you have My full attention."

Have you ever been speaking to someone and pouring out your heart, when you suddenly notice that they are looking right past you? Now, that is disheartening. It makes you feel a little bit devalued, doesn't it? Sometimes we may imagine that's how it is with God. He seems to be looking our way, but then we begin to wonder if His eyes are roaming somewhere else in the universe. Maybe there's a huge supernova going on in the Andromeda Galaxy and He wants to check it out. Or maybe something big is coming down in the Middle East and His attention is diverted. Finally He looks back at us and says, "Now, what were you saying?"

Does He truly pay attention to us? Does He really know what's happening in our lives right now—what we're feeling, what we're wondering, what we're worried about?

The Lord doesn't want us to be concerned about such things. God is a Father who "lifts up His countenance" to us. He looks at us face-to-face, eye-to-eye. He gives us His full attention.

Isn't that one of the essential messages of Christmas? As Matthew recorded for us, "'Behold, the virgin shall be with child, and bear a Son, and they shall call His name Immanuel,' which is translated, 'God with us'" (1:23).

He is *your* Immanuel. He is God with *you*.

You may be at a place in your life where you've convinced

yourself that no one really cares about what you think or feel or dream. But God does. You have His full attention.

Do you suppose Joseph felt God was attentive to him as he sat for two years in that Egyptian dungeon, falsely accused of rape? As the days ran on and on, it must have seemed at times that God didn't care at all. But the fact is, God was watching and attentive at every moment. The Lord had incredible plans for this young man's life. Although Joseph couldn't have known it at the time, the Lord was about to make him the second most powerful man on earth.

In order to prepare Joseph for this crucial role on the world stage, God allowed some time, some disappointment, and some adversity to toughen him up.

Yes, God wants to bless us, but we must learn to handle those blessings. Even if it doesn't feel like it right now, know that God is paying attention to you. He is out in front of you, going before you, preparing future blessings for you. He has not forgotten about you, not even for a moment. He is attentive to you, and when you are ready, He will deliver you.

Truth Number Six: God Wants to Give You Peace

> The LORD lift up His countenance upon you, and give you peace. (Numbers 6:26)

As we consider the fact that the Lord wants to bless us, keep us, and smile on us, it should give us personal peace. When we consider that God is both gracious and attentive to us, a deep-seated contentment should settle over our hearts. This is how Paul could write words like these:

> Don't worry about anything; instead, pray about every-thing. Tell God what you need, and thank him for all he has done. Then you will experience God's peace, which

exceeds anything we can understand. His peace will guard
your hearts and minds as you live in Christ Jesus.
(Philippians 4:6-7, NLT)

Remember, Paul wrote these words *in prison*. These weren't
the words of a madman, but a man who was at peace, knowing
God was in control. And Paul practiced what he preached,
because when he and Silas were beaten severely and thrown
into prison at midnight, they sang praises to God.[7]

What if they had been executed instead of released? No
problem! God would keep and deliver them safely to heaven.
And if they were freed, which they were, they would faithfully
serve the Lord until He was done with them. Paul summed it all
up by writing, "For to me, to live is Christ, and to die is gain"
(Philippians 1:21).

Take It to the Bank!

They shall put My name on the children of Israel, and I
will bless them. (Numbers 6:27)

As He wrapped up this blessing, God was saying to the
priests, "You have spiritual oversight over the people. And I
want you to remember to pronounce this blessing on My people
over and over. I will live up to it in their lives! Don't make
excuses for Me, don't soft-sell this or be afraid that you're going
to put expectations on Me that I won't be able to fulfill. I will do
this, so tell them!"

For the same reason, my reader, I'm telling you these things
today. God has told me to tell you that He will bless you, He will
keep you, He will smile on you, He will be gracious to you, He
will be attentive to you, and He will give you His peace.

You can take that to the bank.

But remember, this is a series of promises only for the child of God. The nonbeliever cannot claim these things. They have no right or portion in this because blessing is really only for the believer.

There's a reason for that. The only reason we can enjoy such blessings is because Christ took the curse that belonged to us! Galatians 3:13 tells us that "Christ has redeemed us from the curse of the law, having become a curse for us (for it is written, 'Cursed is everyone who hangs on a tree')."

Jesus was cursed so that I could be blessed.

Jesus died so that I could live.

Jesus was forsaken so that I might be forgiven.

So, the choice is yours. Do you want to experience this blessing in your life? Then you will, because it's already yours. It's like finding out you have a whole lot more in your bank account than you realized. So make a withdrawal instead of going through withdrawals! Remember, God is blessing you today, smiling on you, listening to you, being gracious to you, and giving you peace.

Or, you can choose a curse.

I don't mean anything mystical by that, and I'm not speaking of any so-called "generational curse" here. I simply mean that if you do not choose His blessings, then you will remain outside the circle of His blessings, facing the full penalty and repercussions of your own sins.

The choice is entirely yours.

Choose wisely, my friend!

4

Who Is Jesus?

A little boy, frightened by a thunderstorm one night, called out from his room, "Daddy, Daddy, come in here! I'm *scared*!"

The boy's father had already settled into bed for the night and didn't really want to get up again.

"Now son, you'll be all right," he called. "Remember, God is with you."

There was a moment of silence, and then the boy yelled back, "Daddy, I need someone with *skin* on right now!"

Jesus is God with skin on.

In the first chapter of John's gospel, we read,

In the beginning was the Word, and the
Word was with God, and the Word was God.
He was in the beginning with God. All things
were made through Him, and without Him
nothing was made that was made. In Him
was life, and the life was the light of men.
And the light shines in the darkness, and the
darkness did not comprehend it. (verses 1-5)

In the original language, there is no definite article before the word *beginning*. That means no one can pinpoint a moment in time when the Word had a beginning. In this passage, John is taking us into the mysteries of eternity past—further than our limited minds can comprehend—and he is telling us that Jesus was *preexistent*.

In other words, Jesus never had a beginning, nor will He ever have an end.

He was never created; in fact, He *is* the Creator.

Bottom line? The Bible clearly teaches that Jesus was and is God. You might say, "Isn't that elementary, Greg?" Perhaps it is, but you would be surprised at how many people miss this simple, all-important truth.

And frankly, to miss this truth is to miss *everything*.

Jesus Christ is God.

When you encounter the various false teachings in our world today, consider carefully what they say about Jesus Christ. If Jesus is not declared to be God, that is all the evidence you need to prove you are dealing with a non-Christian cult.

The divinity of Jesus Christ is one of those foundational truths we cannot fudge on. Before there was a Planet Earth, before there were stars, before there was light or darkness, before there was matter, before there was anything but the Godhead, there was Jesus: coequal, coeternal, and coexistent with God the Father and God the Holy Spirit.

Jesus was with God, and He was and is God.

He also became a human being. As Charles Swindoll has said, Jesus was deity in diapers. In fact, Jesus became a fertilized egg and an embryo. But He never ceased being God. Because of God's plan to rescue you and me, Jesus did not stay in the safety of heaven. He entered our world, breathed our air, shared our pain, walked in our shoes, lived our life, and then died our death. He could not have identified with us any more closely than He did. *It was total identification without any loss of identity.* In other words, He became human, He became one of us, without ceasing to be God.

I love the way the book of Hebrews expresses this:

> Since we, God's children, are human beings—made of
> flesh and blood—he became flesh and blood too by being
> born in human form; for only as a human being could he
> die and in dying break the power of the devil who had the
> power of death. Only in that way could he deliver those
> who through fear of death have been living all their lives
> as slaves to constant dread. (2:14-15, TLB)

In Revelation 22:13, Jesus said of Himself, "I am the Alpha and
the Omega, the Beginning and the End, the First and the Last."

There never was a time when Christ did not exist. Going
back to John 1 again, the text says, "In the beginning was the
Word, and the Word was with God, and the Word was God." In
the original Greek of the New Testament, those words are
stated in what is called the perfect tense. That means He is
continuing. He has always been God, He is God right now, and
He always will be God.

Jesus Is God

As the Son of God, Jesus is a member of the Godhead, or
Trinity. The preposition "with" in John 1:1 carries the idea of
nearness along with a sense of movement toward God. This
demonstrates the deepest equality and intimacy in the Trinity.

It's impossible for finite human beings like you and me to
wrap our minds around the concept of a three-in-one God. It
hasn't been easy for two thousand years, and it isn't easy today.
When we speak of the Trinity, we're not talking about three
Gods; we are speaking about one God in three Persons.

Don't ask me to explain it, because I can't.

People sometimes will use analogies to help them understand
the Trinity, but every analogy ever devised falls short. For
instance, someone will describe water as a type of trinity. It can be

a liquid, a solid when frozen as ice, and a gas, when it is vapor or steam. But whatever form it takes, it's still water. Again, that might give us a rudimentary sense of what a trinity means, but the analogy quickly breaks down, as all the word pictures do.

Sometimes people will even get into arguments over this subject. I read an article in the paper a while back that would have made me laugh, if it wasn't so sad. A husband and wife went to see the movie *The Passion of the Christ*, Mel Gibson's film about Jesus. After they left the theater, however, the couple got into an argument about the nature of the Trinity. The argument boiled over into a fight, and the police were called. The wife suffered injuries on her arm and face, while her husband had a scissor stab wound in his hand, and his shirt was ripped off.

The officer who arrested them said, "You know, it was kind of a pitiful thing to go see a movie like that and then—well, I think they kind of missed the point."

Yes, they did. But to be honest, many people do. So let's put away our scissors and other sharp implements and think a little bit about the Lord Jesus' place in the Trinity.

Jesus Is Creator

As a member of the Trinity, Jesus was present and hands-on at the creation of everything. John 1:3 says, "All things were made through Him, and without Him nothing was made that was made." This verse, along with other Scriptures, asserts that Jesus Himself is the Creator of the universe. In Colossians 1:16-17, we read, "For by Him all things were created that are in heaven and that are on earth, visible and invisible, whether thrones or dominions or principalities or powers. All things were created through Him and for Him. And He is before all things, and in Him all things consist."

Someone will say, "Now wait a second. I thought God the Father created the heavens and the earth." He did. Genesis 1:1 tells us, "In the beginning God created the heavens and the earth." And guess what? The Holy Spirit was in on it too! In Genesis 1:2-3 we read that the "earth was without form, and void; and darkness was on the face of the deep. And the Spirit of God was hovering over the face of the waters. Then God said, 'Let there be light'; and there was light."

So what does this mean?

It means that the Father, Son, and Holy Spirit all played a part in creation. The very word used to describe God in this Genesis passage is *Elohim*, a term that could be translated "more than one."

In several passages in Genesis, we are given some interesting glances, behind the scenes, of God's activity in the world.

- "Then God said, 'Let Us make man in Our image, according to Our likeness." (1:26)
- "Behold, the man has become like one of Us." (3:22)
- "Come, let Us go down and there confuse their language." (11:7)

Us?

Is this a conversation within the Godhead?

As I said, I can't put all these truths together in my finite mind. But as it has been said, if God were small enough for our minds, He wouldn't be big enough for our needs.

Suffice it to say, Jesus is a member of the Trinity. Jesus is God.

Jesus Became Man

Jesus, who is God, became a man. He voluntarily left heaven, was born on earth, and grew up to walk among us. Of course, we celebrate His birth every Christmas.

Isaiah 9:6 gives us an interesting look at this watershed event from two perspectives. It says, "For unto us a Child is born, unto us a Son is given."

From our perspective on earth, a Child was born.

From the Father in heaven's perspective, a Son was given.

The verse goes on to say, "His name will be called . . . Mighty God, Everlasting Father". These are both references to God the Son. And of course, He would also be called Immanuel, which means "God with us" (see Isaiah 7:14; Matthew 1:23).

Jesus Was Born of a Virgin

Jesus was born of a young virgin girl named Mary. Again, this is one of those truths, like the deity of Christ, that cannot be negotiated or compromised.

Is it a big deal?

Yes, a very big deal.

The Bible clearly teaches the Virgin Birth, and it is a truth we must believe. I would take it a step further and say that if you don't believe Jesus was supernaturally conceived in the womb of Mary, then I don't know if you are really a Christian. To question the supernatural birth of Jesus is to question the very deity of Jesus.

The Bible teaches that Mary had other children after Jesus, but she didn't have any before. Joseph played no part in the conception of our Lord; Jesus was conceived by the Holy Spirit.

If Jesus was not supernaturally conceived in the womb of the virgin, then He was not God. And if He was not God, then His death on the cross meant nothing at all. More to the point, He was simply a fraud because the Bible taught that He would be born into the world through a virgin, and Jesus Himself claimed to be God in human form and the only way to God.[1]

The fact that Jesus was God walking among us on earth is the whole point of the *Incarnation*—a word used to describe the supernatural conception of Christ.

It is important to note that although Jesus became man, Jesus never *became* God. He was God before He was born. He was God when He was in the womb. He was God when He was outside of the womb. He was God when He walked the earth. He was God when He hung on the cross. And He was God when He rose again from the dead. The deity of Jesus was pre-human, pre-earthly, pre-Bethlehem, pre-Mary. He was God. He is God.

When Jesus was born as a baby on earth, He laid aside the privileges of deity. He didn't lay aside His deity, but He did lay aside some of the privileges that go with it. Paul tells us in Philippians 2:7-8 that He "made Himself of no reputation, taking the form of a bondservant, and coming in the likeness of men. And being found in appearance as a man, He humbled Himself and became obedient to the point of death, even the death of the cross."

That phrase *no reputation* could be translated, "He emptied Himself." It comes from the Greek word *kinos*. It was a self-renunciation, not an emptying of Himself of deity or an exchange of deity for humanity.

In his book *Laugh Again*, Chuck Swindoll wrote, "In a state of absolute perfection and undiminished deity, He willingly came to the earth. Leaving the angelic hosts who flooded His presence with adoring praise, He unselfishly accepted a role that would require His being misunderstood, abused, cursed, and crucified. He unhesitatingly surrendered the fellowship and protection of the Father's glory for the lonely path of obedience and torturous death."[2]

Why did Jesus empty Himself and lay aside these privileges? The answer is given to us in Hebrews 2:17-18:

> For this reason he had to be made like them, fully human in every way, in order that he might become a merciful and faithful high priest in service to God, and that he might make atonement for the sins of the people. Because he himself suffered when he was tempted, he is able to help those who are being tempted. (NIV)

As you can see, the virgin birth of Jesus Christ is not an optional belief. It is bedrock to one's relationship with God.

But why the Virgin Birth? Why was Jesus born in this way? When you stop and consider it for a moment, it makes good, logical sense.

It would have been possible, for instance, for God the Father to send Jesus as a completely sinless human being without a human parent. He could have come down to earth in a beam of light, appearing as a full-grown man. But of course, if God had chosen that method, it would have been hard for us to think of Him as fully human. We might find ourselves saying, "He may be powerful and wise, but He doesn't really know what we're going through. How could He? He just floated down from heaven and hasn't experienced what we have experienced."

Then again, it could have been possible for God the Father to have Jesus come to us born of two parents and, somehow in the process, had Him retain His full, divine nature intact. The Lord could have done this if He had chosen to. But then we might have said, "He was born of an earthly mother and father just like I was. How can I know that He is really sinless and qualified to be my Savior?"

The way God actually did it just makes sense.

Yes, He was born of a woman, as the Bible says, but super-naturally conceived by the Holy Spirit in the womb.

"But Greg," someone might say, "that's *impossible.*"

Exactly. That's why it's called a miracle. As the Bible says, "With God all things are possible" (Matthew 19:26).

How much did Jesus know about His mission as a child? When He was a little baby in that manger, did Jesus understand what was happening? I don't think so. It would seem to me that His knowledge unfolded over a period of time, as He grew from a baby to a toddler to a young boy to a teenager. Luke 2:52 tells us that "Jesus increased in wisdom and stature." That would appear to say that Jesus went through a learning process like anyone else—without the limitations that sin brings into one's life.

Jesus was a real baby in that rustic manger. He wasn't pretending to be a baby, and He wasn't born with His full speech faculties intact. On the day He was born, He didn't say, "Hello, Mary, Joseph. I am Jesus Christ, the second person of the Trinity and the Creator of the universe."

No! He was a *baby*. He cried. He had to learn how to speak, how to crawl, how to walk, how to count, how to feed Himself, and all the rest.

"Wait a second," you might protest. "Didn't you just tell us that Jesus was God and that God is omniscient, or all-knowing?'"

That's right.

"But now you are saying that as a baby, He didn't know everything. How does that work?'"

I believe Jesus possessed divine attributes without *using* them. Self-emptying is not self-extinction. He humbled Himself. Taking on a human nature was an addition, not a subtraction of His divine attributes. That is such an important distinction! Jesus did not cease to be God or divest Himself of divine attributes to become a man. He took on a human nature, submitting the use of His divine attributes to the will of His Father.

There were times when He exercised omniscience, as in John 4, when He met the Samaritan woman at the well in Sychar and instantly knew all about her, though they had never met. There were other times when He chose not to use His omniscience as He submitted to the will of His Father—but He never lost it.

Jesus was sent to redeem a world that hated Him and largely met Him with cold indifference.

As it says in John 1,

He was in the world,
    the world was there through him,
    and yet the world didn't even notice.
He came to his own people,
    but they didn't want him. (verses 10-11, MSG)

He knew rejection throughout His life, culminating in His death on the cross. We all know there was no room for Him in the inn, when He was about to be born, and that became emblematic of the treatment He received while He walked on earth.

There is one telling verse in the gospel of John where it says, "Then they all went home, but Jesus went to the Mount of Olives" (John 7:53–8:1, NIV).

In other words, Jesus had no home to go to. While everyone else went to the comfort of their residences with a roof over their heads and perhaps a fire to keep them warm, Jesus slept outdoors under the cover of night . . . in the weather . . . in the elements. *There was no room for Him in the inn. Was there room for Him anywhere?* It seems the only place where there ever was room for Jesus was on a cross.

Jesus Veiled His Deity but Never Voided It

Coming back to Philippians 2, we read, "Let this mind be in you which was also in Christ Jesus, who, being in the form of God, did not consider it robbery to be equal with God, but made Himself of no reputation, taking the form of a bondservant, and coming in the likeness of men. And being found in appearance as a man, He humbled Himself and became obedient to the point of death, even the death of the cross" (verses 2:5-8).

So, once again, Jesus was God in human form.

When you really stop to think about it, *isn't that incredible?* Can you imagine what it would have been like to be around Him back then? To have God—the eternal, all-powerful, Creator of the universe—in human form, walking among you? Can you imagine what it would have been like to look at His features . . . to hear the timbre of His voice . . . to catch the scent of His nearness?

I've had the opportunity through the years to meet some well-known and even famous people. Sometimes when I actually see them in person they seem much smaller than I expected them to be. And, without the lighting, makeup, photo touch-ups, and all the rest of it, they don't look like the image you had of them in your mind.

Imagine hanging out with Jesus, day in and day out, over an extended period of time—talking with Him, having breakfast with Him, skipping rocks with Him across the water. It seems to me that I would be staring at Him all the time, thinking, *That is God in human form, right there.* What a privilege that would have been!

The apostle John captured a little bit of that experience in his first epistle when he wrote these words:

That which was from the beginning, which we have heard, which we have seen with our eyes, which we have looked upon, and our hands have handled, concerning the Word of life—the life was manifested, and we have seen, and bear witness, and declare to you that eternal life which was with the Father and was manifested to us—that which we have seen and heard we declare to you, that you also may have fellowship with us; and truly our fellowship is with the Father and with His Son Jesus Christ. (1 John 1:1-3)

John was saying, "Hey, we saw Him with our own eyes." That statement also could be translated, "We viewed and contemplated and gazed upon Him as a spectacle." And when he says, "That . . . which we have heard," it means, "His voice is still ringing in our ears!" In other words, "It was like it all happened yesterday, we remember so clearly."

We think to ourselves, *Oh, those lucky people. Why couldn't that have been me?* But here is some good news. After John declares that he had personally seen and heard Jesus, he then says, "We proclaim to you what we ourselves have actually seen and heard so that you may have fellowship with us. And our fellowship is with the Father and with his Son, Jesus Christ" (verse 3, NLT).

Yes, seeing Jesus with physical eyes and hearing Him with natural hearing was a privilege afforded to a comparative handful of people some two thousand years ago. But at the same time, *we can know God today. We can walk with Jesus today.* In fact, there is a special blessing promised to the person who has *not* seen Him with their eyes, yet has believed. After Thomas saw the risen Lord, Jesus said to him, "So, you believe because you've seen with your own eyes. Even better blessings are in store for those who believe without seeing" (John 20:29, MSG).

What amazes me about the New Testament is that there isn't even one physical description of Jesus. In four gospels, it seems like someone could have given us a little idea. His height, maybe? His facial characteristics? His hair? But there isn't one description of Him in the Bible—except, perhaps, for Isaiah's prophecy that "he had no beauty or majesty to attract us to him, nothing in his appearance that we should desire him" (Isaiah 53:2, NIV).

That last verse suggests to me that He was quite ordinary in His appearance—neither strikingly handsome nor especially unattractive. Maybe He was one of those people who just blended into the crowd. When Jesus appeared to Mary after His resurrection, she at first mistook Him for the gardener. The two disciples on the road to Emmaus took Him to be an ordinary pedestrian. When Judas led the mob to betray Jesus, he had to specify, "The one I kiss is the man." Otherwise, they might not have known which person He was!

Most of us have a certain mental image of Jesus—probably cobbled together from old paintings, movies, and pictures we saw in Bible storybooks or Sunday school papers when we were kids. In some of the older paintings, in particular, He is portrayed as weak and anemic.

I can't see that at all. It took real physical strength to be a carpenter in those days. My hunch is that He was really a man's man, tough, rugged, and strong. Remember that He was able, for a time at least, to carry His own cross after being severely beaten and flogged.

Back in the early 1970s, when Mike MacIntosh (now pastor of Horizon Christian Fellowship in San Diego) and I were just starting out in ministry, we went to do some visitation at a mental institution. Back then I had shoulder-length hair and a full-length beard, as did many young men of my generation in those days. Mike, however, was clean-shaven with well-trimmed hair.

As he was attempting to share the gospel with one of the residents, Mike extended an invitation for the man to receive the Lord, saying, "Would you like to personally meet Jesus Christ right now?"

I was just standing there, watching, and not saying anything. Without missing a beat the guy turns to me, shakes my hand, and says, "Jesus, it's good to meet You."

"Buddy," I said, when I regained my composure, "I am *not* Jesus."

Nevertheless, the real Jesus literally did walk the roads of Israel at one time, leaving sandal prints in the dust.

One of the stories from the Gospels underlines the great paradox of Jesus being both God and man at the same time. One day Jesus and His men were crossing over the Sea of Galilee when a fierce storm arose. Jesus, exhausted from the day's work, was sound asleep in the back of the boat. The storm became so intense that the disciples—several of whom were seasoned sailors—began to fear for their very lives. So they woke Jesus up and cried out, "Lord, we are perishing! Do something!"

Immediately, Jesus stood to His feet and called out to the storm, "Peace, be still." And in that instant a complete calm descended.

Now what could be more human than being asleep because you are exhausted from a day's work? And what could be more divine than stopping a raging storm in its tracks? As the disciples said to one another in Matthew 8:27, "Who can this be, that even the winds and the sea obey Him?"

What kind of man?

The God-man.

Jesus experienced the limitations of humanity without the sinful nature. He was a man in a flesh-and-blood body who became tired, sleepy, and hungry. And finally, He died a physical death. When they thrust the spear into His side, real blood and water gushed out. That may have been because the spear pierced the sac of water surrounding His heart. Blood and water would have indicated a complete heart failure.

Jesus also became angry, saving His most scathing words for the religious hypocrites of His day. He drove the money changers out of the temple — twice. He overturned their tables, scattering their coins, and even used a whip on them.

Yes, He experienced anger — righteous indignation. Yet at the same time He was so tender and approachable that little children would run to sit in His lap and play at His feet. (By and large, kids are a pretty good judge of character.)

Jesus knew deep sorrow during His days on earth. He displayed a broad range of human emotions at the death of His close friend, Lazarus. John 11 tells us what happened when He approached His friend's tomb:

> When Jesus saw [Mary] weeping, and the Jews who came with her weeping, He groaned in the spirit and was troubled. And He said, "Where have you laid him?"
>
> They said to Him, "Lord, come and see."
>
> Jesus wept. (verses 33-35)

Why did Jesus weep?

Could it have been because He knew He was about to call His friend back from Paradise to earth, where he would have to die all over again?

I know that we experience deep sorrow when we lose a loved one. But if that individual died in the Lord — trust me when I tell you this and, more to the point, trust God's Word — they are happier than they have ever been. That is the understatement of the century. Why? Because they are in God's presence, experiencing His immediate comfort.

Why did Jesus weep? I think He wept because He was sharing in the sorrow of His friends. It broke His heart to see what sin had done on earth. As He was considering His friend's death, He might well have thought of a billion other deaths through the centuries and into the future. The simple fact is this: Illness, infirmity, and death were never part of God's plan. God's plan was that human beings would live forever in bodies that never would age or wear out. But because our first parents sinned and sin entered into the human race, we have to suffer the indignities and sorrows of disease, the aging process, and, ultimately, death.

When I read a passage like John 11, it's a good reminder that Jesus has walked in my shoes. He has felt human sorrow and knows what it's like to see a loved one die.

No matter what you have faced, no matter what you are experiencing in your life right now, Jesus has been there. Therefore, as it says in Hebrews 4:16, "Let us then approach God's throne of grace with confidence, so that we may receive mercy and find grace to help us in our time of need" (NIV).

Jesus Experienced Temptation

As a human being, Jesus personally felt the pressure and presence of temptation. Because He experienced these things, He is able to bring encouragement and help to us when we are wrestling with all kinds of temptations.

Hebrews 2:17–18 expresses that truth with these words: "Therefore, it was necessary for him to be made in every respect like us, his brothers and sisters, so that he could be our merciful and faithful High Priest before God. Then he could offer a sacrifice that would take away the sins of the people. Since he himself has gone through suffering and testing, he is able to help us when we are being tested" (NLT).

One of those temptations took place in the wilderness, when Satan made this offer:

Then the devil, taking Him up on a high mountain, showed Him all the kingdoms of the world in a moment

of time. And the devil said to Him, "All this authority I
will give You, and their glory; for this has been delivered to
me, and I give it to whomever I wish. Therefore, if You
will worship before me, all will be Yours." (Luke 4:5–7)

Why would Satan offer something like that? The Bible says
the devil showed Jesus all the kingdoms of the world "in a
moment of time." That makes me wonder if He showed Jesus
all the kingdoms past, present, and future. I wonder if Satan
showed Jesus Rome in its glory, Athens in its prime, and even
flyovers of Los Angeles, New York City, Paris, and Rio de
Janeiro.

Satan was saying, "You can have it all, Jesus. You can have it
right now with no pain, no suffering, no cross. Just bow down
and worship me, and it's all Yours."

Jesus replied to the tempter in the same way that we should
respond to him: with the Word of God.

Jesus answered and said to him, "Get behind Me, Satan!
For it is written, 'You shall worship the LORD your God,
and Him only you shall serve.'" (Luke 4:8)

The truth is, our fate, our eternal destiny, rested on that
moment as well.

If Jesus had succumbed to the temptation to bypass the cross,
there would have been no forgiveness, no salvation, and no
hope of heaven for you and me. But Jesus never wavered from
His goal. As the book of Isaiah prophesied, Jesus set His face
like a flint, keeping His eyes on the prize of bringing salvation
and opening the door of heaven to you and me.[3] Shortly before
His death, Jesus said, "I have a terrible baptism of suffering
ahead of me, and I am under a heavy burden until it is accomplished" (Luke 12:50, NLT).

Through all His days on earth, Jesus lived under the shadow
of the cross. He knew why He had come and what He had to

face. No wonder Scripture called Him a "Man of sorrows" (Isaiah 53:3).

But He also had great joy, knowing that when He cried out on the cross, "It is finished!" that He had purchased our forgiveness and our eternal salvation with His own blood.

Each one of us must decide what we will do with that invitation, with that priceless gift.

In Revelation 3:20, Jesus said, "Behold, I stand at the door and knock. If anyone hears My voice and opens the door, I will come in to him and dine with him, and he with Me."

Receiving the gift of a new life in Jesus is as simple as opening a door.

Part 2

faith and salvation

Why Did Jesus Suffer?

Why did our Lord come to this earth? Why was He born in a stable in Bethlehem? Why did Jesus walk this planet, breathe our air, tread our dusty back roads, and experience life here?

Some would say, "He came to earth to become the greatest teacher in history."

There's no question that Jesus was the greatest teacher who ever lived. The words He spoke and the stories He told are repeated in every corner of our world, even after two thousand years. But that's not the primary reason He came.

Others would say, "He came to give us an example of how to live life at its highest level."

It's true, Jesus certainly was the ultimate example of life at its highest and best. But that is not the primary reason He came.

Someone else might say, "He came to do miracles and heal people."

Yes, He did that, touching many, many lives. But again, that is not the primary reason He came.

Jesus came to buy back the title deed to Earth. He came

to die on a cross for our sins. The Bible says in Hebrews 2:9 "that He, by the grace of God, might taste death for everyone." As our Lord Himself said, He came "to give his life as a ransom for many."[1] That word *ransom* conveys the idea of offering yourself in the place of another. Stating it another way, we could say, Jesus was born to die . . . that we might live.

The birth of Jesus was for the purpose of the death of Jesus.

One of the wise men had it right when he brought the insightful gift of myrrh to the Christ child. Myrrh—an embalming element. That is why Jesus came. The cross was Jesus' goal and destination from the very beginning. He warned His disciples it was coming and described it in detail. Somehow, that whole discussion sailed right over their heads, until it actually happened.

The Day Jesus Died

On the night before He died, in an olive grove in the Garden of Gethsemane, Jesus came under intense, indescribable inward pressure. I don't think any of us can begin to grasp what our Lord endured in those dark hours. Dr. Luke tells us that "His sweat became like great drops of blood falling down to the ground" (Luke 22:44).

Some medical experts have suggested that this may have been hematidrosis, a condition characterized by a unique mixture of sweat and blood when someone comes under the greatest imaginable pressure.

Entering the garden that night, Jesus had said to His three closest disciples, "My soul is exceedingly sorrowful, even to death. Stay here and watch with Me" (Matthew 26:38).

That phrase *exceedingly sorrowful* could be translated, "He was in terrified amazement." In other words, in the face of the dreadful prospect of bearing God's fury against sin, Jesus was in the very grip of terror. Peter, James, and John had often seen their Master pray, of course. But never like this! They watched as He went to His knees, and then to His face, crying out, "My Father, if it is possible, let this cup pass from Me; nevertheless, not as I will, but as You will" (Matthew 26:39).

He didn't say these words quietly. He cried aloud in prayer. Over in Hebrews 5:7, we are told, "During the days of Jesus' life on earth, he offered up prayers and petitions with fervent cries and tears to the one who could save him from death" (NIV).

Jesus knew exactly what was coming. He knew Judas Iscariot was at that moment approaching with the temple guard. He knew He would appear before Annas, Caiaphas, Pilate, Herod, and then back again to Pilate. He knew His tormentors would punch Him in the face and tear out His beard. He knew they would rip His back open with a Roman cat-o'-nine-tails. He knew they would nail Him to a cross.

But something else loomed ahead that was worse than even these horrors.

He knew He would soon have to bear the sin of the entire world for all time. *That* is why He prayed, "Father, if it is possible, let this cup pass from Me."

The Cup of God's Wrath

What cup? The cup of God's white-hot wrath, the cup of God's judgment, which rightly belonged to each and every one of us. Isaiah called it the "cup of [His] fury,"[2] and Jesus had to drink it down to the dregs.

Have you ever eaten something so disgusting that it turned your stomach? Try, then, to imagine looking into *this* cup and all it represented. Imagine contemplating the horrors of bearing all of that sin.

Kent Hughes wrote, "In the greatest display of obedience that will ever be known, Jesus took the full chalice of man's sin and God's wrath, looked, shuddering, deep into its depth, and in a steel act of His will, drank it all!"[3]

Interestingly, when Judas approached Him in the garden with

a kiss of betrayal, Jesus said, "Friend, why have you come?"

Some friend!

That would have been about the last thing I would have said to Judas. I might have said, "You dog! If I'm going down, you're going down with me. Do you understand what I'm saying to you, you filthy betrayer? And after all the time I spent with you, being your friend!"

But that's not what Jesus said or did. He reached out to him in one last act of mercy. I believe it was an opportunity—even then—for Judas to repent. But his heart was too hard at that point, and he missed his opportunity forever.

So Jesus was taken away and hauled to appear before Annas, Caiaphas, and ultimately before the Roman governor, Pontius Pilate.

Pilate was a powerful man, and a hard man. He didn't like to be trifled with. Apparently, he was also a political appointee in quite a bit of hot water. According to some historical accounts, he'd already had a number of run-ins with the Jewish religious leaders and didn't need another major conflict getting back to the authorities in Rome.

Right from the start, it was clear to Pilate what these Jewish leaders wanted: the execution of Jesus Christ. But he didn't want any part of it. He had effectively given them permission to do it themselves, saying, "You take Him and judge Him according to your law." That was another way of saying, "If you guys want to go stone Him to death somewhere, have at it. Just take the responsibility away from *me*."

Those leaders, however, wanted a crucifixion—and nothing less.

In one last-ditch effort to appease the bloodthirsty crowds, Pilate had Jesus scourged. As you may know, this wasn't done with a common whip, but with a Roman cat-o'-nine-tails. This ghastly implement of torture had a wooden base with multiple strands of leather embedded with pieces of metal and glass. Every lash of this whip would rip into the skin, opening up blood vessels and even exposing vital organs. Many men did not survive the scourging. Jesus took the full thirty-nine lashes, and then Pilate paraded Him out before the crowd, looking, perhaps, for a little mercy. "Behold the Man!" he said.

The crowd, however, wouldn't be satisfied. They still cried out, "Crucify Him!" So in the end, after going through a futile show of washing his hands and declaring himself innocent, Pilate gave the command for Jesus to be taken away.

Then they crucified Him, and divided His garments, casting lots, that it might be fulfilled which was spoken by the prophet:

"They divided My garments among them,
And for My clothing they cast lots."

Sitting down, they kept watch over Him there. And they put up over His head the accusation written against Him:

THIS IS JESUS THE KING OF THE JEWS.

Then two robbers were crucified with Him, one on the right and another on the left.

And those who passed by blasphemed Him, wagging their heads and saying, "You who destroy the temple and build it in three days, save Yourself! If You are the Son of God, come down from the cross."

Likewise the chief priests also, mocking with the scribes and elders, said, "He saved others; Himself He cannot save. If He is the King of Israel, let Him now come down from the cross, and we will believe Him. He trusted in God; let Him deliver Him now if He will have Him; for He said, 'I am the Son of God.'"

Even the robbers who were crucified with Him reviled
Him with the same thing.

Now from the sixth hour until the ninth hour there was
darkness over all the land. And about the ninth hour Jesus
cried out with a loud voice, saying, "Eli, Eli, lama sabachthani?" that is, "My God, My God, why have You
forsaken Me?" (Matthew 27:35-46)

No details or explanation are given about crucifixion because
it was far too common in that day. The Romans had viciously
and routinely crucified thousands and thousands of people. It
had become their favorite method of execution throughout the
empire and especially in Judea. It was usually reserved for riot-
ers and insurrectionists—those who specifically wanted to overthrow Rome.

According to the historian Josephus, after the death of Herod
the Great the Roman governor of Syria crucified two thousand
men to quell an uprising. That same historian also tells us that
the Roman general Titus crucified so many people when he
sacked Jerusalem in AD 70 that the soldiers ran out of wood for
crosses—and room to set them up.

Crosses with dead or dying men was a common sight in
Israel. When Matthew simply says, "Then they crucified Him"
(27:35), everybody knew what that meant.

Even so, as Jesus hung there on that instrument of death and
shame, He was fulfilling the very plan and purpose of God.
Scripture had specifically prophesied that not only would the
Messiah die, but that He would die on a cross—even though
crucifixion hadn't even been invented when the Old Testament
prophesies were penned.

Zechariah 13:6 says, "And one shall say unto him, What are
these wounds in thine hands? Then he shall answer, Those with
which I was wounded in the house of my friends" (KJV).

Isaiah 53 is such a vivid description of the Crucifixion that you would think the prophet was an eyewitness. And then there are those famous words in Psalm 22, written a thousand years before the first crucifixion ever took place: "They pierced My hands and My feet" (verse 16).

But this was not just any man being crucified; this was God in human form. This wasn't a man being taken and nailed to a cross against his will; this was the God-man, who willingly went. With one word to the Father, He could have been delivered from that awful death. But if He had done that, if He had chosen to save Himself, He could not have saved you and me. But because He chose to lose Himself, to die in our place, all of us can now be saved from our sins as a result.

Seven Final Words

Death by crucifixion is essentially death by suffocation. It is not the loss of blood that kills the man; it is the inability to breathe. There was a little base placed at the bottom of the cross—a footrest, if you will. By pushing himself up on the footrest with his feet, a crucified person could get air into his lungs.

That's what Jesus had to do in order to make seven statements from the cross. His first statement was, "Father, forgive them, for they do not know what they do" (Luke 23:34).

In Matthew's gospel, we read that the two criminals, crucified on either side of Jesus, joined in the chorus of mockery by the onlookers, until Jesus made that "Father, forgive them" statement.

Right then and there, one of those dying felons placed his faith in Jesus and said, "Lord, remember me when You come into Your kingdom." In response to that plea, Jesus made His second statement from the cross: "Assuredly, I say to you, today you will be with Me in Paradise" (Luke 23: 42-43).

Looking down at the foot of the cross, Jesus saw Mary, the woman who had bore Him, nursed Him, and loved Him, with the apostle John standing next to her. He said to her, "Woman, behold your son" (John 19:26). And then, no doubt nodding to

John, He said, "Behold your mother" (verse 27). With those words, Jesus effectively entrusted the care of His mother to John.

After this, a mysterious darkness fell over the earth for three long hours. Those of us living in Southern California remember the rolling blackouts, when power went off in entire communities. In seconds it would be pitch-dark and seemed very eerie to those of us who were accustomed to seeing the glow of the city.

But the blackout at the cross was at three in the afternoon, with the sun still in the sky. Suddenly it became dark as night, with no light anywhere. And then that eerie darkness was pierced by the voice of Jesus, crying out from the cross, *"Eli, Eli, lama sabachthani?"* or, "My God, My God, why have You forsaken Me?"

At that very moment, I believe that Jesus was bearing the sins of the world; He was dying as a substitute for others. The guilt of our sins and the punishment we deserved fell on Him.

In some mysterious way that we can never fully comprehend, during those awful hours on the cross, the Father was pouring out the full measure of His wrath against sin, and the recipient of that wrath was God's own, much-loved Son. God was punishing Jesus as though He had personally committed every wicked deed ever committed by every wicked sinner for all time. Because of what happened in those moments, God can now forgive us and treat us as though we had lived Christ's perfect life of righteousness. This is what we call justification. It is not merely the removal of sin, amazing as that might be. It is the imputing of the righteousness of Christ into our spiritual bank account.

Scripture clearly teaches that there was a moment when the sin of the world was placed on the Son. Paul wrote in 2 Corinthians 5:21, "For God made Christ, who never sinned, to be the offering for our sin, so that we could be made right with God through Christ" (NLT). Peter wrote, "[He] Himself bore our sins in His own body on the tree" (1 Peter 2:24).

When Jesus cried out, "My God, My God, why have You

forsaken Me?" was it a crisis of faith in His life?

No, it was a declaration of fact.

Jesus was forsaken so that you and I don't have to be. Jesus entered utter darkness so that you and I could walk in the light. Jesus was forsaken so that we might be forgiven.

Here is what we are saying: As the sin of the world was placed on Christ, the Father, who is holy and cannot look at sin, turned away as Jesus became the recipient of His wrath. But because this happened, anyone who cries out to God for mercy in Jesus' name will be received and never forsaken.

Crying Out to God

In the greatest crisis of His earthly life, Jesus cried out, "My God, My God, why have You forsaken Me?"

It was a cry of desolation and great anguish. But Jesus did cry out to His Father, acknowledging Him as "*My* God." The emphasis wasn't on the word *forsaken*. The emphasis was on "My God." He called out to His Father as He bore the sin of the world.

To whom will you cry out when a serious crisis hits your life? What will your cry be? What will happen if tragedy comes to your home? Will you call out to God, or will you close Him out of your mind and heart?

It has been said that character is not made in crisis; it is revealed. In other words, hardships show who you really are. You can say, "I am so angry at God that I will never speak to Him again." Or, you can cry out to Him in your pain and perplexity. You might even say, "Lord, I don't get this. It makes no sense to me at all. I don't like any part of it. Even so, I am looking to You God . . . *my* God."

After this we know that He said, "I thirst," which was the first mention of His physical situation. Why did He say it at this point? Because His task was almost finished. He had borne the sin of the world, and then, as a man whose body was literally hanging in shreds, He responded to the pain and the raging thirst.

This just reminds us that Jesus not only died, but He suffered. Maybe we could understand why Jesus died as a sacrifice for our sins. But why did He have to suffer such agony in the process?

Here's part of the answer: So that we will know beyond all doubt that we serve a God who understands what we're going through here on earth. John W. Stott wrote, "Our God is a suffering God." And I think he is right.

Listen to Isaiah's description of what Jesus, the Son of God, went through at Calvary:

> He was despised and rejected—
>   a man of sorrows, acquainted with deepest grief.
> We turned our backs on him and looked the other way.
>   He was despised, and we did not care.
> Yet it was our weaknesses he carried;
>   it was our sorrows that weighed him down.
> And we thought his troubles were a punishment from God,
>   a punishment for his own sins!
> But he was pierced for our rebellion,
>   crushed for our sins. (53:3-5, NLT)

He suffered because of us. He suffered for the love of us.

If you are suffering today, you need to know that you do not suffer alone. Maybe you feel like you are the only person who has to endure your pain or sorrow. Jesus, however, was called a "Man of sorrows" and is "acquainted with grief." No matter how great your difficulty or need, know that He understands. As the apostle Peter reminded us, "Cast all your anxiety on him because he cares for you" (1 Peter 5:7, NIV).

Is your body wracked with pain? So was His.

Have ever been misunderstood, misjudged, or misrepresented? So was He.

Have you ever had those who are nearest and dearest to you

turn away? So has He.

So why did Jesus have to suffer and die? In the following paragraphs, I offer four brief answers to that question . . . although I know that many more reasons could be given.

Why Did He Have to Suffer and Die?

To show God's love for us.

Jesus said, "For God so loved the world that He gave His only begotten Son." Paul said in Ephesians, "Christ also loved the church and gave Himself for her." Paul also said that He "loved me and gave Himself for me."[4] It is a demonstration of love.

If you are ever tempted to doubt God's love, take a long look at the cross of Calvary because that is where you will see God's love on display.

To absorb the wrath of God.

I have broken God's commandments and fallen short of God's standards. Because I have offended a holy God, there was a judgment that had to be meted out. The Bible clearly says, "The soul who sins shall die" (Ezekiel 18:20). So who is going to pay that price? Jesus essentially said, "I will. I will absorb the judgment and wrath of God in your place." And that is exactly what happened.

If God were not just, there would be no *demand* for His Son to suffer and die. If God were not loving, there would be no *willingness* for His Son to suffer and die. But God is just and willing. And because God's love was willing to meet the demands of His own justice, Jesus took the full impact of that judgment on Himself, in our place.

To cancel the legal demands against us and disarm the devil.

We have all broken some or all of the Ten Commandments. The Bible tells us that if we offend in one point of the law, we are as guilty as if we had offended in all of it (see James 2:10). This shows the utter absurdity of the claim, "I don't really need Jesus Christ because I live by the Ten Commandments." No, you don't! You do not live by the Ten Commandments, and the fact that you have broken them means that you deserve God's judgment. But Jesus died to cancel the legal demands against us and disarm the evil one, the enemy of our souls. Colossians 2:14-15 tells us that "He canceled the record of the charges against us and took it away by nailing it to the cross. In this way, he disarmed the spiritual rulers and authorities. He shamed them publicly by his victory over them on the cross" (NLT).

So here is what it comes down to: Not only did He cancel the legal demands against us, but He disarmed the devil. The devil says, "You are mine. I will do what I want to do in your life, and you never will be free. You always will be bound by these addictions. You always will be trapped in this lifestyle. You always will do the same stupid things again and again."

Here is what you can say in reply: "Satan, you are a liar. What you are saying is not true, because Jesus died in my place on the cross and dealt a decisive blow against you."

Yes, the devil may be powerful.

But Jesus is infinitely more powerful.

As the apostle John put it, "The one who is in you is greater than the one who is in the world" (1 John 4:4, NIV). In other words, the power of Christ cancels out the power of Satan. If you want to be free from that addiction, free from that sin, free from whatever it is that holds you down, you can be if you *choose* to be—if you will take hold of what Jesus purchased for you at the cross of Calvary.

To provide our forgiveness and justification.

We are told in Romans 5:9 that we have "been justified by His blood." To be justified means you have been forgiven of the wrongs you have done. But as I pointed out earlier, it also means that God has placed the righteousness of Jesus Christ into your spiritual bank account. As a result, you don't ever need to say, "I'm not worthy to pray to God" or "I'm not worthy to attend church."

In one sense, you're right. You *aren't* worthy. But you never were. Sometimes we will think to ourselves, *I've done pretty well this week. I read the Bible, prayed a little, and didn't sin as much as I usually do.* Well, that's good if you've had that kind of week. But even on your *best* week, your *best* day, you still fell short. Your approach to God never has had anything to do with your worthiness. It has everything to do with what Jesus has done for you.

Because of the Cross, we have instant access into His presence. There is nothing, ever, that should keep you from calling on Christ and placing your trust in Him.

6

What Is Faith?

W hat exactly is this thing that we call faith? What does it mean when the Bible says we should have faith in God?

I like to define it like this: *Faith is belief plus action.*

This is what we do when we initially come to Jesus Christ. We act on something we have accepted as true. The Bible says, "For it is by grace you have been saved, through faith—and this is not from yourselves; it is the gift of God— not by works, so that no one can boast" (Ephesians 2:8-9, NIV).

I've heard some people say, "I can't have faith. I'm a practical person. I believe in science and need to *know* something is true before I can believe it."

But that's not really true, is it?

You and I apply faith every single day of our lives.

When you order a meal at a restaurant and eat what they bring you, that is faith! When it comes right down to it, you really don't know what's in that sandwich or in that gravy. You don't know whether that is what you ordered. Unless you're one of those paranoid people who walk back into the restaurant kitchen to check things out before they dine, you're not sure of the sanitary conditions where the food was prepared. You don't know!

You apply faith when you pick up your prescription at the pharmacy. You *assume* those little pills the pharmacist gave you are the actual ones you ordered and not a placebo, the wrong dosage, or even the wrong medication. You trust your life to that pharmacist, and that, too, is faith.

When you submit to surgery, go under anesthesia and allow the surgeon to work on you, that is complete faith in those professionals.

How about when you board a 747 and taxi down the runway? Do you understand aerodynamics? Most of us don't. We just take it by faith that the massive jet with all that fuel and weight will somehow lift itself off the ground and soar up to thirty thousand feet. And we also take it by faith that the pilots have had enough sleep, aren't distracted, and haven't been drinking.

My point is simply this: You apply faith each and every day, in a thousand ways. We couldn't really live and function other-wise and remain sane. Do you have a mechanic check out your car before you get behind the wheel every morning? Do you examine the structural reliability of a chair before you place your weight on it?

No, you don't.

You acknowledge, at least to that degree, that you have to live by faith.

Why is it so hard, then, to place faith in the living God? You can put faith in a waiter, pharmacist, surgeon, and pilot, and you won't put faith in God Almighty?

Why is it so amazing that someone would put their faith in the all-knowing, all-powerful, everywhere-present Creator of the universe? Faith is the means by which the infirmity of man takes hold of the infinity of God, where the weakness of man taps into the unlimited resources of God.

Now some would say to us, "Faith is a force. You must harness it and speak things into existence."

No, that is not what the Bible teaches.

A. W. Tozer wrote, "Faith in faith is faith astray."[1] We don't put our faith in *faith*; we put our faith in God Himself.

What Is Faith?

The Bible defines faith this way in Hebrews 11:1: "Faith is the substance of things hoped for, the evidence of things not seen."

Wuest's Expanded Translation of the Greek New Testament puts it this way: "Now faith is the title deed of things hoped for. It is the proof of things that are not yet seen."

The New Living Translation renders the passage, "Faith is the confidence that what we hope for will actually happen; it gives us assurance about things we cannot see."

The Message paraphrases the passage with these words: "Faith . . . is the firm foundation under everything that makes life worth living. It's our handle on what we can't see."

We know from the stories of the early church how many courageous men and women, and even children, were martyred for their faith. The accounts tell us that even as they were being executed—burned alive or fed to wild animals—they called on the Lord to forgive the people who were killing them. There are many accounts of the persecutors coming to faith in Christ after witnessing the faith of those believers as they went into God's presence.

In Acts 16, we read of Paul and Silas enduring a brutal beating, being thrown into a dungeon, and then singing praises to God at midnight. Before the night was over, the jailer and his whole family had come to faith in Christ. That wasn't a result of mind over matter; it was *faith over circumstances*. The two missionaries had no guarantee they would ever get out of that prison alive. But because of their faith in God, they were able to see things in perspective and even find reason to be joyful in the bleakest of circumstances.

How Does Faith Come?

In one sense, everyone has a little faith. The Bible even says, "God has dealt to each one a measure of faith" (Romans 12:3).

But how does faith *develop*?

Faith develops by listening to, studying, and immersing yourself in the Word of God. Romans 10:17 clearly tells us, "So then faith comes by hearing, and hearing by the word of God."

So you made a decision today to read a Bible-based book about the essentials of your faith, or you went to church last Sunday to hear what God's Word has to say. Those decisions will strengthen and build up your faith.

It isn't, however, logging so many minutes in church or turning the pages of your Bible that will increase your faith; it is truly *listening* to what God has to say to you. You need to pay attention. That is why Jesus said, "He who has ears to hear, let him hear!" (Luke 8:8). It's another way of saying, "Listen up!" It is attention with intention. If we truly hear the Word of God, our faith will grow.

Hearing God's Word also will enable us to put everything else in life in its proper perspective. When we read Scripture, we see God for who He is—which helps us to see life and all its challenges for what they are. Paul says of the study of Scripture that it "is useful to teach us what is true and to make us realize what is wrong in our lives; it straightens us out and helps us do what is right. It is God's way of making us well prepared at every point, fully equipped to do good to everyone."[2]

Having said that, faith also is developed by use. Hearing the Word of God bolsters my faith, and using it further strengthens my faith. Some of us treat faith as though it were a fragile little egg made of priceless crystal: "Oh . . . be careful with my faith! Don't bump it. Don't jostle it. Don't drop it. Put it where it will be safe!"

No, that is not the character of faith. Faith is tough, resilient, and gets stronger — like a muscle — through constant use.

Here in Southern California, quite a number of people drive four-wheel-drive vehicles, though I'm not really sure why. You see them on the freeways all the time with those gleaming, big lights, a powerful winch on the front, and the huge, knobby, gnarly tires.

"Hey, that's a great rig," you might say to one of those drivers. "Where do you go four-wheeling?"

And he probably would reply, "I don't go four-wheeling."

"So where are you headed now?"

"To the car wash."

"So, you never take it up to the mountains or power up some hillside or something?"

"Are you kidding me? Do you know how much money I have invested in this thing? I don't want to tear it up on some back road in the middle of nowhere!"

So they maintain an expensive vehicle that was made for tackling dirt roads and rough terrain, but they never use it that way. They keep it gleaming, as though they had just driven it off the showroom floor.

That's how many people are with faith. They talk about it. They listen to messages about it. They sing about it. They study the word *faith* in Hebrew and Greek. But they never actually *use* their faith. They never put it to the kind of work it was made for.

Real faith, however, is the consent of the will to the assent of the understanding. Faith always has in it the idea of action. It is movement toward its object. Faith is a restless, living thing and cannot remain inoperative.

Faith *moves*.

Faith *acts*.

Faith *does*.

C. H. Spurgeon said, "Believing and obeying always go side by side."

Faith Can Make All the Difference

Faith can make all the difference between something happening and not happening.

Our God is sovereign; He can do whatever He wants whenever He wants with whomever He wants. He doesn't need our opinion, our approval, or our vote of confidence; He just does it.

But here is the interesting thing: This sovereign God whom we worship and follow has chosen to primarily accomplish His purposes through fallible human instruments. Now if I were God, I would not have made that choice. If I were God, I would never use failing, unreliable people like you and me to accomplish my purposes. I would just do it myself. Why mess around with humanity? They're only going to make a mess of things.

Nevertheless, God has primarily chosen to do His work on this planet through people.

When God wanted to part the Red Sea, He certainly didn't need Moses to hold up his staff, did He? No, God was doing the work. Even so, the Lord had said, "Okay, Moses, you go out there and stand in front of the Red Sea and hold up that staff of yours, believing that I'm going to work." So Moses obeyed and the sea parted, with a path right through the middle of it.

God didn't need Elijah to pray for fire to fall from heaven and burn up the sacrifice on the altar atop Mount Carmel. God didn't need Noah to build an ark. In the blink of an eye, He could have created His own ocean-going craft for the animals and Noah and his family. In each case, however, the Lord chose to work through human instruments to accomplish His purposes.

In the New Testament, it's interesting to note that Jesus did not heal everyone. Most people weren't raised from the dead or healed from their infirmities. The ones who called out to Him, however, were touched and healed by His power.

I think of blind Bartimaeus, sitting along the Jericho road, who heard that Jesus was coming his way. When the Lord came near, Bartimaeus called out, "Jesus, Son of David, have mercy on me!"

Someone basically told him, "Hey, knock it off! Don't yell so loudly. You're drawing undue attention to yourself."

Really? And then Bartimaeus yelled and screamed with all his might, "Son of David, have mercy on me!"

And what happened? Jesus heard the blind man's cry, stopped, and went over to him and touched him. Bartimaeus was healed that day.[3]

Not everyone in the New Testament was as vocal about it as Bartimaeus, but others were just as persistent. Think of the desperate woman with a medical condition that resulted in constant bleeding. She had spent all of her money on doctors, and nothing had come of it. In fact, she was only becoming worse. And then she saw Jesus walking through a crowded marketplace one day and said to herself, "If only I may touch His clothes, I shall be made well." Armed with that faith, she got up close to Him, reached through the crowd, and just brushed the tip of her finger across the edge of His robe.

In a heartbeat she was healed.

In the same moment Jesus came to a complete standstill and said, "Who touched Me?"

"Who touched You? Seriously? Who *didn't* touch You? Everybody has been touching You on all sides!"

"No . . . someone touched Me. I have perceived that power has gone out of Me."

At that, the crowd probably parted, and there was the lady—frightened, but joyful too. She was afraid that Jesus was going to rebuke her for what she had done, but instead He commended her for her active faith.[4]

God responds to faith.

Remember, the gospel of Matthew tells us that when Jesus came to His own hometown, "He did not do many mighty works there because of their unbelief" (13:58).

Unbelief hinders the work of God. Faith unleashes it.

And we build our faith on what the Word of God says.

Remember the story of Peter walking on water? Here's how it reads in the gospel of Matthew:

Immediately after this, Jesus insisted that his disciples get back into the boat and cross to the other side of the lake, while he sent the people home. After sending them home, he went up into the hills by himself to pray. Night fell while he was there alone.

Meanwhile, the disciples were in trouble far away from land, for a strong wind had risen, and they were fighting heavy waves. About three o'clock in the morning Jesus came toward them, walking on the water. When the disciples saw him walking on the water, they were terrified. In their fear, they cried out, "It's a ghost!"

But Jesus spoke to them at once. "Don't be afraid," he said. "Take courage. I am here!"

Then Peter called to him, "Lord, if it's really you, tell me to come to you, walking on the water."

"Yes, come," Jesus said.

So Peter went over the side of the boat and walked on the water toward Jesus. But when he saw the strong wind and the waves, he was terrified and began to sink. "Save me, Lord!" he shouted.

Jesus immediately reached out and grabbed him. "You have so little faith," Jesus said. "Why did you doubt me?" (14:22-31, NLT)

How many times have we heard Peter used as an example of doubt and lack of faith? But let's give the man some credit. Climbing out of that boat at night in a howling storm was an amazing act of faith. This is what we would describe as muscular faith, or believing faith.

Yes, Jesus had told Peter to come, but it took faith on Peter's part to do it. These were crazy circumstances, and Peter had never been in a situation like that in his whole life. He had floated on water, swam in water, fished in water, and sank in water, but he had never even dreamed of *walking* on water. Faith, however, is the refusal to panic, even in fearful situations. Faith has no backup door, no safety net.

Peter didn't have a life jacket on, and he wasn't wearing water wings. No, this was a sink-or-walk situation. But Peter had his eyes on Jesus and just went for it, literally doing the impossible. But notice that he wasn't acting presumptuously here. He waited for a command from Christ.

> Then Peter called to him, "Lord, if it's really you, tell me to come to you, walking on the water."
> "Yes, come," Jesus said. (verses 28-29, NLT)

This is my point: We build our faith on what the Word of God says. We don't just start making wild claims: "By faith I want this. By faith I demand that." No, we say, "What does Scripture teach? What should I be praying for? What should I be asking for?" And we pray accordingly. That is exactly what Peter did.

As long as he kept his eyes on the Lord, he was able to do the impossible. The moment he took his eyes off Jesus, he began to sink.

Years ago my youngest son Jonathan wanted to learn how to scuba dive. We were in Hawaii at the time, and we went over to a place that will teach you how to do this in a day. They don't certify you to dive on your own, but they teach you the basics so that you can go down twenty or thirty feet, with an instructor right by your side.

The instructor asked me, "Would you like to go through the training with him?"

"No," I said, "I'm already certified. Just train him, and when we go out for the dive, I'll go along." So Jonathan went through the training, and the plan was to go out the next morning for a dive.

When morning came, the water was rough and the waves were pitching. I thought to myself, *Oh man, this is not great weather for diving.* I thought about canceling, but then decided, *No, we'll go for it.*

We climbed into the boat, loaded down with all our gear. I had forgotten how much gear you had to wear! You've got your inflatable vest, your weight belt that pulls you to the bottom, your very heavy tanks, your mask, your flippers. And the way you get in the water is to fall backward off the boat.

With a hundred pounds of gear on, going over backward doesn't feel natural at all. And it's not what you *feel* like doing at all. So we got into the water, not quite under, but with the waves breaking over our heads. I was getting a little panicked and glanced over at Jonathan, who was *totally* panicked. I could see it in his eyes, but I looked away. I didn't want him to see that I was as frightened as he was.

The instructor handled it so well. He said, "Jonathan look at me. *Look at me now.*" Jonathan looked at him. Then the instructor said, "Remember your training. Remember what I told you."

Immediately, Jonathan calmed down. Then the instructor had us put our regulators in, and we began to breathe. Shortly after that, we slipped below the surface, where everything was calm and serene, with beautiful tropical fish darting by.

That's pretty much what Jesus was saying to Peter that stormy night. "All right, Peter, step out. Look at Me. Keep looking at Me. Keep your eyes on Me, and you will be fine."

Peter was thinking, *Oh yeah, this is good, this is good, this is . . . CRAZY! What in the world am I doing? Oh no, I'm going to sink! Is that a great white shark over there? Help! I'm in trouble!*

He took his eyes off the Instructor. He stopped listening to the Instructor's voice. He saw the waves churning beneath his feet, lost his nerve, and began to sink.

Have you ever done that? Have you ever stepped out in faith and lost your nerve, right in the middle of some scary venture for the Lord?

You have?

Well, welcome to the club.

Our fear and inconsistent faith are no great news to God. I like what it says in Psalm 103, where we are told:

As a father has compassion on his children,
  so the LORD has compassion on those who fear him;
for he knows how we are formed,
  he remembers that we are dust. (verses 13-14, NIV)

We all have those moments when we feel unsure, unstable, and afraid. What should you do when you have a lapse of faith?

Call Out to Jesus

When he saw the strong wind and the waves, he was terrified and began to sink. "Save me, Lord!" he shouted.
  Jesus immediately reached out and grabbed him. "You have so little faith," Jesus said. "Why did you doubt me?" (Matthew 14:30-31, NLT)

Notice for a moment what the text *doesn't* say. It doesn't say, "Peter called out to the Lord, and Jesus replied, 'Hey, you made your own bed, now sleep in it! This is all your fault!'"

No, Jesus immediately reached out His hand and caught His man.

In the New King James Version, Jesus says, "O you of little faith, why did you doubt?"

Those two words *little faith* are one word in the original Greek. *Littlefaith.* I think Jesus was almost using a term of affection here, almost like a nickname. "O Littlefaith . . . why did you doubt?" In other words, "Come on, man. You were doing so well. Why did you doubt?"

Verse 32 says, "And when they got into the boat, the wind

ceased." *They* got into the boat. Jesus lifted Peter up and walked with him—on the water—back to the place of safety. Apparently, the storm didn't stop until they reached the boat. The wind and the waves were still raging. But Peter had his focus back, and with his eyes on Jesus, he was once again able to do the impossible.

Here's the bottom line: We should never doubt our beliefs or believe our doubts. Peter started out with faith, had a lapse, and then got it back again. Yes, he failed. But it was a spectacular failure, wasn't it? If you are going to fail, this is the way to do it!

Have you ever tried to do something for God and had your efforts fail?

There is no disgrace in that.

I would rather try and fail than never try at all. In fact, most of us learn lessons through our so-called failures that we would not learn otherwise. Sometimes, achieving success is just the process of elimination. You say, "Okay, next time I'm not going to try A, B, C, or D because I tried those, and they don't work."

It has been said that the doorway to success is often entered through the hallway of failure. Maybe you attempted something for God, and it didn't go all that well. I remember when a guy came up to me who was really nauseated. He said, "Oh, Greg, I'm so sick. Pray for me."

So I prayed for him, and immediately after that he threw up. He said to me, "Don't ever pray for me again." But guess what? I still pray for people who are ill, and sometimes God chooses to heal those people.

Maybe you tried to start a Bible study and no one showed up. Maybe you tried to engage someone with the gospel and they blew you off. You said to yourself, *I'm such a failure*. It's true that you might not have done it as well as you wish you had. But what did you learn through the experience?

Keep trying. Keep reaching. Keep taking steps of faith. Because as you do this, you will see God work in and through your life.

I think the apostle Paul had the best perspective of all:

I don't mean to say I am perfect. I haven't learned all I
should even yet, but I keep working toward that day when
I will finally be all that Christ saved me for and wants me
to be.

No, dear brothers, I am still not all I should be, but I
am bringing all my energies to bear on this one thing:
Forgetting the past and looking forward to what lies ahead,
I strain to reach the end of the race and receive the prize
for which God is calling us up to heaven because of what
Christ Jesus did for us. (Philippians 3:12-14, TLB)

7

What Is Salvation?

A reporter did some research for a *USA Today* article about people who had won the lottery but, for whatever reason, had never collected their prizes. In other words, they bought winning tickets but somehow became distracted or weren't paying attention and never bothered to collect the enormous prizes that were theirs for the taking.

According to the article, "About $570 million in lottery prizes went unclaimed [in 2006]." And in 2002 the winner of a $51.7 million Powerball ticket in Indiana never stepped forward to claim his or her winnings.[1]

This is no endorsement of the lottery. My point is simply this: People with winning tickets entitling them to great fortunes have lost those opportunities because they didn't claim what was theirs.

Here is something even more mind-boggling than that: God has a prize waiting for you that is of greater value than all the money of all time. It is called salvation, and for some, it remains unclaimed. For others, it is unused. And for many of us, it is unappreciated—and perhaps taken for granted.

Do we really grasp all that salvation is? Do we even begin to understand what God has given to us when we put our faith in Christ?

Salvation

Maybe at some point you have been approached by some stranger with a wild-eyed look on his face who said to you, "Are you *saved*?"

It might have been just a little bit of a turnoff. Somehow, the word seems a little overdramatic, doesn't it?

Saved.

Do we really have to use that term? It makes it sound like a Coast Guard helicopter dropping a line to someone drowning in the open sea or a firefighter carrying an unconscious body out of a burning house.

Does it really have to be so . . . intense?

Yes, in some ways it does.

Before we met Christ, our fate was infinitely worse than drowning at sea or being trapped in a burning house.

Saved is actually a perfect term to use. In fact, it may not be intense and dramatic enough to convey what Jesus Christ did for us when we placed our trust in Him.

Think of it! Salvation covers your past, your present, and your future.

Salvation Covers Your Past

When you are saved, God forgives you of all your sins.

That may be the first place where Satan launches his attack against your decision to trust Christ. Just as he tempted our first parents in the Garden of Eden, he will whisper in your ear, "Did God really say what you thought He said? Do you really believe God could forgive someone like you? After all the stuff you have done?"

And then he may play a few mental movies, plucked from your own memory, reminding you of some of the sins in your life that you're most ashamed of. "Do you honestly believe you will go to heaven when you die?" he hisses. "Seriously? There is no way that you deserve that. You're completely unworthy!"

In moments like those, we need to remember that our salvation isn't based on our feelings in the moment, but on the fact of what the Word of God says.

The Bible is adamant in saying that if you have believed on the Lord Jesus Christ, you *are* saved. It is your present possession, and you can rest in that.

- "All who believe in the Son of God know in their hearts that this testimony is true." (1 John 5:10, NLT)
- "The Spirit Himself bears witness with our spirit that we are children of God." (Romans 8:16)
- "You were dead because of your sins and because your sinful nature was not yet cut away. Then God made you alive with Christ, for he forgave all our sins. He canceled the record of the charges against us and took it away by nailing it to the cross." (Colossians 2:13-14, NLT)
- "Very truly I tell you, whoever hears my word and believes him who sent me has eternal life and will not be judged but has crossed over from death to life." (John 5:24, NIV)

In that last passage, Jesus doesn't say, "Whoever hears and believes *might* have eternal life" or "*hopes* to have eternal life." Rather, He says that the one who believes *has* eternal life!

Similarly, in 1 John 5:13 we read, "I write these things to you who believe in the name of the Son of God so that you may *know* that you have eternal life" (NIV, emphasis added).

Salvation covers your past. If you have believed on the Lord Jesus Christ, you have been saved.

Salvation Covers Your Present and Future

God not only has *saved* you (past), but He is *saving* you (present), and He will *save* you (future).

What is He saving you from today, in the present? He is saving you from the power and control of sin. In 2 Corinthians 1:10 Paul writes, "He has delivered us from such a deadly peril, and he will deliver us again. On him we have set our hope that he will continue to deliver us" (NIV).

Yes, God has saved me in the past, He is saving me every single day of my life, and He will save me in the future as well.

His salvation delivers us from future judgment. Romans 5:9-10 says, "And since we have been made right in God's sight by the blood of Christ, he will certainly save us from God's condemnation. For since our friendship with God was restored by the death of his Son while we were still his enemies, we will certainly be saved through the life of his Son" (NLT).

God has saved me. God is saving me. And God will yet save me in the future.

But what does it mean to be saved? What does that encompass? What does that include?

What Salvation Includes

In Romans 5:1-2, Paul writes, "Therefore, having been justified by faith, we have peace with God through our Lord Jesus Christ, through whom also we have access by faith into this grace in which we stand, and rejoice in hope of the glory of God."

First off, Paul tells us that we are *justified*.

Now before I speak to that very important word, let me contrast it with another word we need to know about: *regeneration*. When you believe in Jesus, you are regenerated. To be saved is to experience regeneration. We use interchangeable terms like *born again, believe in, saved, regenerated*. So when you put your faith in Christ, God has regenerated you. You have passed from darkness to light, from the power of Satan to God, and from hell to heaven.

Now contrast that with this word *justification*. Regeneration has to do with what takes place in the believer's heart; justification concerns our standing before God. Regeneration is God's answer to the problem of spiritual death; justification is the answer to the problem of guilt.

The word *justified* carries a twofold meaning. First of all, to be justified means you are forgiven of all of your sins. When you put your faith in Jesus Christ, all evidence of sin and guilt is completely wiped out.

Let that sink in for a moment.

Have you ever done something you are ashamed of? I have, too! I've done things I wish I hadn't done and said things I wish I hadn't said—things I wish I could somehow take back. But I can't.

"So," I might say, "I guess that's that. That stain will always be there."

No, it won't! Because when a person is justified, God forgives that offensive thing. He wipes it out. Acts 13:38-39 says, "Brothers, listen! We are here to proclaim that through this man Jesus there is forgiveness for your sins. Everyone who believes in him is declared right with God—something the law of Moses could never do" (NLT).

Speaking of our sins, God says in Hebrews 10:17, "I will never again remember their sins and lawless deeds" (NLT). Over in Jeremiah 50:20 it says, "In those days and at that time . . . they'll look high and low for a sign of Israel's guilt—nothing; search nook and cranny for a trace of Judah's sin—nothing. These people that I've saved will start out with a clean slate" (MSG).

Wouldn't you love a clean slate? Don't you long for a fresh start? That is what happens when you believe in Jesus. We are told in Micah 7:18-19, "Where is another God like you, who pardons the guilt of the remnant, overlooking the sins of his special people? You will not stay angry with your people forever, because you delight in showing unfailing love. Once again you will have compassion on us. You will trample our sins under your feet and throw them into the depths of the ocean!" (NLT).

A number of years ago I remember scuba diving in Hawaii with some friends. We weren't down that deep—maybe fifteen feet under the surface—and we could see the ocean floor down below us. Even though we stayed at the same depth, the ground below us kept getting further and further away. And then it was as though we came to a massive cliff: The ocean floor just disappeared, and you couldn't see the bottom. I went out a few more feet, looking down at that nothingness, and it freaked me out a little. It didn't really change my situation, but it was so deep it scared me. I also began to wonder, *What lives down there?*

That mental image comes to my mind when I read that God has thrown our sins into the depths of the sea. They're not just forgiven, they are forgotten. That doesn't mean God has a lapse in memory; it just means that He has chosen not to remember.

In our marriages, we say to our spouse that we've forgiven him or her for old offenses. But isn't it funny how those "forgotten" things seem to pop back up again? Maybe you'll be having a little disagreement, and the wife or husband will bring up something from twenty years ago!

We might say, "Hey, I thought you forgave me."

And our spouse will reply, "I did. But I don't forget!"

That's not real forgiveness, is it?

The truth is, you and I should never choose to remember what God has chosen to forget. Why do we do that? Why do we tend to keep reliving those things again? We need to accept the fact that when we have salvation in Christ, we are justified, which means that God has forgiven and forgotten your sins. As Corrie ten Boom used to say, "God has taken our sins, thrown them into the sea of forgetfulness, and He has posted a sign that says, 'No fishing allowed.'"

So let those things go. Stop thinking about your old sins, as well as the mistakes and offenses of others in years gone by. As Paul said, "Forgetting those things which are behind and reaching forward to those things which are ahead, I press toward the goal" (Philippians 3:13-14).

On my computer keyboard I have a key that has the word *delete* on it. You have that key as well. So what happens when you highlight a paragraph and hit the delete key? Where does that text go? I have no idea. And I don't really care. It probably goes to the same place where all my missing socks go.

I don't know where old sins, mistakes, and offenses go. I'm just glad they're gone. I am more grateful than I can express that God forgives and forgets my sins.

But that is only part of justification—the negative part.

Justification also has a vastly positive side, which includes all that God has done for us and given to us. A technical definition of the word *justified* is "to put to one's account." When God justifies a man or woman, He not only wipes away all their sins, giving them a clean slate, but He also places the very righteousness of His Son, Jesus, in their account.

Philippians 3:9 tells me that I have been "found in him, not having a righteousness of my own that comes from the law, but that which is through faith in Christ—the righteousness that comes from God on the basis of faith" (NIV).

That is not a gradual process; it doesn't take place over a period of time. It is instantaneous. God removes your sin and then immediately deposits His own righteousness into your account.

Let's imagine that you had somehow accumulated a debt of ten million dollars. Let's also imagine that because of what you owed, you were being sent to prison. An article appeared in the local paper with your picture in it, detailing how you were in debt for all that money and that you were going to be sentenced that day.

So there you are in the courtroom, awaiting your fate. Suddenly, before the hearing begins, billionaire Bill Gates himself slips into the room and comes to sit by you and your public defender. Having heard of your plight, Mr. Gates informs you that he has arranged a deal with the judge in which he will pay all that you owe your creditors, including interest. You say, "Oh, Mr. Gates, thank you! How wonderful!"

Then, as he is about to leave the courtroom, Bill Gates turns to you and says, "Oh, by the way. You might want to check your bank balance."

"Why would I want to do that?" you ask. "I already know what it is."

"Check it again," he says with a smile.

So on your way home you stop at an ATM and punch in your code. And there in your account is a positive balance of twenty million dollars.

"Well," you say, "that would never happen."

But something more shocking and mind-blowing than that really did happen! God has, in actual fact, deposited the righteousness of Christ into your spiritual account.

How is this done? Does this have anything to do with my good works somehow outweighing my bad works? Absolutely not. This is only accomplished through the sufficient death of Jesus Christ on the cross when He met the righteous demands of God. In 2 Corinthians 5:21 we are told, "For [God] made Him who knew no sin to be sin for us, that we might become the righteousness of God in Him."

Dr. John MacArthur defined justification like this: "On the cross God treated Jesus as if He had personally committed every sin ever committed by every person who would ever believe. . . . God treated Jesus as a sinner so that He could treat us as if we were righteous."[2]

And that is how God sees me now! He doesn't see me wrapped in my good works or accomplishments; He sees me in Christ with His righteousness in my spiritual bank account.

Those are truths that bring such peace to my life!

In Romans 5 we read, "Therefore, having been justified by

faith, we have peace with God through our Lord Jesus Christ, through whom also we have access by faith into this grace in which we stand, and rejoice in hope of the glory of God" (verses 1-2).

You see, I don't have to live in constant fear of what God thinks about me. I don't have to always be doing things to earn His approval. I don't have to worry and be anxious about where I will spend eternity. This is all covered in Christ! And that gives me peace—a deep inner peace that says no matter what else happens in my life, the big things are covered. So I don't have to sweat the small stuff.

Yes, of course we all have our trials, tribulations, disappointments, and heartaches. You've had tragedy visit your life, just as I have. But we know that we are saved and safe in the Lord's protective care. And we also know that the Lord can take these odds and ends of life that seem so difficult and sad, and He can bring glory to His name through them. He has promised in Romans 8:28 that He can cause all things to work together for good to those who love Him and are the called according to His purpose.

Adopted into His Family

Not only has God justified me and forgiven me, but He has adopted me, bringing me into His family circle.

Regeneration has to do with a change in nature. Justification has to do with a change in standing. Adoption has to do with a change in *position*. When I am adopted into God's family, I become His child, as though I were born into that family. In fact, the word *adoption* used in Scripture means the placing of a son or a daughter. Ephesians 1:5 says, "God decided in advance to adopt us into his own family by bringing us to himself through Jesus Christ. This is what he wanted to do, and it gave him great pleasure" (NLT). Galatians 4:4-6 tells us, "When the right time came, God sent his Son, born of a woman, subject to the law. God sent him to buy freedom for us who were slaves to the law, so that he could adopt us as his very own children. And because we are his children, God has sent the Spirit of his Son into our hearts, prompting us to call out, 'Abba, Father' " (NLT).

Slavery was common in biblical times. If you had enough money, you could go down to the slave market and purchase a man or woman to work for you. So this is the picture in Galatians 4:4-6. Jesus Christ went down to the slave market, saw you on the auction block, and paid the price for you. From there, He marched you straight to the courtroom, where He adopted you as His son or daughter. So not only did He purchase you, buying you back from bondage, but He also took you into His own home as His own child. How amazing! I stand in awe of a God who would have the power and the desire to do something like that for me.

After His resurrection, Jesus said to Mary, "Find my brothers and tell them, 'I am ascending to my Father and your Father, to my God and your God'" (John 20:17, NLT).

It was unthinkable to a Jew living in this time to address God Almighty as "Father." But this is the privilege we have been given in Christ. He has adopted me into His family, and I can call out, "Abba, Father."

I don't know what kind of father you have or had on earth. For the most part, I never really had a dad when I was growing up. My mom married and divorced seven times, and there were lots of guys in between those husbands. I remember coming to the point where I got tired of calling strange men "Dad."

My mom would say, "Call him Daddy." And I think after the second or third one, I said to myself, "Nah. I'm not going to do that." Most of these men in my life either mistreated me or indulged me or ignored me. There was only one man in my life growing up who ever treated me as a father ought to treat a son, and his name was Oscar Laurie. In fact, he adopted me and gave me my name. Because of that, I think of him as my dad, even though he wasn't my biological father. (He is now in heaven — along with my mom and my son.)

I'm very grateful that Oscar Laurie cared enough about me

that he adopted me. But it's even greater to know that I have been adopted by my Father in heaven.

Three Important Truths About Being Adopted by God

1. God understands you.

Psalm 103:13-14 says, "As a father has compassion on his children, so the LORD has compassion on those who fear him; for he knows how we are formed, he remembers that we are dust" (NIV).

Most parents know their children. We can look at our kids and know what's up. We know when they're not doing so well or when they have done something wrong. We know these things. We understand, and we care. Even when our children have failed, we care for them. We hurt for them, and their pain becomes our pain. We also want the best for them, look out for their welfare, think about them, pray for them, and even sometimes lose sleep over them. So we have compassion on our children.

How much more does our heavenly Father have compassion on us, His adopted sons and daughters!

2. God will take care of you.

Because you have been adopted by God, He will take care of you. In Matthew 6:31-33 Jesus said, "So do not worry, saying, 'What shall we eat?' or 'What shall we drink?' or 'What shall we wear?' For the pagans run after all these things, and your heavenly Father knows that you need them. But seek first his kingdom and his righteousness, and all these things will be given to you as well" (NIV).

You are God's own child, and He knows how to take care of His kids.

3. God loves to bless you.

In Matthew 7:11 Jesus said, "If you then, being evil, know how to give good gifts to your children, how much more will your Father who is in heaven give good things to those who ask Him!" And again in Luke 12:32, Jesus said, "Do not fear, little flock, for it is your Father's good pleasure to give you the kingdom."

Your Father is not stingy! I don't know what your earthly father may have been like, but your heavenly Father is generous. Your heavenly Father loves to lavish things on you and bless you.

Since I've had little granddaughters, I have begun to explore those mysterious pink aisles in the toy stores. Raising two sons as we did, I had never tried those aisles before. Nothing there really interested me because it was all stuff for little girls, and all that pink stuff and princess stuff mystified me a little.

But now I'm having fun with it. It's my joy. It's my delight. In fact, I have to *restrain* myself because I don't want to spoil those granddaughters. In the same way, the Lord loves to bless us with all kinds of blessings. "See what great love the Father has lavished on us, that we should be called children of God! And that is what we are!" (1 John 3:1, NIV).

What Do I Do with This Salvation?

We are justified. We are forgiven. We are adopted. And we have a Father who delights to lavish His love on us.

What am I supposed to do with all of this, this great thing called salvation? Should I just put it up on a shelf like a trophy and admire it when I walk in and out of the room?

No, we need to explore it, to understand it, to appreciate it.

But then do you know what we need to do?

We need to *work it out* in our lives.

I didn't say work *for* your salvation. It is a gift from God to you and can't be earned. But you need to work it out in your life. Philippians 2:12-13 tells us, "Work out your own salvation with fear and trembling; for it is God who works in you both to will and to do for His good pleasure."

You have to work it out for yourself; someone else can't work it out for you.

I'd love to have someone do workouts for me while I receive the benefit. Wouldn't that be nice? I could pay someone to run twenty laps around the track or do one hundred crunches and all of those uncomfortable things that hurt and make me sweat. But it doesn't work that way. If Greg Laurie wants the physical benefit, then Greg Laurie has to do the exercise.

What does it mean to "work out" our own salvation? A better translation of that verse would be, "Carry to the goal and fully complete." The phrase Paul used here in the original language referred to working a mine. It would be like owning a gold mine and exploring what's in there, bringing out gold nuggets from time to time.

In the same way, we are discovering all that God has for us and learning how to let it affect and benefit our lives. And bear this in mind: If you are saved, that salvation *will* affect the way you live.

But that doesn't mean we concentrate on other people's lives, speculating on whether they are saved or not. Instead, we should examine our own lives. As the apostle Paul said to the Corinthians: "Examine yourselves to see whether you are in the faith; test yourselves" (2 Corinthians 13:5, NIV).

The book of 1 John gives us six quick litmus tests to apply in our lives, helping us to consider the question, *Am I bringing forth the fruit of salvation—the evidence that I have really encountered Christ?*

1. If I am truly saved, I will confess Jesus as Lord.

> Whoever confesses that Jesus is the Son of God, God abides in him, and he in God. (1 John 4:15)

Have you done that? Have you confessed that Jesus Christ is your Lord? Someone might reply, "Well, people know I am a Christian by the way that I live. I try to be moral. I try to be compassionate. I try to be caring." All of those things are good and commendable. But there needs to be a moment when you say,

"I believe in Jesus Christ. I confess Him as my Savior and Lord."

It may be walking forward in an evangelistic meeting. It may be a testimony you give at your baptism. It may be in some other public setting. It is important for a believer to declare his or her faith in Jesus Christ.

2. If I am truly saved, I will obey the commands of Christ.

This is the love of God, that we keep His commandments. And His commandments are not burdensome. (1 John 5:3)

Do you obey the commands of Christ? This is the problem for some. They say they are Christians, but in their day-to-day lives, they disregard what the Bible says. They simply don't obey God's commands. Jesus said in John 15:14, "You are My friends if you do whatever I command you."

He didn't say, "You are My friends if you do whatever you are comfortable with." Or, "You are My friends if you do whatever you personally agree with." Or, "You are My friends if you do whatever you find easy."

No, friendship with Christ is linked to obedience to His commands.

3. If I am truly saved, I will love and obey the Word of God.

Whoever keeps His word, truly the love of God is perfected in him. By this we know that we are in Him. (1 John 2:5)

If you are really a Christian, you will love and obey the Word of God. That begins, of course, with *reading* God's Word, the Bible. I have to read God's Word to know what His commandments are, and then I can live accordingly. That is why Bible memorization is so important. The psalmist told us, "Your word I have hidden in my heart, that I might not sin against You" (Psalm 119:11). When you commit the Word of God to memory, it will be there for you to draw upon in times of temptation and trial. I think of Bible verses I memorized forty years ago as a seventeen-year-old kid that I still remember and draw upon today. What a great thing for all of us, especially those of us who are young, to fill our minds with the Word of God. And those Scriptures will be there for your lifetime.

4. If I am truly saved, I will be unhappy and miserable when I sin.

Those who have been born into God's family do not make a practice of sinning, because God's life is in them. So they can't keep on sinning, because they are children of God. (1 John 3:9, NLT)

If you are really a Christian, you will be unhappy and miserable when you are sinning. The Bible doesn't teach that a Christian is sinless, but it does teach that if you are a real follower of Jesus, you will sin less—and less and less and less with the passing of time. All of us sin; let's be clear about that. The Bible even says, "If we claim we have not sinned, we are calling God a liar and showing that his word has no place in our hearts" (1 John 1:10, NLT). But we shouldn't use that as an excuse for godless behavior. The fact of the matter is, true believers should be unhappy and conflicted when they are sinning. If, on the other hand, you can break God's commands without any discomfort or conviction of sin in your heart, then I suggest to you that you may not be a child of God. At the very least you are a very disobedient child of God who is going in the wrong direction.

5. If I am truly saved, I will keep myself from the devil.

We know that whoever is born of God does not [habitually] sin; but he who has been born of God keeps himself, and the wicked one does not touch him. (1 John 5:18)

If we are really saved, we will keep ourselves from the devil. When John wrote that the child of God "keeps himself," he wasn't suggesting that Christians keep themselves saved. No, that is the work of the Holy Spirit who has sealed us. The Scripture clearly teaches that it is God who keeps us. First Peter 1:5 says that we "are kept by the power of God through faith for salvation ready to be revealed in the last time."

Yes, thank the Lord, we are kept by God.

However, the Bible also teaches that we should *keep ourselves* in the love of God (see Jude 21). We don't keep ourselves saved, but we do keep ourselves *safe*. There is a difference. God saves me and keeps me saved. But I keep myself safe when I make sure I'm living in His presence and protection.

In the Lord's Prayer, Jesus taught the disciples to pray, "And do not lead us into temptation, but deliver us from the evil one" (Matthew 6:13). Another way of saying that is, "Lord, help me to have the good sense to stay away from situations in which I know I could fall. Help me to be careful, Lord. I know You are keeping me, and I thank You for that. But help me to keep myself as close to You as I can possibly be."

Coming back to that phrase we read earlier in Philippians 2:12, "Work out your own salvation with fear and trembling," another way to say that is, "Carry your salvation to the goal and fully complete it." But then the passage goes on to say, "For it is God who works in you both to will and to do for His good pleasure" (verse 13).

In other words, there is God's part, and there is Greg's part.

There is His part, and there is your part.

God does the saving, but you need to stay as close to Him as you possibly can.

6. If I am truly saved, I will love other Christians.

Everyone who believes that Jesus is the Christ is born of God, and everyone who loves the father loves his child as well. (1 John 5:1, NIV)

Finally, if you are really saved, you will love other Christians. Do you love Christians? Do you love to be around Christians? In my own life, I find that my relationships with other people affect me in different ways. And there are certain people who, whenever I am around them, just make me want to get closer to God.

Just last night I had a ten-minute conversation with a friend of mine. And when we went our separate ways, I felt closer to the Lord just for having been around him. Why? Because this man represented Christ so well in what he said to me.

Then there are other people who, for whatever reason, seem like a drag on my walk with the Lord. Without even intending to, they have the effect of pulling me away from God. A person like that may or may not be outright hostile toward your faith, but there is something about what they say or do that makes the world look a little more attractive and your faith seem a little less important. As the apostle Paul said, "Do not be misled: 'Bad company corrupts good character'" (1 Corinthians 15:33, NIV).

It's good to be around people who strengthen your faith and remind you of the most important truths of life. On the other hand, the Lord doesn't want us to so isolate ourselves from the world that we never have conversations with people outside of Christ. We want to influence and affect people and call others to Christ. But again, we also want to be careful and to keep ourselves in the love of God. In 2 Timothy 2:22, the Bible tells us to "run from anything that stimulates youthful lusts. Instead, pursue righteous living, faithfulness, love, and peace. Enjoy the companionship of those who call on the Lord with pure hearts" (NLT).

We need to love one another. And God will use His people to bring you closer to Him and build you up.

As I've traveled to different parts of the world, it always amazes me how I can meet brothers and sisters in Christ and feel an immediate connection. It's as though we've known each other our entire lives. And I think to myself, *Only the Lord could do this.*

The truth is, we should be looking for more opportunities to be with God's people instead of looking for ways to avoid times of fellowship. We need more time together, not less.

That special bond we feel with fellow believers is one of the sweetest benefits of what the writer of Hebrews called "so great a salvation."

8

Can You Lose Your Salvation?

Have you ever heard of the Hope Diamond? It is described as the most perfect blue diamond in all of the world and one of the most valued gems on the planet, with an estimated value of $250 million.

This diamond has an amazing history and has passed across oceans, from country to country, and through the hands of numerous kings, queens, and colorful characters. Despite its incredible value, however, one of the more eccentric owners of the Hope Diamond often strapped it to her dog's collar while living in Washington, D.C. What's more, she would often misplace it at parties and make a children's game of "finding the Hope Diamond."

Eventually it came into the possession of a diamond merchant named Harry Winston, who ultimately donated it to the Smithsonian Institute, where it remains on display.

But here is the interesting thing. Harry Winston sent the Hope Diamond to the Smithsonian Institute by regular U.S. mail, in a box wrapped with a brown paper bag. Can you imagine being the person at the museum who opened the mail that day?

What's so amazing is that something so amazingly valuable would be treated in such a careless way. Placed on a dog collar? Lost at a party? Wrapped in a brown paper bag? Are you kidding me? Is that any way to treat the most valuable gem in the world?

As careless as those actions might be, I can think of something even more amazing than that. I speak of our personal salvation, that incalculably valuable gift God gives to every person who puts his or her trust in Jesus Christ. It is the greatest gift God could ever give to us, and (let's face it) we often take it for granted.

"Your Names Are Written in Heaven"

In Luke chapter 10, we read the account of Jesus sending out seventy of His disciples, two by two, empowering them to do miracles and cast out demons. They returned from their ministry trip excited and overjoyed, exulting that "even the demons are subject to us in Your name" (verse 17).

But the Lord said to them, "Do not rejoice in this, that the spirits are subject to you, but rather rejoice because your names are written in heaven" (verse 20).

In other words, "Get some perspective, guys. Here's the big picture: You are saved, and you are going to heaven when you die. Nothing is more important than that."

Ephesians 2:8-9 tells us, "For by grace you have been saved through faith, and that not of yourselves; it is the gift of God, not of works, lest anyone should boast."

Salvation, then, is the gift of God. When you have received that invaluable gift, you are not only saved, but you are also safe. God protects and keeps His own children. The Bible says that you are "kept by the power of God through faith" (1 Peter 1:5). In Romans 8:38-39, Paul declares, "And I am convinced that nothing can ever separate us from God's love. Neither death nor life, neither angels nor demons, neither our fears for today nor our worries about tomorrow—not even the powers of hell can separate us from God's love. No power in the sky above or in the earth below—indeed, nothing in all creation will ever be able to separate us from the love of God that is revealed in Christ Jesus our Lord" (NLT).

We are saved. And we are safe.

Nevertheless, remember this: *God does not save anyone against his or her will. Nor will He keep anyone against his or her will.* Now that we have been saved, we should never presume upon the grace of God. We should seek to live as followers of Jesus Christ because it is possible for us to depart from the faith, even as believers.

Writing to Christians, the author of Hebrews says, "Beware, brethren, lest there be in any of you an evil heart of unbelief in departing from the living God; but exhort one another daily, while it is called 'Today,' lest any of you be hardened through the deceitfulness of sin" (3:12-13).

Again, that was written to believers. And the author was warning them, saying, "Brothers, don't depart from the living God."

In a similar way, the apostle Peter warns believers about those who would lead them astray, saying, "Therefore, dear friends, since you have been forewarned, be on your guard so that you may not be carried away by the error of the lawless and fall from your secure position" (2 Peter 3:17, NIV).

Departing from the living God . . . falling from your secure position.

Those sobering words bring us to the big question of this chapter: Can a Christian lose his or her salvation? Once you are saved, can you become "unsaved"?

Some Bible scholars take one point of view, while others are just as adamant, taking the opposite point of view.

My question is simply this: *Why would you want to push the envelope?*

People Who Concern Me

Here is what concerns me. There are people who want to know how they can be saved—and still live as though they are not saved. They want to know they are going to heaven yet continue to live like hell. They basically want to live in two worlds and want to know how much they can get away with and still technically remain a Christian.

Frankly, I don't know about such people. That seems like a precarious attitude to me.

If you have really been saved, it seems as though your life should change dramatically. We are told in Titus 2:11-14:

> The grace of God has been revealed, bringing salvation to all people. And we are instructed to turn from godless living and sinful pleasures. We should live in this evil world with wisdom, righteousness, and devotion to God, while we look forward with hope to that wonderful day when the glory of our great God and Savior, Jesus Christ, will be revealed. He gave his life to free us from every kind of sin, to cleanse us, and to make us his very own people, totally committed to doing good deeds. (NLT)

Is that a description of your life today as a follower of Jesus? Are you totally committed to doing what is right? In other words, if you really have been saved, there will be *results* in your life.

What did Jesus say? "You will know them by their Christian bumper stickers"? No. "You will know them by their Bibles"? No. What He said was, "You will know them by their *fruits*" (Matthew 7:16, emphasis added).

People should be able to see spiritual fruit in your life. People ought to be able to discern changes in your life that would indicate to them that you are a true follower of Christ. In 2 Corinthians 5:17 we read, "For if a man is in Christ he becomes

a new person altogether—the past is finished and gone, everything has become fresh and new" (PH). Is that a description of
your life right now? Or are you one of those persons who is
trying to live in two worlds at the same time?

Here is what Jesus thinks about that. Writing to the church of
Laodicea in Revelation 3:15-16, Jesus said, "I know your deeds,
that you are neither cold nor hot. I wish you were either one or
the other! So, because you are lukewarm—neither hot nor
cold—I am about to spit you out of my mouth" (NIV).

The Message version of the same verse goes as follows: "I
know you inside and out, and find little to my liking. You're not
cold, you're not hot—far better to be either cold or hot! You're
stale. You're stagnant. You make me want to vomit."

"Well," you say, "that's a harsh translation."

It also happens to be accurate. That is exactly what Jesus is
saying.

Years ago, Cathe and I were about to leave on a trip overseas.
Our youngest, Jonathan, was just a two-year-old at the time. We
didn't want to haul a car seat and a stroller along on the plane,
so we purchased something I had seen advertised somewhere
called a "backpack stroller."

When we got overseas, I realized what a worthless item I had
purchased. The problem with this "backpack stroller" was that
it was neither one. When I attempted to put it on my back, the
wheels dug into my back muscles, making it impossible to wear.
When I took it off and made it into a stroller, it didn't have back
wheels, so I had to prop it up the whole time. It was easier to
just carry Jonathan.

I remember saying in frustration, "This thing is totally worthless!" It has since become a family proverb, a phrase for
anything that doesn't work quite right. Someone will say, "Oh,
that's another backpack stroller, isn't it?"

Maybe you know some "backpack stroller" Christians in your
life. They try to live with one foot in one world and one foot in
another, and they don't do either very well. They're not living

fully for the Lord, but they're not wholly immersed in the non-Christian world either.

Jesus said that we are to be salt in our world, but salt that has lost its saltiness isn't good for much of anything. We need to make up our minds who we are and who we want to be. Rather than trying to live on the edge, we should choose to live as close to Jesus as we possibly can.

Were They Really Saved at All?

Can a person lose his or her salvation?

I think the better question might be: Was this person ever a Christian to begin with? Sometimes we will see people make a commitment to Christ, but then, after a period of time, they go back to their old lives and never return again.

Did they lose their salvation? *Or did they ever have salvation at all?*

It seems to me that if they go away, they were never really Christians to begin with.

The apostle Peter, who could be pretty blunt sometimes, made this statement about some people who had turned back from following the Lord:

> It would have been better for them not to have known the way of righteousness, than to have known it and then to turn their backs on the sacred command that was passed on to them. Of them the proverbs are true: "A dog returns to its vomit," and, "A sow that is washed returns to her wallowing in the mud." (2 Peter 2:21-22, NIV)

So a pig returns to the mud.

Well, yes, that is in a pig's nature. The reason pigs like to hang out in the mud is because they don't have sweat glands, and that is how they cool themselves. Just as a dog will cool itself by panting, a pig will cool itself by rolling around in the mud. Pigs also sunburn easily, so that's another reason they like lounging around in a mud bath.

Some people claim that pigs can be domesticated. So you take your pig outside for a walk on a sunny day, and maybe you rub him down with sunscreen, give him little sunglasses, tie a ribbon to his curly tail, and put some perfume behind his ears. But as soon as you turn your back, he'll make a beeline for the biggest, sloppiest mud puddle he can find.

Why? Because a pig is a pig. That's what a pig does. That is a pig's essential nature.

So how do we apply that to believers and nonbelievers?

When a believer goes astray (and we all do), he or she won't be able to stand the loss of fellowship with Jesus for very long and will hurry back to Him again, desiring His nearness, His cleansing, and His companionship.

A nonbeliever won't.

A nonbeliever doesn't miss the Lord's fellowship and is in no hurry to return to a Christian lifestyle that never really felt right to him or her anyway.

To me, the big question is, Where does such a person end up?

In 1 John 2:19 we read, "They went out from us, but they did not really belong to us. For if they had belonged to us, they would have remained with us; but their going showed that none of them belonged to us" (NIV).

The true test is where you wind up in life.

When people speak of an individual who has "fallen away" and wonder if that individual has "lost their salvation," I would suggest they never were saved to begin with.

My own mother was raised in the church and made a profession of faith as a young girl living in Friendship, Arkansas. As time went by, however, my mom rebelled against her faith and her upbringing. She always "believed," but she didn't want to live the life of a Christian. At the very end of her life, not long before she passed away, my mom came back to the Lord and made a recommitment. And I believe she is in heaven today and that I will see her again.

Was she a long-term prodigal who came back to the Lord after a lifetime away from Him, or had she ever really received the Lord as a young girl? Who can say? The important thing is that she turned to Him in her last days and came to faith.

As I said, the big question in my mind is, "Where do you end up?"

Backsliding

The fact is, any of us can backslide, and no one usually plans on doing it. You don't call up your Christian friend and say, "Hey, dude, want to backslide tonight? Pick you up at nine o'clock. It will be so cool."

No, that is not the way it usually works. It usually starts with making small, seemingly insignificant compromises . . . that somehow lead to bigger compromises. And the next thing you know, you find yourself in a place you never thought you would be. According to 1 Timothy 4:1, one of the signs of the end times is that "some will depart from the faith." It could happen to you. It could happen to me—if I became careless and didn't take precautions.

I believe there are many believers who are backslidden and aren't even aware of it because they don't understand what the term *backslide* means. It's a biblical term. In Jeremiah 3:22 God says, "Return, faithless people; I will cure you of backsliding" (NIV). And in Jeremiah 2:19 He says, "Your own wickedness will correct you, and your backslidings will rebuke you."

Here is something to think about. The Christian life is one of progression, growth, and constant change. The simple fact is that you are either moving forward as a believer, or you are moving backward. You are either gaining ground, or you are losing ground.

Are you moving forward in your spiritual life today? Because if you aren't, you are potentially backsliding. You might protest and say, "Hey, I'm still a Christian! I still go to church when I feel like it. I still read the Bible if it occurs to me. I still obey God . . . unless it conflicts with something I want to do. Cut me some slack!"

Here's the problem, however. *You are not what you once were.* You are slipping away from the place in your walk with God that you used to be. And that is why we need to take practical precautions. The fact is, anybody can fall away from the Lord. Anyone can depart from the faith. I don't care how long they have been a Christian. I don't care how much of the Bible they have memorized. I don't care if God has even spoken through them and used them.

You could fall away. I could fall away. Anyone could fall away. And the moment we begin to doubt, that is the moment we are taking a step toward doing it.

Peter's Story

Simon Peter, in one crucial season of his life, was a backslider. This is the same Peter who was one of the handpicked disciples of the Lord Jesus Christ and spent three concentrated years of walking and talking with Jesus. Peter not only was part of the Twelve, but also was included in the Three — the trio of disciples who were closest to Jesus and were granted special privileges. Peter had an unprecedented exposure to what was right and true.

But we also know that Peter fell away from the faith.

Why?

In Luke 22, in an upper room, the ministry of Christ was coming to a great crescendo. Within hours, He would be arrested, tried, and sentenced to die on a Roman cross. He knew it was coming. He had predicted it, spoken of it, and specifically warned His men that the time was drawing near.

On the very night when it would all begin, Jesus turned to Peter with a startling assertion:

The Lord said, "Simon, Simon! Indeed, Satan has asked for you, that he may sift you as wheat. But I have prayed for you, that your faith should not fail; and when you have returned to Me, strengthen your brethren."

But he said to Him, "Lord, I am ready to go with You, both to prison and to death."

Then He said, "I tell you, Peter, the rooster shall not crow this day before you will deny three times that you know Me." (verses 31-34)

Can you imagine how frightening that would be? Jesus turns to you, looks you in the eyes, and says, "Satan has been asking for you . . . by name." From the original Greek, it could be translated like this: "Simon, Simon, Satan has been asking excessively that you would be taken out of the care and protection of God."

I don't know that I have ever been tempted by the devil himself. We know that the devil is not omnipresent and can only be in one place at a time. Nevertheless, he has an army of demons at his command who can harass and tempt God's children.

In this particular instance, however, the devil, Satan himself, comes personally calling for Peter. He actually says to Jesus, in so many words, "I want that fisherman. I want him bad. I want You to give him to me." And so Jesus reveals this to Peter.

But then the Lord tells Peter: "I have prayed for you, that your faith should not fail; and when you have returned to Me, strengthen your brethren" (Luke 22:32).

What a great comfort that is—to know that Jesus Christ Himself is praying for and interceding for us! Romans 8:34 says, "Who then will condemn us? No one—for Christ Jesus died for us and was raised to life for us, and he is sitting in the place of honor at God's right hand, pleading for us" (NLT).

If it were not for the personal intervention and intercession of Jesus Christ in our lives, none of us would make it. As Robert Murray M'Cheyne once said, "If I could hear Christ praying for me in the next room, I would not fear a million enemies. Yet the distance makes no difference; he is praying for me!"[1]

The Steps Leading to Peter's Fall

Downward Step 1: Self-confidence.

He said to Him, "Lord, I am ready to go with You, both to prison and to death."

Then He said, "I tell you, Peter, the rooster shall not crow this day before you will deny three times that you know Me." (Luke 22:33-34)

In Matthew's gospel, we have these additional words from Peter: "Even if all are made to stumble because of You, I will never be made to stumble. . . . Even if I have to die with You, I will not deny You!" (26:33,35).

Why did Peter make this statement? Because Christ had revealed that one of the disciples was about to betray Him. So Peter thought this would be a good opportunity to boast of his own rock-solid commitment. He was saying, "Hey, even if all the rest of these guys turn traitor, You can count on me! Don't forget that nickname You gave me, Lord: Peter the Rock. I don't know about these other guys, but I won't let You down, no matter what."

I am always suspicious of anyone who makes himself look better at someone else's expense. If you find someone who has to cut down others to lift himself up, something is wrong. Another thing is, I don't think we should ever boast of our love for God. Rather, we should boast of His love for us. If you love the Lord, there is nothing wrong with saying that. But I would rather talk about how much God loves me.

John the apostle described himself as the disciple whom Jesus loved. I like that.

That's my story, too.

Greg Laurie is the man Jesus loves.

My own love, for all my good intentions, can be fickle,

unsteady, and inconsistent. But the love of God is flawless, completely consistent, and never stops.

In this instance, Peter is boasting of his dedication and his commitment. If this was self-confidence, it was misplaced self-confidence. Paul wrote, "Therefore let him who thinks he stands take heed lest he fall" (1 Corinthians 10:12). Solomon said the same thing in different words: "Pride goes before destruction, and a haughty spirit before a fall" (Proverbs 16:18).

In other words, just when you think you are out of danger and that you're not going to fall, you are in the greatest danger of falling.

It is interesting to note that some of the great men of the Bible who were known for certain admirable character qualities *fell in those very areas.*

Elijah was very courageous. We remember him standing up against the four hundred prophets of Baal on Mount Carmel and walking into the court of Ahab and Jezebel and saying, "It won't rain again until I say so." Later in his life, however, we read about how he ran and hid in a cave because Jezebel put a contract out on his life. The man of courage hid in fear.

Or how about Samson? We remember him for his super-human strength, how he could kill Philistines with whatever object happened to be laying on the ground at the time. Yet Samson, the strong man, couldn't resist a woman and was brought down by immorality.

How about Abraham? We know him for his faith. Yet on at least two occasions he lied, saying that his wife, Sarah, was his sister, out of fear of what would happen to him.

Here's what it comes down to. Sometimes we stumble in the areas we consider our greatest strengths. If I am weak in a certain area of my life, I will cry out to God for help and make sure I keep my guard up so I won't fall. But if I think I'm strong and invulnerable to a certain sin, I may lower my guard — and get hammered by the evil one. The fact is, *an unguarded strength is a double weakness.* Think about that. An unguarded strength is a double weakness. I may keep a close watch in the area of my vulnerability but lower my guard in the area where I think I am strong. And that might be the place where I will fall on my face.

So we all need to be very careful . . . and humble before the Lord.

Downward Step 2: Following at a distance.

Having arrested Him, they led Him and brought Him into the high priest's house. But Peter followed at a distance. Now when they had kindled a fire in the midst of the courtyard and sat down together, Peter sat among them. And a certain servant girl, seeing him as he sat by the fire, looked intently at him and said, "This man was also with Him."

But he denied Him, saying, "Woman, I do not know Him."

And after a little while another saw him and said, "You also are of them."

But Peter said, "Man, I am not!"

Then after about an hour had passed, another confidently affirmed, saying, "Surely this fellow also was with Him, for he is a Galilean."

But Peter said, "Man, I do not know what you are saying!"

Immediately, while he was still speaking, the rooster crowed. And the Lord turned and looked at Peter. Then Peter remembered the word of the Lord, how He had said to him, "Before the rooster crows, you will deny Me three times." So Peter went out and wept bitterly. (Luke 22:54-62)

Jesus and the Eleven had left the Upper Room in the darkness and walked to the Garden of Gethsemane. In the hours that followed, the Lord was in great agony as He contemplated the cross and its horrors. He had asked Peter, James, and John to stay awake with Him and pray with Him, but they were exhausted with sorrow and soon fell asleep. In the meantime, Judas and a mob of guards and temple police came to the Garden with torches, arrested Jesus, and led Him away in chains to the high priest.

Luke notes that Peter followed Jesus and the mob "at a distance."

He might have said, "At a *safe* distance." Peter was heading in the right direction as he followed Jesus, but he was leaving plenty of room for escape or changing his mind. It was what you might call a half-hearted commitment.

There are numerous people like this today. They follow at a distance. They still have a foot in the church, but they have a foot in the world as well. They "follow" the Lord, but not so closely that they will be identified with Him.

Downward Step 3: Hanging out with the wrong people.

When they had kindled a fire in the midst of the courtyard and sat down together, Peter sat among them. (Luke 22:55)

It was cold in those early morning hours, and Peter warmed himself at a fire in the courtyard of Caiaphas, who, at that very moment, was trying Jesus for His life. The fire was surrounded by nonbelievers. We might call it "the enemy's fire." At that point, Peter was worn down, exhausted, defeated, and more vulnerable than he knew. That fire was the last place where he should have been.

Matthew's gospel tells us that he sat down with the guards to see the end. He was resigned now to the fate of Jesus and felt there was nothing he could do. The bottom line, however, was that Peter was with the wrong people at the wrong time in the wrong frame of mind and about to do a greater wrong than he ever imagined possible.

This may or may not come as a revelation to you, but when

you hang around the wrong people in the wrong places, you end up doing wrong things.

That is why we need to give a lot of thought as to whom we spend the bulk of our time with. We might think we are influencing those non-Christian friends for the Lord, but the truth is, they may be influencing us, pulling us down.

Psalm 1 speaks wisely when it says, "Blessed is the man who walks not in the counsel of the ungodly, nor stands in the path of sinners, nor sits in the seat of the scornful; but his delight is in the law of the LORD, and in His law he meditates day and night" (verses 1-2).

Did you notice the progression (or regression) illustrated in this psalm? First it speaks of the guy walking in the counsel of the ungodly. Then he stands in the way of sinners, and before long, he's sitting in the seat of the scornful—walking, standing, and then sitting.

It's like being on a diet and walking by your favorite bakery. You know you shouldn't be within a block of that place. But you just walk by . . . and then you are standing in the doorway . . . then you are sitting at the counter with a doughnut in each hand.

Peter was with the wrong people at the wrong place at the wrong time. And it shouldn't have surprised him that he did the wrong thing.

Downward Step 4: His first denial.

> A certain servant girl, seeing him as he sat by the fire, looked intently at him and said, "This man was also with Him."
>
> But he denied Him, saying, "Woman, I do not know Him." (Luke 22:56-57)

After these words left Peter's mouth, you would have thought that he would come to his senses. I can imagine him saying, "Whoa! What did I just say? Didn't Jesus warn me about this in the Upper Room? I've got to get out of here before I do even more damage."

But that is not what happened. Peter already was beaten down.

Downward Step 5: His second denial.

> After a little while another saw him and said, "You also are of them."
> But Peter said, "Man, I am not!" (Luke 22:58)

Notice that a little time had passed since that first denial. Peter would have had plenty of opportunity to slip away from the enemy's fire and vacate that place. Instead, he stayed where he was.

Downward Step 6: His third denial.

> Then after about an hour had passed, another confidently affirmed, saying, "Surely this fellow also was with Him, for he is a Galilean."
> But Peter said, "Man, I do not know what you are saying!" (Luke 22:59-60)

Busted!

They told him, "Hey, you've got a Galilean accent. You can't fool us!"

Sometimes when I travel to different parts of the country, they will tell me that I have an accent. Are you kidding? A California accent? We're the ones who are normal, and everyone else has an accent. I'm not sure what a California accent would sound like. Maybe they think we all sound like surfer dudes.

Calling Peter out on his accent was really just a way of putting him down. The more cultured, affluent, educated Jerusalemites looked down on those who were from the more rural area of Galilee. It might be like calling someone a country bumpkin or trailer trash.

Whatever they said to Peter, it brought about his third denial. And this one was much worse than his first two. Matthew's gospel says "he began to curse and swear, saying, 'I do not know the Man!'" (26:74).

Does this mean that Peter let loose with a string of profanity—that he swore like a sailor? I'm sure he knew all the words; he wasn't a sailor, but he was a fisherman. But I don't think that is what's being said here.

The term used here for *curses* is a very strong expression that involved pronouncing death on oneself at the hand of God if he were lying. So instead of simply using salty language, Peter was essentially saying, "I swear to God, I never knew Jesus. I take an oath before God that I was never one of the followers of Jesus."

And then we read these words:

> Immediately, while he was still speaking, the rooster crowed. And the Lord turned and looked at Peter. Then Peter remembered the word of the Lord, how He had said to him, "Before the rooster crows, you will deny Me three times." So Peter went out and wept bitterly. (Luke 22:60-62)

Peter heard the rooster and looked up to see Jesus looking right at him. By the way, that last phrase could be better translated, "Jesus looked right through Peter."

Have you ever had someone look right through you? Let me restate that question: Do you have a mother? You know how it goes . . .

"Where have you been?"

"Nowhere."

"Look at me. I'm going to ask you one more time: *Where have you been?*"

It's so intense that you start confessing things you didn't even do!

What do you think the Lord's expression really showed in that moment? Was He angry and accusing? Did He roll His eyes, as if to say, "What an idiot. Why did I ever choose you?" No, I don't think that was our Lord's expression right then. After all, Jesus had predicted this and knew it was coming. And as soon as Peter saw His face, he went outside and wept.

I think that Jesus looked at Peter with love and compassion, and it broke the man's heart. In an instant he was asking himself, *Oh, how could I have done that? I've just ruined everything, lost everything. God will never be able to use me again.*

So here is the question. Did Simon Peter fail? *Yes.* Did he fail big? *Without question.* Did he openly deny the Lord? *Yes. Three times, as a matter of fact.* Was he still a believer? *Yes, he was.*

And in that moment he also needed to remember something else Jesus had said to him: "When you have returned to Me, strengthen your brethren."

In other words, Jesus had already seen Peter's restoration. It wasn't "if" you come back to Me; it was "when" you come back to Me.

The Three Rs

Have you lost ground in your walk with Christ? Have you opened your eyes at some point and realized that you have drifted a long way from your earlier commitment and your love for Jesus? How do you get back to the place where you are right with God?

In the second chapter of the book of Revelation, Jesus gave the church of Ephesus—and all the rest of us—a three-step process for coming back to God. After commending the church members for their hard work and their discernment, the Lord made this statement: "Nevertheless I have this against you, that you have left your first love. Remember therefore from where you have fallen; repent and do the first works, or else I will come to you quickly and remove your lampstand from its place—unless you repent" (verses 4-5).

Remember. Repent. Repeat.

First, I have to *remember*. Can you recall a time when your commitment to Christ was stronger than it is today? Can you recall seasons of your life when your walk with Jesus was more close and sweet and satisfying than it has been in recent days, weeks, or months? Think about it! Remember those times. Remember what was important to you and how you pursued your relationship with God. It's a valuable point of reference.

Second, *repent*. Change your direction. Stop doing what you are doing and go back to doing what you were doing before.

Third, *repeat*. Repeat what? Let's imagine that your marriage is in trouble—and even beginning to unravel. You say, "There is nothing that can be done to save my marriage."

Yes, there is! You can get your marriage back to where it needs to be. How do you get romance back into your marriage? It isn't rocket science: *You do romantic things.* If you are a husband, what did you used to do before you were married and were taking your future wife out on a date? You probably took a shower. (Always a good idea.) Then you took her out for dinner. Maybe you opened the car door for her or helped seat her at the restaurant. You probably told her how nice she looked and gave her a little gift that you'd brought along.

Do those things again.

Tell her how beautiful she is. Tell her you love her. Give her a gift.

"What if I don't feel like it?" you ask.

Do it anyway, because these are the right things to do. Go back and do those "first things" again.

So let's come back to our relationship with Christ. Let's say that you have lost that feeling of nearness and warmth and love for Him. What do you do? Jesus Himself tells you, "Remember therefore from where you have fallen; repent and do the first works." What did you used to do as a Christian that you aren't doing now?

"Well," you say, "I used to get up every morning and read my Bible."

Good. Start doing that again. What else did you do?

"I prayed a lot. I even used to take long walks and talk to the Lord."

Start doing that, too. What else?

"I used to love going to church. I went on Sunday morning and went to a midweek Bible study. I listened to Christian radio teaching programs. I read Christian books."

Work those things back into your life. You loved them once, you can love them again. What else did you do?

"Honestly, I tried to look for opportunities to share my faith a little."

Those opportunities are still there. Take them!

"But what if I'm not feeling it?"

Feelings come afterward. Just do the right things and the emotions will catch up later.

Remember. Repent. Repeat.

It will restore the bloom of love to a strained marriage, and it will bring back a walk with your Savior, Lord, and Friend that's better than anything else in life.

Good News in a Bad World

I t was a dark period in the history of the nation of Israel, a time that, in many ways, parallels our own.

On the surface, things could have not been more bleak.

But then God broke through with some very, very good news.

The Problem

First, let's identify the problem. The city of Samaria in Israel had been completely besieged by the forces of Syria, creating a crushing famine.

How bad was the famine?

The Bible tells us just a little bit more than we want to know. Second Kings 6:25 tells us that a pint of dove droppings—basically pigeon poop —sold for five shekels of silver. A donkey's head went for eighty.

In one shocking passage, we're told of two women who decided to kill and eat their own sons. They struck an agreement that they would eat one boy on one day and the other on the next. And so they killed the first boy and ate him. And then the next day, the mother of the second boy changed her mind and hid him.

The lady who had killed her son the day before was so upset that she took her problem to the king, saying, in effect, "King, this isn't right. It's her turn to kill her boy so we can eat him. What are you going to do about it?"

The king couldn't believe his own ears. He was so upset that he ripped his clothing, which was a biblical way of showing that you were *really* upset, frustrated, or angry.

So what did this king do? Did he drop to his knees and call out to God for help? *"God, what is wrong? What have we done to bring this calamity upon us? Lord, have mercy on us."*

No, that's not what he said. Instead, he focused all his anger on Elisha, the prophet of the Lord and God's representative.

The king said, "May God punish me terribly if the head of Elisha son of Shaphat isn't cut off from his body today!" (2 Kings 6:31, NCV).

Instead of turning to God, the king struck out at God's representative. Why? Because Israel was reaping the consequences of their sinful actions and their worship of false gods. God had withdrawn His blessing from the nation.

Was idolatry such a big deal?

We really have no idea how big it was or what an offense it was (and is) to God. I read a poll some time ago where people assessed the Ten Commandments, listing them in order of importance. Most people agreed that murder was the worst thing you could do, with adultery right behind it. As far as most of the respondents were concerned, idolatry wasn't so bad.

But God begs to differ with that.

In fact, the first two commandments zero in on the topic of idolatry. Why is it so important to God? Because if you aren't worshiping God, you will be worshiping someone or something in His place. In reality, all of the sinful activities you can imagine in our world are simply the result of not having God in His proper place in our lives.

God cares about being number one. And that bothers some people.

Media superstar Oprah Winfrey once said that she couldn't worship a jealous God, a God who wanted to be praised. "Her god" would never be that way. I'm not sure who her god might be, but I can speak for the God of Scripture. He *is* a jealous God, and He will not share His glory with another.

You say, "Isn't that a little paranoid on God's part?"

Let me ask you a question. If you're a husband, how would you feel if your wife was going out with a different guy every night of the week? Would you be good with that? If you are a wife, how would you feel if your husband had a girlfriend for every day of the week? You wouldn't put up with it. Of course you wouldn't! When you enter into a marriage relationship, you expect your spouse to be faithful to you. And that is what you *should* expect.

In the same way, when we enter into a relationship with God, He expects our faithfulness to Him. He is faithful, certainly, to us. And He says, "I don't want you to have any other gods before Me" (see Exodus 20:3).

This Israelite king, however, worshiped other gods. And the consequences came to him in the form of a besieging army and a killer famine. But instead of turning to the Lord for help, he turned in anger on God's servant.

It's something we see all the time, isn't it? People sin against God, reap the natural consequences of their sin, and then get mad at God for letting these things happen to them (as though He were somehow responsible)! The truth is, God has warned us again and again about the results and consequences of our sins, so we have only ourselves to blame.

The king was powerless. He didn't have the answers, and he knew it. The answers were neither economic nor military nor political. Israel needed to turn back to the God of their fathers.

It isn't difficult at all to see a parallel between this period of Israel's national story and our own. It has been said that he who refuses to learn from history will be forced to repeat its mistakes. Malcolm Muggeridge said, "All new news is old news happening to new people."

Our own nation faces a set of seemingly critical, insoluble problems. But the reality is that we have faced such things before in our history. And we have seen what can happen if we as a nation turn to the true and living God, the God of the Bible, for help.

I came across an interesting verse in Psalms just recently. It says,

> They never call on God.
> But there they are, overwhelmed with dread,
>   where there was nothing to dread. (53:4-5, NIV)

The problems that seem to be so overwhelming and terrible to us could melt away overnight if we as a nation cried out to the living God for help.

"A Day of Good News"

> The king said, "All this misery is from the LORD! Why should I wait for the LORD any longer?"
>
> Elisha replied, "Listen to this message from the LORD! This is what the LORD says: By this time tomorrow in the markets of Samaria, five quarts of choice flour will cost only one piece of silver, and ten quarts of barley grain will cost only one piece of silver."
>
> The officer assisting the king said to the man of God, "That couldn't happen even if the LORD opened the windows of heaven!"

But Elisha replied, "You will see it happen with your own eyes, but you won't be able to eat any of it!" (2 Kings 6:33–7:2, NLT)

Now the story shifts:

There were four men with leprosy sitting at the entrance of the city gates. "Why should we sit here waiting to die?" they asked each other. "We will starve if we stay here, but with the famine in the city, we will starve if we go back there. So we might as well go out and surrender to the Aramean army. If they let us live, so much the better. But if they kill us, we would have died anyway."

So at twilight they set out for the camp of the Arameans. But when they came to the edge of the camp, no one was there! For the Lord had caused the Aramean army to hear the clatter of speeding chariots and the galloping of horses and the sounds of a great army approaching. "The king of Israel has hired the Hittites and Egyptians to attack us!" they cried to one another. So they panicked and ran into the night, abandoning their tents, horses, donkeys, and everything else, as they fled for their lives.

When the lepers arrived at the edge of the camp, they went into one tent after another, eating and drinking wine; and they carried off silver and gold and clothing and hid it. Finally, they said to each other, "This is not right. This is a day of good news, and we aren't sharing it with anyone! If we wait until morning, some calamity will certainly fall upon us. Come on, let's go back and tell the people at the palace." (7:3-9, NLT)

We have already identified the problem: It was sin, and specifically idolatry. Israel had abandoned God. But God had not abandoned Israel. What follows is His promise.

The Promise

Out of the blue, God promised that He would change things.

Dramatically.

Almost instantly.

And He would do it in a way no one could have imagined.

Elisha said that by the next day, food—real food, not pigeon poop and donkeys' heads—would be affordable to the common person. You can almost see the royal official's mouth curl up into a sneer.

In *The Message* version, the conversation goes like this:

"Listen! GOD's word! The famine's over. This time tomorrow food will be plentiful—a handful of meal for a shekel; two handfuls of grain for a shekel. The market at the city gate will be buzzing."

The attendant on whom the king leaned for support said to the Holy Man, "You expect us to believe that? Trapdoors opening in the sky and food tumbling out?"

"You'll watch it with your own eyes," he said, "but you will not eat so much as a mouthful!" (2 Kings 7:1-2)

God made a promise, and this man was simply unwilling to believe it. He couldn't comprehend God's solution so he rejected it. Why did he reject it? Because it was a *spiritual* solution.

Does this sound just a little familiar?

God has spiritual solutions for our lives as well. Let's say your marriage is struggling. There is a spiritual and biblical solution for that. Let's say that you are a single person trying to find that right man, that right woman. There is a spiritual and biblical solution for that too. Let's say your finances are a mess. There is a spiritual and biblical solution for that also. There are always spiritual and biblical solutions to life's problems and dilemmas.

You say, "I've already tried that. It didn't work."

No, you didn't! Because if you had tried it and kept pursuing it, you would indeed find the answers you need. I have never yet counseled a couple with a troubled marriage who were doing what God wanted them to do. I have never seen a marriage fall apart in which the husband was loving his wife as Christ loves the church, as Scripture commands. Nor have I seen a marriage falling apart in which the wife was submitting to her husband as unto the Lord, as the Bible tells us.

The problems and heartaches always arise when there is an ignorance of what the Bible says or a refusal to embrace God's solutions.

God says to us, "Call on me in the day of trouble; I will deliver you, and you will honor me" (Psalm 50:15, NIV).

Does He mean it? Yes, He actually does.

Aren't those just nice words? No, they are truth, and they are life.

Whether it's your job or your marriage or family troubles or loneliness or addictions or enslaving habits, God will deliver you, one way or another.

The king's official we read about earlier, however, was too cynical to believe God's promise of provision and bounty and deliverance. He said, in essence, "Oh please. That just won't work. I refuse to believe that."

It isn't always a bad thing to be a little skeptical. I think sometimes we can be a little too gullible and too willing to believe anything that is written or said. In fact, the Bible tells us to be discerning—to "test all things; hold fast what is good" (1 Thessalonians 5:21).

Having said that, however, there is a difference between skepticism and unbelief. Skepticism might be a sign that you are thinking something through or turning it over in your mind. Even the Lord, in Isaiah 1:18, says, "Come now, and let us reason together. . . ." The Hebrew word for *reason* could include the meaning of arguing or disputing.

By nature, I tend to be of this frame of mind, so I can

understand a little healthy skepticism. Unbelief, however, is different. Unbelief says, "I refuse to believe." Unbelief declares, "I choose to not believe what God says in His Word. No, that is simply not true."

That is what this king's official was doing. He wasn't just skeptical, he was contemptuous. He didn't believe a word of it, and he was full of unbelief.

Hebrews 11:6 says, "Without faith it is impossible to please God, because anyone who comes to him must believe that he exists and that he rewards those who earnestly seek him" (NIV).

If you want a relationship with God, you need to come to Him in faith. And the Bible is replete with stories of men and women who had their lives transformed because they reached out in believing faith and took God at His Word.

Will you? What is your problem? What is troubling you today? What are the issues that weigh down your heart or keep you up at night?

Call upon the name of the Lord. Scripture says, "Cast your cares on the LORD and he will sustain you. . . . Cast all your anxiety on him because he cares for you" (Psalm 55:22; 1 Peter 5:7, NIV).

God is the One who will do it. God is the One who will complete it and bring it about, but the way He works in my life is through faith.

The king's aide in our story wasn't buying any of this. He said, in essence, "What a joke. That couldn't happen even if God opened up all the windows of heaven."

And Elisha replied, "Oh, it will happen all right. But it won't happen for *you*."

There always will be people in your life who predict your failure—people who tell you that "you will never amount to anything." I remember a teacher who actually wrote on my report card, "Greg Laurie will never amount to anything because all he does is sit in class all day long and look out the window and daydream and draw cartoons."

Now, was that true? Yes, I did daydream and doodle. But what did she know about God's plans to enter my life and use me for His glory?

Throughout my ministry I've heard the same thing. I started a church at age twenty, and people told me, "You can't start a church. You're too young. It will never work, and you're not qualified." When we started our crusade ministry, people told me, "Oh, that won't work. Crusades are over with. No one wants to go to crusades anymore."

Everything we have done in our ministry has been discounted and dismissed by naysayers and people who opposed us. At this point in my life, I've actually come to expect it. In fact, if I don't get opposition, I start wondering what I've done wrong!

I am not saying that a person should be presumptuous or reckless. But I am saying, "Let's take some steps of faith and see what the Lord will do." I would rather try and fail at something than never try at all. Let's face it, there are always people out there ready to throw a wet blanket on everything new people want to try. We hear, "No, no, no. Don't try that. That will never work."

And sadly, for those people, it never does work.

But for the ones who are willing to step out in faith and take some risks, God can and does do some amazing things.

God's Provision

We have considered, thus far, Israel's *problem* and God's *promise*. Now let's consider God's astounding *provision*.

The Lord brought unbelievably good news to the starving, besieged citizens of Samaria. But to whom did He choose to deliver that message? That's probably the biggest surprise of all.

He chose four men with leprosy.

People afflicted with leprosy were the lowest of the low on the socioeconomic ladder. In fact, they were at rock bottom.

People with leprosy had an incurable, highly contagious,

eventually fatal disease. They usually were isolated and quarantined, and if anyone with leprosy was out and about, they had to cry out, "Unclean!" Everyone kept their distance from them.

So God basically said, "Let's see, I've got some great good news to share with my hurting, starving people. Whom should I choose to herald this important message? I know! I will choose four men with leprosy."

The men slipped out of the city and made their way to the Syrian camp to surrender. They basically had come to the place where they were saying, "Pick your poison. We die if we stay, and we'll probably die if we go. But getting killed with a sword isn't the worst thing that could happen to us. What do we have to lose?"

What they found, as we already read in 2 Kings 7, was a completely abandoned camp, well-stocked with food and all kinds of valuables. The Syrian army was nowhere to be seen.

Why did the Syrians flee? Because God had caused them to hear the noise of a vast army approaching their camp. Thinking that Israel had somehow managed to hire an army from another country, the Syrians ran for their lives in the night—and kept on running.

This is a great example of how God can work both naturally and supernaturally at the same time. On the supernatural side, God cleared out the Syrians with the noise of an approaching army. Was it just an illusion or a trick? No, I believe God allowed them to hear an army of angels drawing near, around the city.

If we could somehow get a glimpse behind the veil of God's angelic armies—and the demon hosts that oppose them—we never would see life in the same way again. Frankly, it probably would freak us out a little bit.

Remember the story when Elisha and his servant were in the town of Dothan and got up in the morning to find that they were encircled by the Syrian army, sent to apprehend them?

When the servant of the man of God got up and went out early the next morning, an army with horses and chariots had surrounded the city. "Oh no, my lord! What shall we do?" the servant asked.

"Don't be afraid," the prophet answered. "Those who are with us are more than those who are with them."

And Elisha prayed, "Open his eyes, LORD, so that he may see." Then the LORD opened the servant's eyes, and he looked and saw the hills full of horses and chariots of fire all around Elisha. (2 Kings 6:15-17, NIV)

The Bible says that "the angel of the LORD encamps all around those who fear Him, and delivers them" (Psalm 34:7). Scripture also assures us that angels are "ministering spirits sent forth to minister for those who will inherit salvation" (Hebrews 1:14).

You might say, "You have no idea, Greg. I've got some pretty big problems. Are there enough angels to go around?" Yes, as a matter of fact there are. Daniel 7:10 speaks of well over one hundred million angels who stand ready to do the bidding of God. So that ought to do the job, don't you think?

The Lord used supernatural means to clear out the Syrian army. But he used simple hunger to draw those lepers into the abandoned Syrian camp. Have you ever found yourself right in the middle of God's will when you were doing a rather mundane thing?

Here is the way it works. I'm driving my car when the "idiot light" on the dashboard reminds me that I'm almost out of gas. So I pull over to the first gas station and stand there with the nozzle inserted into my car, pumping away.

Someone at the pump ahead of me is also standing there, and he turns around and says, "Hey, how's it going today?"

And I say, "It's going well. I didn't run out of gas."

He laughs, and we begin talking. Somehow, I have the opportunity to slip something spiritual into the conversation or maybe invite him to church. And just that quickly I realize that I'm in the middle of a divine appointment. That's how it works for me most of the time.

Sometimes when we're seeking God's will, we're looking for visions of angels or pillars of fire and audible voices. Meanwhile, without any fanfare, the Lord has dropped an opportunity right into our laps. He will lead you both supernaturally and naturally. But for the most part, the Christian life is one of faith where you study His Word, pray for direction, apply His principles, and hold your course until He gives you fresh directions.

I once asked my mentor, Pastor Chuck Smith, "If you could travel back in time and meet yourself when you were a young man, just entering the ministry, what counsel would you give to that younger Chuck Smith? What would you say?"

"I would say, 'Hold your course,'" he replied.

"That's it?"

"Yes, just 'Hold your course.'"

In other words, keep moving forward. Keep on keeping on until God releases you from that task, gives you a new assignment, or takes you home to heaven. Sometimes holding to that course will seem almost effortless, but at other times it becomes very, very difficult. Either way, God wants us to remain true to our commitments and keep a steady hand on the wheel.

The Proclamation

Finally, they said to each other, "This is not right. This is a day of good news, and we aren't sharing it with anyone! If we wait until morning, some calamity will certainly fall upon us. Come on, let's go back and tell the people at the palace." (2 Kings 7:9, NLT)

Can you picture those four men just chowing down on all the food in the Syrian camp, walking around laughing—with a drumstick in each hand? And just moments before they had been starving and not caring much whether they lived or died.

Suddenly one of them said, "You know, this just isn't right. Just inside those walls, people are starving. Little kids are crying for food. I know those people in the city haven't been very good to us, but if we keep our mouths shut now, something really bad might happen to us. We've got to go back and give them the good news." They recognized that to fail to share with others at that point would have been criminal for them, even sinful.

In the same way, for you and me to fail to share the good news of salvation in Christ with a lost world can actually be a sin. When we think of sin, we usually think of acts of disobedience or of specific broken commandments. And those things certainly are sin. Sin, however, is not only doing what is wrong, it is *not* doing what is right. The Bible speaks of both sins of commission and sins of omission. James 4:17 tells us, "If anyone, then, knows the good they ought to do and doesn't do it, it is sin for them" (NIV).

You and I ought to tell others about Jesus Christ.

Let's imagine you were a brilliant scientist who had discovered a cure for cancer. Just think of how many lives have been devastated by this dreaded disease! And you found a cure—a pill that you took one time and the cancer would be permanently erased.

What would you do? I would hope you would share the cure with as many people as possible.

"Well," someone might say, "I just don't know. I'm really not very comfortable talking to strangers."

That would be wrong, wouldn't it? It would be wrong when men and women and children at this very moment are sitting in chemotherapy rooms across the world, taking poison into their systems in the hope of extending their lives.

You would *have* to tell them about your miracle cure. To do less would be a great wrong.

The fact is, Christians have a cure for something that is even worse than cancer, as horrible as that disease is. It is a cure for eternal separation from God, a cure that will deliver an eternal soul from hell. *We have the answer that everyone needs.* We have the best of all news in a sad, mixed-up world, and it is the gospel of Jesus Christ.

"Greg," someone might say, "can't you come up with something new every now and then?"

Actually, no. There is nothing new. If it is new, it is not true, and if it is true, it is not new. We don't need "something new." We need to get back to the gospel and offer it to an increasingly hopeless world.

When the four men with leprosy went to the gatekeepers at Samaria and gave them the good news about the vacated Syrian camp, the king couldn't bring himself to believe it. That's the way it can be sometimes with someone who has heard bad news so often, for so long: They become cynical to the fact there even could be such a thing as "good news" in the world.

The king said, in effect, "It must be a trick. It must be a trap. This can't really be happening. This is just too good to be true."

But it was true. And after the king investigated and found everything just as the men had said, he opened the gates of the city and said to the people, "Have at it."

That pronouncement, of course, set up a wild stampede among the starving residents. They headed for the gates . . . and guess who was standing in the way and got trampled to death? The very official, the king's aide who had said, "This could never happen." Elisha had said to that disbelieving man, "You shall see it with your eyes, but you shall not eat of it." And that is exactly what happened.

There are people like that today. With their own eyes they see the lives of others transformed through a living relationship with Christ, but they never reach out to receive it for themselves. They remain slaves to their addictions, their lifestyles, and their sins, and in the end they throw their lives away.

Perhaps you are that person. You've seen the undeniable

power of Christ in the lives of people you know, and you're
hungry for the same thing. It's never too late to reach out for that!

Just pray something like this: "Lord, I want my life to change
this coming year. I want to be a real Christian, living in the
power of Your Holy Spirit. I want all that You have for me.
Please transform my life."

Are you ready for some good news?

He will!

10 Leading Others to Christ

I had been up early, my body clock thrown into confusion by a trip to Israel and the resulting jet lag.

Instead of sitting around for an hour drinking coffee, however, I decided to maximize the moment and take an early morning walk. The air was fresh and cool, and much to my surprise and delight, a magnificent rainbow arched across the sky in front of me.

We don't see all that many rainbows in Southern California, so the sight truly thrilled me. On an impulse, I pulled out my little iPhone with its two-megapixel camera and snapped a quick shot.

The resulting picture, however, wasn't anything to talk about. You really couldn't even tell there was a rainbow. *Oh well,* I told myself, *I'll just enjoy the journey. That's the best I can do.*

But was it? I wasn't that far from home, and I could run back and get my good camera. What a shot that would be! And even as I hesitated, the rainbow grew more beautiful, the colors more vivid. On a one-to-ten scale, it had started at a five and had now soared to a six.

Then—even as I stared at it—it became a seven!

That made my decision for me. I had to run home and get my camera and try to capture this. Breathless and back at the house, I remembered that I had left the camera in the car. Perfect! I jumped behind the wheel, driving back to the spot where I had been walking. Was the rainbow still there? Yes, it was. By now it was an eight, a fiery swath of colors across the morning sky.

Then I thought of an even better place that would give me a perfect angle for the shot. As I drove, the rainbow burned even brighter. Now it was a nine or ten. I could have just pulled off the road right then (if only I had!), rolled down my window, and snapped a picture of it. But I wanted to get to that "perfect" place.

Arriving at the place I had envisioned, I jumped out of the car with my camera and . . . it was gone. The rarest and most perfect of rainbows had burned itself right out of the sky, and there was no bringing it back. Getting back into the car, I thought, *This is why people should not chase rainbows.*

Trying to be Ansel Adams, trying to get the shot of the century, I ended up missing the whole thing. How frustrating! It would have been far better to just continue with my early morning walk, worshiping and praising the Creator for the beauty He had brought across my path.

Later it occurred to me that my experience had been a pretty good metaphor for life—especially our tendency to chase after things that are always just out of reach.

You know how it goes. When you're really young, you think to yourself, "When I finally get into high school, that will be really cool. I can't wait."

And then . . . "When I graduate from high school, I'll be on my way."

And then . . . "When I get through college, life will really begin for me."

And then . . . "When I get into my career, it's going to be great."

And then . . . "When I move up the ladder in this company and make a little more money, I'll be ready to roll."

And then . . . "When I own my own business, I'll be set."

And then . . . "When I get married, I'll be happier."

And then . . . "I was happier single. I think I'll get a divorce."

And then . . . "But I'm lonely now. I'll get married again."

And then . . . "Maybe what I needed was some kids to raise. That will make me happy."

And then . . . "How can I get away from these kids? They're driving me crazy."

On it goes. Life flies by, and you find yourself chasing rainbows, never quite catching up to them. Then one day you wake up and realize there is more of life behind you than there is in front of you. And you ask yourself the question, "What happened to my life? Where did it go?"

Hole in His Heart

When I read the story of the Ethiopian official in Acts chapter 8, I have to wonder if he had been a man who had chased a few rainbows. Here was a man with influence, power, and wealth. In his own nation, he probably was a renowned and well-respected man.

Here is how Scripture introduces him:

Behold, a man of Ethiopia, a eunuch of great authority under Candace the queen of the Ethiopians, who had charge of all her treasury, and had come to Jerusalem to worship, was returning. (verses 27-28)

He was secretary of the treasury of a powerful nation, second only to the queen in his power and influence. Yet for all of that, he had an emptiness in his heart that had sent him on a long journey in search of the true and living God.

His search led him to Jerusalem, the spiritual capital of the world at that time. Yet even there, though he had the opportunity to learn more about Judaism and marvel at the great temple, he did not find what he had been looking for.

But he had come away with a very precious possession—a scroll of the book of Isaiah. It's evident from the story that he was committed to search that scroll from one end to the other, seeking clues and knowledge about this great God of the Hebrews.

God will always respond—someway, somehow—to a seeking heart. And unbeknownst to this African official as he rode along in his chariot on a bright, sunny day in the desert, he was about to meet his heart's desire.

It's always a great story when a person gives his or her heart to Christ. And we can see quite clearly from this story that when a person really believes in Jesus Christ, his life changes—because this man went from emptiness and misery to overflowing joy. In fact, the story ends by saying, "He went on his way rejoicing" (verse 39).

The Bible says that when we believe in Jesus Christ, we pass from darkness to light, from the power of Satan to the power of God (see Acts 26:18). God's Word is describing what takes place in an individual's life.

But here's what we need to recognize: No two people will come to faith in the same way—different individuals, possessing different temperaments, will experience conversion in different ways. Some have an intense emotional response when they come to put their faith in Jesus. Others don't. But the emotions of the moment have little to do with the *reality* of that transforming moment. As we all know, feelings come and go; tears and goose bumps are no guarantees that an individual's decision for Christ will stand the test of time.

In His parable of the sower and the soils, Jesus spoke about seed sown in rocky soil that sprouted and shot up quickly. But it withered just as quickly in the hot sun because it had no root. As the Lord explained, "These likewise are the ones sown on stony ground who, when they hear the word, immediately receive it with gladness; and they have no root in themselves, and so endure only for a time. Afterward, when tribulation or persecution arises for the word's sake, immediately they stumble" (Mark 4:16-17).

An emotional experience, then, does not guarantee that you have really met God. When I prayed and asked Christ to come into my life, I felt nothing at all. Because of that lack of a defining experience, I falsely concluded that God had rejected me. It was only later that I discovered the Christian life is a walk of faith, not of feeling.

Even though emotions and experiences may vary for those who come to Christ, certain things remain true about every genuine conversion. As we look more closely at how this Ethiopian official found salvation out on a desert road, we will consider five principles common to every genuine conversion.

Philip's Surprise Assignment

In Acts 8, we see how Philip led an influential foreign official to faith in Christ. Have you ever had the privilege of leading someone to the Lord?

"Well, Greg," you might say, "I just can't see God using me in that way. I don't have that gift."

Perhaps you have believed that leading someone to Jesus is an experience reserved for a few, specially anointed people with the spiritual gift of evangelism.

But if that were the case, why is the Great Commission given to every Christian? The fact is, all believers in Christ are called to go into all of the world and preach the gospel. We are all called. We all have a part to play.

The primary way God has chosen to reach people who are not yet believers is through verbal communication. I have always found that a little bit amazing.

In a recent media interview, the writer said to me, "You seem to be very natural when you speak. It must come easily to you."

"Nothing could be further from the truth," I told him. "Before I was a Christian, I wasn't a public speaker at all. Far from it!" After I came to faith in Jesus Christ, however, I realized the best way to help people believe was through verbal communication. So as I began to speak a little bit here and there, in front of people, I came to realize it wasn't about *me* anyway. It was all about the message.

As I pointed out in the previous chapter, what if you had somehow come across a surefire cure for cancer — a remedy so effective that it reversed and eventually eliminated every form of the disease in every patient? Beyond any shadow of a doubt, you knew this cure would work for every cancer patient everywhere.

Now imagine that you meet an individual with stage four cancer — someone with only weeks, perhaps even days, to live. And in your heart you knew very well that if that individual would only accept your cure, he or she would be instantly healed.

What would you do?

"That's a dilemma," you say, "because I'm really not comfortable talking to strangers. And I don't know if I want to leave my comfort zone, engage this person in conversation, and actually say, 'I have found a cure for cancer.' They might think I was being forward. Or maybe I wouldn't word it right and they wouldn't like the way I said it. Or maybe they would reject me and send me away. Besides, the whole thing is a little bit embarrassing."

Obviously, you would have to get over such feelings because that individual's life would be infinitely more important than your temporary discomfort.

You already know where I'm going with this! The message we have as Christians is even more important than a cure for cancer because this is the cure for *sin*. This is the only way to get right with God and determines the destiny of an eternal soul. There has to come a moment when we say to ourselves, "You know what? It's not about me. It's not about whether I feel comfortable or don't feel comfortable. It's about my obeying the Lord."

No matter what we might think about it, the primary way that God reaches people who do not yet know Him is through verbal communication—God's children talking to people who aren't yet His children. Romans 10:14 says, "But how can they call on him to save them unless they believe in him? And how can they believe in him if they have never heard about him? And how can they hear about him unless someone tells them?" (NLT).

Who is that "someone"?

It might very well be you . . . or me.

God chooses to reach people through people. And that brings us to our first principle.

God (Not Us) Saves People

No matter how many times we may have heard this, I'm not sure it really sinks in. We still find ourselves thinking that some-how everything depends on our performance or technique or Bible knowledge or winning personality. But it just isn't true. Of course, God can use any or all of those things, but He is in no way limited by their presence or absence. In the final analysis, He must be the One who touches a heart, prepares a heart, and draws a heart to Himself.

In John 6:65 Jesus reminds us, "No one can come to me unless the Father has enabled them" (NIV).

So just for good measure, let's say it again.

It isn't something I do.

It isn't something I bring about.

It isn't dependent on my clever arguments or power of persuasion.

Sometimes all I will be able to do is sow the tiniest little seed of truth about Jesus. At other times, maybe I'll have a quick opportunity to add just a little water to a seed that someone else sowed already—perhaps a long time ago. At another time—who knows? I may be in the right place at the right time to simply help someone take that final step into the kingdom.

Remember Paul's words to the Corinthians?

> Each of us did the work the Lord gave us. I planted the seed in your hearts, and Apollos watered it, but it was God who made it grow. It's not important who does the planting, or who does the watering. What's important is that God makes the seed grow. The one who plants and the one who waters work together with the same purpose. And both will be rewarded for their own hard work. (1 Corinthians 3:5-9, NLT)

Believe me, I know that it can be discouraging when you talk to people or when you try to reach family members, and they won't listen or respond. And sometimes you feel like saying, "Oh, just forget about it. No one wants to hear this anyway. I'll just keep my mouth shut."

It's like a farmer who invests his resources and plants a crop, only to see his little seedlings destroyed by a storm or drought. But when he replants and then enjoys a bumper crop, it becomes worth it all, and his discouragement is forgotten.

In the same way, we can maintain a faithful witness for the Lord and nothing ever seems to happen. And then one day, the seed takes root. One person gets it, gives his or her life to Jesus, experiences the joy of salvation, and all the angels of heaven cheer from the celestial grandstands.

Jesus affirmed there is "joy in heaven over one sinner who repents" (Luke 15:7). The psalmist agrees, saying, "Those who sow tears shall reap joy. Yes, they go out weeping, carrying seed for sowing, and return singing, carrying their sheaves."[1]

We Need to Have a Heart for Nonbelievers

> Then Philip went down to the city of Samaria and
> preached Christ to them. And the multitudes with one
> accord heeded the things spoken by Philip, hearing and
> seeing the miracles which he did. For unclean spirits,
> crying with a loud voice, came out of many who were
> possessed; and many who were paralyzed and lame were
> healed. And there was great joy in that city. (Acts 8:5-8)

Before the incident with the Ethiopian royal official ever
takes place, we already know from Scripture that Philip had a
heart for nonbelievers.

Remember that Philip, along with Stephen and five other
Spirit-filled men, was called to be a deacon in the Jerusalem
church, backing up the apostles by taking care of day-to-day
church operations.

But you never know where the wind of the Spirit will blow a
Spirit-filled man or woman, do you? When a storm of persecution broke out after the death of Stephen, Philip grabbed his
suitcase and headed for Samaria with the gospel.

Samaria? That's a name that may not mean a lot to you and
me, but when you understand the culture of that day, it was
something of a shocking destination for Philip. To begin with, he
was a Jew, and Jews and Samaritans *hated* each other. With a
generational enmity that had persisted for centuries, Jews were
taught from their youth to hate the Samaritan people, regarding
them as illegitimate before the Lord. After all, the Jews reasoned,
the Samaritans worshiped God in the wrong way and in the
wrong place. Besides all that, their ancestors had intermarried
with Gentiles, so they weren't true Jews anyway.

But Philip had deliberately set his eyes on the city of
Samaria, and God had placed the desire in his heart to reach
them with the good news.

It makes a simple point: If you want to be an effective communicator, you need a willingness to approach people who are different from you. Most of us prefer to hang around people who are most like us, don't we? We feel naturally inclined toward people who look like us, talk like us, and have the same interests as us. We're uncomfortable when we find ourselves in a group that holds different values from ours and speaks or dresses in ways so very different from our own circle of friends and acquaintances.

But what if God calls you to such a group or such an individual? Would you be willing to make yourself uncomfortable for His sake? Would you be willing to acknowledge that all prejudice is wrong and that everybody needs Jesus? Are you prepared to represent your Lord without embarrassment in front of people who may not accept you or cheer you on?

Philip was. And that's just what he did.

The truth is, we can talk all day about the latest evangelism techniques and methodologies. I was listening to a Christian radio broadcast the other day, and some guy announced that he had come up with a set of clever, new conversation-starters designed to steer everyday encounters toward sharing the gospel. That's fine. I applaud his efforts. But the fact is, none of that will matter if you really don't care much about people.

Don't kid yourself. People can tell right away whether you care about them or not. My goodness, even a dog can tell that! A person knows within seconds whether you are sharing with him or her out of sincerity or out of a mere sense of duty.

The Samaritans must have sensed Philip's heart for them right away—or he never would have made it to first base with them when he went to preach Christ.

We Need to Be Open and Obedient to the Holy Spirit

In Acts 8:26, an angel came to Philip and said, "Arise and go toward the south."

Angels are fascinating creatures, working behind the scenes, doing the work of God in this world. The book of Hebrews calls them "ministering spirits sent to serve those who will inherit salvation."[2] In the Psalms, we learn that "the angel of the LORD encamps all around those who fear Him, and delivers them."[3]

So this means that all of us have angels that have been involved in our lives. The Bible says it's even possible that you have met an angel without knowing it.[4]

But here's the thing about angels. They're very careful about not drawing attention to themselves. They are instantly obedient to God and do His work quietly and effectively. Billy Graham once described them as "God's secret agents."

So we read that an angel came to Philip and said, "Here's your assignment: Get up and go toward the south." And that was the end of it.

But there is another way Acts 8:26 could be translated. Instead of reading (as it does in the New International Version), "Go south to the road—the desert road—that goes down from Jerusalem to Gaza," the passage could just as easily read, "Go to the desert at noon."

So the angel's instructions to Philip might have been, "I want you to go to this desolate part of the wilderness, and I want you to do so during the hottest part of the day."

The angel specifically directed him onto the desert road, a seldom-used route between Jerusalem and Gaza. It would be like God coming to you and saying, "Go out into the Mojave Desert in July at twelve noon, and I'll tell you what to do next."

How easily Philip could have argued with the angel. "You want me go where and do what? Preach to lizards? Hey, that place is too hot, even for them! You want me to leave this place of revival, blessing, joy, and miracles to head off by myself into the middle of nowhere? Really, does that even make sense?"

Notice that the angel did not tell him what was going to happen when he got there. There was no blueprint, no itinerary, no vision statement or set of objectives. He was being led one step at a time.

Philip discovered what you and I may also discover: *God's way becomes plain when we start walking in it.* Obedience to revealed truth guarantees guidance in matters unrevealed.

Has the Lord shown you something He wants you to do? Then just do it—because there is a time to sit and there is a time to move. There is a time to sow and there is a time to reap.

So Philip, the one-time-deacon of the First Jerusalem Church, simply saluted, strapped on his sandals, and obeyed. It would have been totally understandable if he had run in the other direction, as the prophet Jonah had done (the original chicken of the sea) when he received baffling directions from the Lord.

But to Philip's credit, he left everything and headed south.

"Sorry guys, I've got to leave the revival now."

"What? Are you kidding? This thing is about to explode! Where are you going?"

"To the desert."

"Why the desert?"

"Because an angel told me to."

"By yourself?"

"Yes, by myself."

"Why? What will you do there?"

"I have no idea. But God said to go, so I'm going. See you down the road."

Sometime later, Philip stood on that deserted wilderness road in the blazing sun, probably thinking to himself, *Okay, Lord. What's next?*

Suddenly he saw a cloud of dust in the distance—a caravan lumbering south from Jerusalem. As the procession drew nearer, he saw mounted men and bodyguards surrounding a man in an ornate chariot. Evidently, the man was reading something.

Suddenly it dawned on Philip. "Oh! I think I get it, Lord. This must be what You want me to do."

Who was this man from Ethiopia? In New Testament days, Ethiopia was a large kingdom located south of Egypt. To the Greeks and Romans, it represented the outer limits of the known world. And this particular Ethiopian, identified as the eunuch, was very possibly second only to Candace the queen. (Candace, by the way, wasn't the queen's name; it was her title, like "Caesar" or "Pharaoh.")

This African official had gone to Jerusalem looking for answers and had apparently found none. But as we mentioned, he had somehow come away with a copy of the scroll of Isaiah. Back in those days, people didn't have shelves full of Bibles like many of us have today. They read from scrolls that had been meticulously copied by hand.

As Philip approached, the Ethiopian just happened to be reading from the passage we know today as Isaiah 53, which contains a vivid prophetic description of the death of Jesus, written hundreds of years before our Lord walked this earth.

So the traveler read, reread, and pondered.

This was Philip's moment of opportunity. And just in case he might have missed it, the Spirit nudged him and said, "Go near and overtake this chariot" (Acts 8:29).

In verse 30 we read,

> Philip ran to him, and heard him reading the prophet Isaiah, and said, "Do you understand what you are reading?"

In that moment, Philip utilized something that is often lacking in many presentations of the gospel.

That something is called *tact*.

Tact has been defined as the intuitive knowledge of saying the right thing at the right time. Some Christians don't seem to have much of this quality at all or even see its importance.

Jesus was so tactful. Think back to His encounter with the woman at the well in Sychar, Samaria, described in John 4. Here was a woman who had been married and divorced five times and was currently cohabiting with yet another man. And this was back in the day when a lifestyle like that was considered scandalous. (Today we celebrate it.) So this social outcast went at noon to draw water from the community well because that was the time when she least expected to meet anyone.

As she approached the well, however, she saw a Man sitting there—and not just a man from the village, but a *Jewish* man. I can just imagine how she must have braced herself for a confrontation. She probably thought, *Oh no, this is going to be trouble. He's going to say something mean to me or treat me like dirt. For sure He's going to insult me.*

Trying her best to ignore this Stranger, she lowered her bucket into the well and began to fill her water pot. That's when the Man at the well shocked her to the core by looking right into her eyes and asking her a question.

"Will you give me a drink?"

Surprised as she was, she answered, "You are a Jew and I am a Samaritan woman. How can you ask me for a drink?"

Jesus replied, "If you knew the gift of God and who it is that asks you for a drink, you would have asked him and he would have given you living water."

"Give me this water."[5]

Just that quickly, a conversation developed as Jesus had tactfully built a bridge of communication to this woman. Far too often we burn our bridges when we ought to be building them and establishing a dialogue.

I use that word *dialogue* deliberately. Many of us have imagined sharing our faith to be more of a monologue—a one-way information dump. In a real conversation, however, you ask questions, you listen, and you respond appropriately, seeking to build a bridge of communication so that you might bring a word of witness to that individual.

That is what Jesus did, and that is what Philip was doing when he said, "Excuse me, sir. Do you understand what you're reading?"

The official said, "How can I, unless someone guides me?" And he asked Philip to come up into the chariot and sit with him. That was all the introduction Philip needed. He knew the man's heart had already been prepared and made ready by the Holy Spirit.

We Need to Give the Gospel Accurately

We've all heard about quack doctors who attempt surgeries they have never been properly trained to perform. Sadly, there are some quack preachers out there, too, offering false assurances to people seeking spiritual help.

Some of these ministers are guilty of spiritual malpractice. Why do I say that? Because they give a gospel message that lacks the true essentials. They tell people, "Just believe," but they don't warn them of a hell or impress on them the need to repent. Some don't even give much weight to the death of Jesus on the cross.

They offer Jesus as though He were just a product you could buy off a shelf, a commodity that will make your life just a little bit better. They don't make it clear that Jesus is the only way to God, and that there is "no other name under heaven given among men by which we must be saved" (Acts 4:12). People who listen to such teachers may embrace an incomplete, watered-down version of the gospel and thus have a false hope based on a false premise.

That is why God says of the false prophets in Jeremiah 6:14, "They offer superficial treatments for my people's mortal wound. They give assurances of peace when there is no peace" (NLT).

In *The Message* paraphrase, the words are rendered, "My people are broken—shattered!—and they put on Band-Aids, saying, 'It's not so bad. You'll be just fine.' But things are not 'just fine'!"

Why was Philip's message accurate?

First, *because it was centered in Scripture*. In Acts 8:35 we read, "Philip opened his mouth, and beginning at this Scripture, preached Jesus to him."

Any effective presentation of the gospel must be biblical. Why? Because God's Word says of itself that it will not return void.[6]

Second, *it was centered on Jesus*. Philip preached Jesus to him. He didn't preach prosperity or positive self-image or the dangers of global warming or politics or world peace; he opened the Scriptures and zeroed in, like a laser, on Jesus Christ.

It's all about Jesus. The gospel *is* Jesus. It is Jesus prophesied, born, crucified, resurrected from the dead, and coming again. It is Jesus who can change a life, not philosophy, not religion, not even "Christianity." The gospel message is about a relationship with God through Jesus Christ, the only way to the Father.

That is what Philip preached to the official in his chariot as they bounced down that desert road under the hot desert sun.

And the man believed.

In 1 Corinthians 15 Paul says,

Let me now remind you, dear brothers and sisters, of the Good News I preached to you before. You welcomed it then, and you still stand firm in it. It is this Good News that saves you if you continue to believe the message I told you—unless, of course, you believed something that was never true in the first place.

I passed on to you what was most important and what had also been passed on to me. Christ died for our sins, just as the Scriptures said. He was buried, and he was raised from the dead on the third day, just as the Scriptures said. (verses 1-4, NLT)

Embed that thought deeply into your mind. The gospel in a nutshell is this: Christ died for our sins and was raised again on the third day.

Someone once asked C. H. Spurgeon, the great British preacher, if he could put his Christian faith into just a few words. Spurgeon said, "It is all in four words: Jesus died for me!"[7]

The Gospel Must Be Responded to Appropriately

It's important to have a heart for people outside of the faith, to be led by the Holy Spirit, to know Scripture, and to focus on Jesus.

But no heavenly transaction is actually completed unless and until the listener *responds* to the gospel message. And we need to ask people if they want to respond.

Here's an example that is pretty typical. A young man came up to me after one of our services a few weeks ago. He had some questions about Christianity, and we talked a little bit. My impression was that he was open to the gospel and that he might like to receive the Lord.

So I simply asked him.

"Would you like to accept Jesus Christ into your life right now?"

He looked a little surprised and paused for a moment. "You mean," he said, "like *right here?*"

"Yes," I said. "Right here. Right now. It would be my privilege to lead you in a prayer to ask Christ into your life."

I never push people to do this; I just offer it to them. I will say, "You have a choice. If you don't feel like you want to do this right now, then you don't have to. But if you would like to do this, I would love to lead you in a prayer."

While my young friend was thinking about this, I just stepped back a bit and silently prayed, *Lord, just work in his heart. Right now.* And I waited for him to respond.

Finally, stammering a little, he said, "Well . . . uh, I . . . okay."

"Good," I said. "Let's pray right now." And I led him in a prayer, and he prayed with me. Sometime later, I checked in with a friend who knows him and said, "How is he doing?"

"He's doing well," this friend replied. "He's beginning to grow spiritually."

That is not to say that I always get a yes, because I don't. But what is the worst-case scenario? Maybe someone will say, "No, I don't want to do that."

"Okay," I'll reply. "I'll be praying for you, then, that you will see your need for Jesus."

Then I just leave it at that. I leave it in the Lord's hands. But at least I will know that I gave that individual an opportunity to respond, if he or she was ready.

I love the way Philip's story concludes:

> As they went down the road, they came to some water. And the eunuch said, "See, here is water. What hinders me from being baptized?"
>
> Then Philip said, "If you believe with all your heart, you may."
>
> And he answered and said, "I believe that Jesus Christ is the Son of God."
>
> So he commanded the chariot to stand still. And both Philip and the eunuch went down into the water, and he baptized him. Now when they came up out of the water, the Spirit of the Lord caught Philip away, so that the eunuch saw him no more; and he went on his way rejoicing. (Acts 8:36-39)

Saying "he went on his way rejoicing" is a pretty wonderful way to end any story. There is another story of another man in the New Testament that ended with some different words. The Bible says of the man known as the rich young ruler that "he went away sorrowful" (Matthew 19:22).

Why did he do that? Because he was unwilling to do what Jesus asked him to do and could not bring himself to let go of his old life and embrace a new life in Christ.

So one man heard the message and believed, and he went on his way changed, transformed, and full of joy. But another man had the same opportunity and turned away, going home sad, dejected, and empty.

That's the way it always will be. Some will respond, and some won't. It isn't our responsibility to make that eternal decision for them. All we can do is give them the opportunity.

And that is all our Lord asks of us.

chapter

11

Secrets of the Early Church, Part 1

S tella, my little granddaughter, loves secrets. Even when she's in a bad mood or maybe fussing about something, I can kneel down in front of her and say, "Stella, want to hear a secret?"

She will say, "Yeah!" and eagerly lean over for me to whisper into her little ear.

Now at this point in her life, the secret doesn't have to be particularly profound. She's not all that particular about it. Not long ago, for instance, I gave her the secret, "Chicken before bread."

Maybe I should explain. Stella loves bread, and when we go out to eat, she wants to eat all the bread on the table, just filling up on it. Then, of course, when it comes time to eat her main course, she's too full. So my secret for her was "chicken before bread."

She got it.

The next time I said, "Stella, want to know a secret?"

"Yeah," she said, leaning again.

I whispered, "This happy feeling comes from

Jesus." And she smiled because that's a little song we like to sing together.

Stella is not alone in loving secrets. Most of us do. If you're in a restaurant and someone in the booth next to you says to someone else, "Hey, I want to tell you a secret. Make sure you don't share this with anyone else," what do you do? Do you keep listening?

Of course you do. You'll do your best to tune in without being too obvious about it. Because we all like to hear a secret or two.

In the next two chapters, we will consider some secrets of the early church.

But it isn't as though these truths are hidden. In fact, they are plain as day to anyone reading the Scriptures. But we still might refer to these points as "secrets" because they seem to be unknown—or ignored—by so many people today.

Hypocrites in the Church?

So often in contemporary church circles, we hear people say, "We need to reenvision the way that we do church."

No, we don't.

There is no need to recast or redefine what God has already clearly defined in the pages of Scripture. What we need to do is to get back to the church that Jesus Himself set up.

Granted, it's all too easy to be critical of the church these days—and some of that criticism has been well-earned. But don't forget this: In the years that Jesus Christ walked this earth, He started only one organization, and it is called the church. And He said, "The gates of [hell] shall not prevail against it" (Matthew 16:18).

Some might dismiss the church with a wave of the hand and say, "Aw, the church is full of hypocrites."

But so what? There is certainly nothing new in that comment. *Any* organization made up of human beings will be laced with hypocrites. There are hypocrites in Congress, in the White House, in Buckingham Palace, and in your own city council. That's just the human condition. There were plenty of hypocrites to go around in the first-century church as well. In fact, one of our Lord's handpicked disciples turned out to be a notorious hypocrite. Hypocrisy is nothing new. It's been around since there were two fallen human beings to rub shoulders. I'm not excusing hypocrisy, just explaining it. I have heard people say, "If I find a hypocrite-free church, I'll join it!"

Please don't, because you would only spoil it!

Jesus once told a story we have come to know as the parable of the wheat and tares.[1] In this story He talks about a farmer who plants wheat in his field, and then one night an enemy comes in and sows the seeds of tares, or weeds, among the wheat. The particular weed Jesus described, also known as darnel seed, is virtually indistinguishable from wheat as both sprout from the soil. In fact, it continues to look just like wheat through most of its growth process. But in the end, along toward harvest, the darnel uproots and destroys the wheat.

Jesus was saying to them, "Do you see how this works? In the kingdom of God here on this earth, you'll find the fake right next to the real, the counterfeit side by side with the genuine."

And so it is in the church today. The tares and the wheat will grow together, and we won't necessarily know who is who and what is what until that final day. But God knows.

I have often said there will be three surprises when we get to heaven. The first surprise will be the people there who we never thought would be there. The second surprise will be the people who won't be there that we thought for sure would be there. And the third surprise? *We* will be there! But really, that isn't true; I fully expect to be in heaven because I have placed my faith in the Lord Jesus Christ.

So yes, there are certainly hypocrites among us, destructive tares growing alongside the genuine wheat. And only God knows which is which. As the Holy Spirit told the prophet

Samuel in the early days of David, "The LORD does not see as man sees; for man looks at the outward appearance, but the LORD looks at the heart."[2]

Each one of us, of course, has our own moments of hypocrisy. (We would be hypocritical to deny it!) So don't worry too much about the hypocrites in the church because there's always room for one more. Come on in and join the family!

Jesus was committed to the church, and we should be, too. There is nothing this world offers that is even close to it. The church may have many critics, but it has no rivals!

When I travel around the world, the special bond between followers of Jesus Christ transcends all others—even the bonds of race and nationality. Yes, I am certainly proud to be an American and believe the United States of America to be the greatest country on the face of the earth.

But I am a Christian first and an American second. I will sit down with people from different countries, and though we might see the world a little bit differently and might not agree on every political fine point, we can agree on the fact that Jesus Christ is the Savior of the world and that He has changed our lives.

The Bible calls us fellow members of the body of Christ, and that is just what we are. We are His church.

Everyone Doing His or Her Part

In the book of Acts, we encounter the church that changed the world, the church that turned the world upside down. What was their secret?

It is the simple fact that every Christian believed they were called to do his or her part. Every person mattered.

A Spartan king once boasted to a visiting monarch about the superb, impenetrable walls of Sparta. The visiting king, however, was somewhat confused by these claims. As he looked around, he could see no city walls at all. "Where are these walls you speak of?" he asked.

For a reply, the Spartan king gestured around him at his bodyguard of magnificent troops. "Just look around you," he said. "Here are the walls of Sparta. Every man is a brick."

In the same way, in the church every man and every woman is a brick—or as the Bible terms it, "living stones."[3] It's easy for someone to stand on the sidelines and be critical of the church, pointing out all the areas where it is falling short. But God never called us to stand on the sidelines. He called us to be involved in His church, fighting the battles, standing toe to toe with enemies in the arena. Perhaps those who are so critical would have a different perspective if they were a living part of the living church.

President Theodore Roosevelt made this statement:

> It is not the critic who counts, not the man who points out where the strong stumbled or how the doer could have done better. The credit belongs to the man who is in the arena, his face marred by dust and sweat and blood, who strives valiantly, who errs and falls short again and again. There is no effort without error.[4]

So yes, we in the church have our shortcomings. But we are in the arena, attempting to do the work of God in a Christ-rejecting world.

Over in Ephesians 4:15-16 we read that we should hold to the truth in love because the whole body is perfectly fitted together as each part does its special work. Each part helps the other parts grow so that the whole body is healthy and growing and full of love.

We are living in a time, however, when people are saying, "We need to reinvent the church."

Again I say, "No, we don't." I agree that we need to be relevant to the culture we are living in, adapting to changing styles or design or music or peripheral things. We want to make sense to the people we are seeking to speak to. But our core beliefs and our mission must not change one iota. At Harvest Christian Fellowship, where I pastor, we are essentially still doing today what we were doing thirty-five years ago. And by God's grace, we *still will be doing* these things thirty years from today if the Lord doesn't return for us first. Styles change, terms change, approaches change, and music changes, but undergirding all that, we hold to core principles that must never change.

There is no better place to find such core principles than in the pages of Scripture. Here in Acts chapter 2 are the secrets of the effective and successful, or — better yet — *biblical* church.

Is Bigger Better?

The church described in Acts 2 was a very large church. Today we might call it a megachurch.

We usually think of successful as "big," don't we? (Especially here in America.) That has been our philosophy: Make it bigger, and it will be better. I love the way that mentality affected our car design back in the fifties. Many feel that the golden era of car design was between 1955 and 1957. (I would have to agree with that.) Detroit built some really cool cars in those years, and everything kept getting bigger. (Especially the fins on the Cadillacs!) Now you see some of those cars on the road, and they look like the Millennium Falcon.

When people from other countries come to visit, that is often their impression of America: everything is bigger here — especially our food portions. In many countries where I have traveled overseas, the portion sizes served in restaurants seem uniform — and uniformly small. Then you go to some of the more popular restaurants here in Southern California, and one entrée could feed an entire family.

And if it isn't big enough, you can always "super-size" it.

So it is not surprising that we would take some of that bigger-is-better mentality and apply it to the church, assuming that the larger a church is, the more successful it is.

But that is not necessarily true. You can have a big church and yet not have a *strong* one. The fact is, there are many things you can do to draw a crowd. You could go out and start a fight and draw a crowd! So it isn't about just being big. It's about being *strong*, and it is about being biblical.

On the other hand, some people are automatically critical of a church just because it happens to be well-attended. You'll hear people say, "I hate these megachurches. You drive in there and have to wait for parking! They have parking lot attendants! Can you imagine that?"

Let's think about that for a moment.

It would be like someone saying, "There are two restaurants I can choose between. One restaurant has a line around the block, and the other never has anyone in it, except the people who work there. Where do you think we should go eat?"

Can you hear someone replying like this? "Well, let's go to the place with no line because we won't have to wait." Probably not! Did you ever stop and think there might be a *reason* there is no line? Maybe the food in the other place is better than the place with no people inside.

So sometimes a large church is that way because a large number of people are finding their souls fed, love the worship, and love the fellowship they find there.

Even so, it's never been my objective to have a large church. But it always has been my desire to pastor a biblical church and a strong church. As to the size, we've always felt that we should just leave the growth up to God. There is no virtue in being small, in and of itself.

Not every church is going to be a large church, but every church should be a *growing* church. And the fact is, if you don't have new people coming into your church, it will begin to stagnate. In the book of Acts, we read that "the Lord added to the church daily those who were being saved" (2:47).

That first-century church recorded daily growth as a constant flow of new converts were coming in. New converts are the lifeblood of the church! And if a church doesn't have *that* kind of growth, I have to say to you right now that there is something wrong with it.

So why is the church here? To just be big? No. The objective of the church is to be as *faithful* as we can be to what God has called us to be. Because on that final day, Jesus is *not* going to say, "Well done, good and *successful* servant. Oh, and by the way, how many numbers were you running on Sunday mornings?"

So what is the purpose of the church? I believe the church exists for three reasons: the exaltation of God, the edification of believers, and the evangelization of the world. Or to put it another way, our directions are to be upward, inward, and outward.

Reason 1: To Exalt God (Upward)

The church of Jesus Christ exists to honor and glorify God. That is why at our church, we put a lot of emphasis on singing, praise, prayer, and worship. The New Testament tells us that "we, who were the first to put our hope in Christ, might be for the praise of his glory."[5] We are here to praise our glorious God.

This idea may come as a revelation to some people. Why? Because they actually think their purpose on earth is to find personal happiness.

Isn't that why I exist?

No, that is not why you exist. And if you chase after personal happiness, you will never really find it.

Wait a minute. What about finding that right person, getting married, and raising a family? Isn't that what I live for?

Marriage and family are both very good — priceless blessings from the Lord Himself. But even as wonderful as they are, these are not the primary reasons you draw breath. You have been put on earth to honor and glorify and praise God.

A poll was taken among young people recently in which they were asked what their primary goal in life was. The number one response was "to be rich and famous." For a few people, that may happen. (And then after it happens, they really don't like it very much.) But that is not why you are here. That is not why you open your eyes each morning to a new day.

You are here to glorify and exalt and honor God. That is why every one of us has been placed on this earth: to bring glory to the God who made us. Jesus said, "By this My Father is glorified, that you bear much fruit. . . ."[6] In his first letter to the Corinthians, the apostle Paul tells us, "You do not belong to yourself, for God bought you with a high price. So you must honor God with your body" (6:19-20, NLT).

I spoke with a man the other day who had just gone through major, life-threatening surgery. Coming through that experience has caused him to reevaluate his life. He has a good career in sales, but he said to me, "You know, I'm beginning to wonder if this is what I should be doing with my life."

Knowing that God graciously spared his life and kept him on earth for a reason has prompted this man to think deeply about why he is here and what his life is supposed to mean.

I told him, "God put you here to glorify Him. That is why you exist."

He was already beginning to realize that life was more about significance than success. Significance. *What am I doing with my life? What impact is my life making on others?* Sometimes people will go through a near-death experience like that and think, *Maybe I need to quit my job and go out on the mission field or be in full-time ministry.*

That may indeed be what the Lord is saying to you. Then again, maybe He would have you stay exactly where you are and honor Him there. Wherever you are, whatever you are doing, make sure you can glorify God while you are doing it.

Whatever you do [no matter what it is] in word or deed, do everything in the name of the Lord Jesus and in [dependence upon] His Person, giving praise to God the Father through Him. (Colossians 3:17, AMP)

Reason 2: To Edify Believers (Inward)

The apostle Paul said his goal was not merely to evangelize but, according to Colossians 1:28-29, to "[warn] everyone and [teach] everyone with all the wisdom God has given us. We want to present them to God, perfect in their relationship to Christ. That's why I work and struggle so hard, depending on Christ's mighty power that works within me" (NLT).

That is why we are here as the church of Jesus Christ.

We don't exist to just pop into church on Sunday morning, sing a few songs, hear a (hopefully) quick message, and then go on our merry way. We are here as the church to exalt and worship the Lord, to be taught and equipped, and to equip one another. Yes, we want people to come forward and receive Christ. But we also want those people to *go forward* and follow Christ for the rest of their lives.

Jesus gave the command to "go into all the world and preach the gospel. . . ." Then Jesus said, "Teaching them to observe all things that I have commanded you."[7]

So His commission involves both an element of proclamation *and* the element of teaching and discipleship. We are here to build up one another.

Reason 3: To Evangelize the World (Outward)

This is the natural outgrowth of the first two reasons. If we are glorifying God and building up one another, we will naturally want to share the hope of salvation with others through our loving actions and words. As Pastor Chuck Smith has often said, "Healthy sheep will reproduce themselves."

It is essential that we keep these three principles in their proper balance. The church is not to emphasize one of these things at the expense of the others or take them out of their order. For instance, you might have one church that says, "We're called to evangelize. We don't care about teaching Christians or making well-fed believers even fatter."

I heard it said once by a pastor, "We are not called to be keepers of the aquarium but fishers of men!"

Well, that is a clever saying, but no, that is not your *whole* mission. The purpose of the church is to glorify God, to build up believers, *and* to preach the gospel.

Another church will say, "We're not called to evangelism. We are called to in-depth Bible study. We are called to study deeply and learn more."

Yes, that is part of your calling. You are truly called to Bible study. But you are also called to edify one another and evangelize the world. You see, it isn't part of our calling to *customize* the church. Our objective is to follow the original template in the book of Acts and ask ourselves, "How can we get as close to *that* church as possible?" That is our objective. Why? Because *that* is the church that changed the world. *That* is the church that turned the world upside down.

First Steps of the Baby Church

Gathered together in an upper room, the believers waited together for that which Jesus had promised just before He ascended into heaven:

> Behold, I send the Promise of My Father upon you; but tarry in the city of Jerusalem until you are endued with power from on high. (Luke 24:49)

They knew the Holy Spirit would come, but they had no idea what to expect or what to look for. When the Spirit suddenly arrived, no one had to wonder whether He had come or not! His entrance was dramatic: a mighty, rushing wind; divided tongues of fire resting above each head; and an outpouring of languages they had never learned before, declaring the wonderful works of God.

Stunned by all of this, a huge crowd formed. Looking at each other in sheer amazement, they were saying, "What in the world does all this mean?" That is when Simon Peter, who once cowered before a stranger when asked if he was one of Jesus' disciples, stood up and gave a very bold and brilliant presentation of the gospel, resulting in the salvation of three thousand people.

And what did they do *then*? Let's read about it:

They continued steadfastly in the apostles' doctrine and fellowship, in the breaking of bread, and in prayers. Then fear came upon every soul, and many wonders and signs were done through the apostles. Now all who believed were together, and had all things in common, and sold their possessions and goods, and divided them among all, as anyone had need.

So continuing daily with one accord in the temple, and breaking bread from house to house, they ate their food with gladness and simplicity of heart, praising God and having favor with all the people. And the Lord added to the church daily those who were being saved. (Acts 2:42-47)

The church that turned the world upside down was alive, healthy, and vibrant. And here's why. . . .

They Were a Learning Church

They continued steadfastly in the apostles' doctrine. (Acts 2:42)

This is a consistent trend we see throughout the book of Acts: the Spirit of God working through the Word of God in the hearts of the people of God.

Were these believers filled with the Holy Spirit? You'd better believe it! They had experienced the Day of Pentecost together. So what is the sign of a Spirit-filled church? Check out the very first thing that Dr. Luke brings to our attention: *They were studying the Word of God.*

When you think about it, it could have been a real temptation for these believers to say, "Wow! What an experience we had on the Day of Pentecost! The wind! The fire! Speaking in tongues! Lord, give us more supernatural phenomena. Let us experience that all over again!"

But that's not what we read. Instead, we find them just reveling in the Word of God. And what is true of a church is also true of individuals because the church is made up of people. If you are really Spirit-filled, you will love the Word of God. If you have no interest in the Bible, if you find Scripture boring and uninteresting and don't really care about reading and studying it, then I have to wonder if you've been filled with the Holy Spirit at all—or if you even know the Lord Jesus as your Savior.

It's a trend in many contemporary churches today to disregard the study of Scripture—to no longer have Bible study as the centerpiece of a service. For some groups—including the so-called emergent church—you might say that questions are the new answers. They will say, "Let's not have a sermon. Let's instead have a discussion, a dialogue. We're on a journey together, and isn't it rather arrogant for anyone to say that he or she actually understands what the Bible teaches? No, let's instead discuss our doubts as we travel through life together. We can talk about the latest books and movies and our own spiritual journeys. Better still, we can sit around and criticize the evangelical church! In fact, let's not even go to church on Sunday. Let's just go down to the local coffee place, order some espresso, and talk about the ups and downs of our spiritual journeys."

Those first-century believers loved to assemble, loved to worship, and loved to study the Word of God.

Another trend in the church today is to simply marginalize

Scripture. The Bible is there, yes, but it's off to one side, half out of sight. You attend a service, and there's a lot going on: songs, drama, film clips, testimonies, maybe even a dance or two. There might be a brief sermon, usually topical in nature, with very little Scripture involved. Instead of a meaty message from God's Word, we have a "sermonette." (The only problem with this is that "sermonettes" often produce "Christianettes.")

That is not the template of the book of Acts church. They valued preaching and the apostles' doctrine.

Acts chapter 20 gives us a revealing instance of this that took place in the city of Troas, where Paul had come to preach one evening.

> On Sunday, we gathered for a communion service, with Paul preaching. And since he was leaving the next day, he talked until midnight! The upstairs room where we met was lighted with many flickering lamps; and as Paul spoke on and on, a young man named Eutychus, sitting on the window sill, went fast asleep and fell three stories to his death below. (7-9, TLB)

Paul rushed out with the rest of the crowd, prayed for this young man, and raised him up from the dead. Now you'd think that after a traumatic incident like that, the preacher might have called it a night and sent everyone home. Not Paul! The Bible says, "They all went back upstairs and ate the Lord's Supper together; then Paul preached another long sermon — so it was dawn when he finally left them!" (verse 10, TLB).

The Word of God was their focus, and they loved it.

Something wonderful happens when believers study the Bible together. It's great to study it individually, and we need to do that daily. But when we all come together for Bible study and turn together to a passage in our Bibles, reading the words and making discoveries together, that is a special thing.

God has ordained preaching as a primary function of the

church. In some of the last words Paul would ever write, he told his young disciple Timothy,

> Preach the word of God. Be prepared, whether the time is favorable or not. Patiently correct, rebuke, and encourage your people with good teaching. For a time is coming when people will no longer listen to sound and wholesome teaching. They will follow their own desires and will look for teachers who will tell them whatever their itching ears want to hear. They will reject the truth and chase after myths. (2 Timothy 4:2-4, NLT)

I like that phrase *itching ears.* Another way to say it might be, "An itch for novelty." That certainly sounds a lot like today, doesn't it? *Hey, what's new? What's cool? What's different?*

We need to get back to the reading, study, teaching, and preaching of the Word of God. And what is preaching? Dr. Martyn Lloyd-Jones defined it as "logic on fire." I like that.

We've all encountered sermons that were all logic and no fire—the kind that will put you to sleep. The teaching may be sound, solid, and theologically correct, but it's also B-O-R-I-N-G. Then you have other sermons that are all fire and no logic. The message gets you excited, but afterward when someone asks you, "What was the sermon about?" you really have no idea!

We need passion and content, logic and fire. The world certainly needs to hear it. Why? Because preaching is God's primary way of reaching lost people. Don't ask me why. It was God's choice. We're told in 1 Corinthians 1:21, "For since, in the wisdom of God, the world through wisdom did not know God, it pleased God through the foolishness of the message preached to save those who believe."

According to some leaders of the "emergent church," we shouldn't even be using the term *Word of God*. One such leader stated, "To say Scripture is the word of God is to employ a metaphor. God cannot be thought of as literally speaking words, since they are an entirely human phenomenon that could never prove adequate as a medium for the speech of an infinite God."[8]

Yet the Bible itself says that God chose the medium of preaching the Word to reach and save lost men and women. We are to declare a known God to a world that does not know Him. *God can be known.* That should be the message of His church today.

Paul wrote: "I want to know Christ and experience the mighty power that raised him from the dead" (Philippians 3:10, NLT). Don't tell me God is a mystery and can't be known. God can be known. God should be known. God *must* be known. And it will happen as His Word is proclaimed with passion and authority.

That is not to say that each of us doesn't wrestle with our personal struggles and doubts from time to time. But it isn't our job to indulge and wallow in our doubts with a lost world on its way to hell. Our job is to point people in the right direction, to point them to Christ.

Paul didn't get up at Mars Hill in front of the Athenian intellectuals and say to them, "I see you worship an unknown god. So do I! We're all on a journey together. So pour me an espresso, and let's talk about it!"

No, Paul said, "I see you worship an unknown God, and this is the God I want to proclaim to you. You can know Him just as I do!" (see Acts 17:22-32).

Dr. Martyn Lloyd-Jones said it this way: "Come to the Word of God. Stop asking questions. Start with the promises in their right order. Say, 'I want the truth, whatever it costs me.' Bind yourself to it. . . . We are not meant to be left in a state of doubt and misgiving, of uncertainty and unhappiness."[9]

They Were a Steadfast Church

While it is true that we need preaching and teaching that has been anointed by the Spirit of God, we also need anointed listening!

Acts 2:42 says that the people "*continued steadfastly* in the apostles' doctrine" (emphasis added).

Those are two important words, speaking of both *attention* and *intention.* They had a hunger and a desire for the Word of God and an openness to receive it.

In later years, perhaps the apostle Peter was remembering that hunger for the Word of God in the book of Acts church when he wrote, "Like newborn infants, long for the pure spiritual milk, that by it you may grow up into salvation" (1 Peter 2:2, ESV). Peter was saying, "Just like a little baby craves his mother's milk, so you should crave and desire the Word of God." Healthy believers are hungry believers.

We should come to the Word of God with a desire to not only hear its truths, but to also apply them to our lives. Get yourself a notebook and jot down the thoughts that God brings to your heart as you read. Then review them again later in the day or maybe at night before bedtime.

Come to the Bible with a wide-open heart, saying, "Holy Spirit, what do You want to say to me today?"

If you want to be a strong Christian, you need to be someone who loves the Word of God.

chapter

12

Secrets of the Early Church, Part 2

The church portrayed in the pages of the book of Acts was strong, vibrant, and healthy.

That is our model, and I'm so glad that it is.

Why? Because I don't much like dead churches or dead services or dead preachers. And we have far too many of all three out there today, where people sit in pews like expressionless mannequins, or preachers get up and somehow manage to take the dynamic, life-changing, power-packed message of the Word of God and make it as dull as watching hubcaps rust.

I heard a story about a pastor who spoke to his congregation one Sunday and really had to wonder how the message went over because he had so little feedback. Standing in his traditional place at the back of the auditorium after the service was over, he smiled and shook hands with people, waiting for someone to say something.

People were polite and smiled, but no one said a word about the message.

Finally, he found himself shaking hands with a lady who usually could be counted on to say something thoughtful. So he said to her, "Tell me, Martha, what did you think of my sermon today? How was it?"

"Oh, Pastor," she said, "your sermon reminded me of the peace and love of God."

He was pretty relieved to hear that. "Wow," he said, "I've never had anyone actually say that to me before. Tell me, how did my message remind of you of the peace and love of God?"

She said, "Well, like the peace of God, it passed all understanding, and like the love of God, it endured forever!"

Sometimes you're better off just receiving the compliment and not asking for specifics.

The book of Acts church, however, had passion and excitement to spare, blended with a strong commitment to love and serve one another. Acts 2:42 tells us, "They continued steadfastly in the apostles' doctrine and fellowship, in the breaking of bread, and in prayers."

I like that word *steadfastly*. These men and women were living in a first-love relationship with Jesus Christ, and their hearts burned with love for Him. This was no casual attitude like you might find at a social club, sales meeting, or political rally—it was a spiritual excitement that went right to the core. As a result, they diligently applied themselves to what was taught from the Word of God.

As we noted in the previous chapter, they were *a learning church*, a group of people who believed in the teaching and preaching of the Bible. That's the way it is with genuine believers who have been filled with the Spirit of God: They will love the Word of God. As John Stott said, "The Spirit of God leads the people of God to submit to the Word of God."

But beyond being a well-instructed church, they were deeply committed to one another as well.

They Were a Loving Church

Acts 2:42 says they continued steadfastly in fellowship.

What does this word *fellowship* mean? It's a word Christians like to throw around a lot.

"We'll meet in the fellowship hall."

"Let's have some fellowship."

"Come for food, fun, and fellowship."

But what does that really mean? What is fellowship, anyway? It comes from the Greek word *koinonia*, and that is the term used here. They continued in *koinonia*.

In fact, it isn't the easiest term in the world to translate. It could be translated "fellowship" or "partnership" or "communion." It also carries the sense of being *generous*.

Koinonia is far more than socializing, far more than cookies and coffee. Anyone can socialize. People can get together and rally around their passions, be it sports or cars, quilting or kung fu. This is different altogether. This is where people get together to talk about their shared life in Christ. And how the Lord loves that!

Have you ever been in a room and heard your name mentioned in some conversation by someone who didn't know you were there? Have you ever noticed how your ears perk up? *What? Did someone just say my name?* Or maybe you've been someplace and heard a conversation going on, and you heard the name of Jesus Christ mentioned. You're immediately interested to know what they are saying about your Lord.

Listen to what God said in the Old Testament about a small group of believers who met together to seek the Lord and talk about Him during a time of national cynicism and decay:

Then those who feared the LORD spoke to one another,
And the LORD listened and heard them;
So a book of remembrance was written before Him
For those who fear the LORD

And who meditate on His name.

"They shall be Mine," says the LORD of hosts,

"On the day that I make them My jewels." (Malachi 3:16-17)

The text says that *"the LORD listened and heard them."* That phrase could be translated, "to prick the ear, to bend down so as not to miss a single word."

When we say the name Jesus, He listens.

Sometimes I will hear people use His name as profanity, and I will say, "Be careful. He listens when you say His name."

People may think you're crazy when you tell them that, but it's completely true. God listens with special attention when someone speaks His name. The Bible says that "whoever calls on the name of the LORD shall be saved" (Romans 10:13). Why? Because He is paying attention.

When those who love Him, then, call His name, when His own sons and daughters speak His name in honor and love, having fellowship around His name, He loves that. It isn't just socializing; it's in an entirely different category than that. It's *koinonia.*

My little granddaughter Stella calls me "Papa" (which started because she couldn't say "Grandpa"). And I'll tell you this: whenever I hear "Papa," I'm all ears. I pay complete attention to her. Am I busy? Sure, I'm busy. But I make time for her. Papa always has time for Stella.

And so it is with the Lord. "Busy" as He might be, running the universe and answering the prayers of billions, He makes time for you. He listens when you speak His name.

In an earlier chapter, we looked at Numbers 6, where God gave the priests a blessing to pronounce upon God's people:

The LORD bless you and keep you;

The LORD make His face shine upon you,

And be gracious to you;

The LORD lift up His countenance upon you,

And give you peace. (verses 24-26)

Notice again the phrase *The Lord lift up His countenance upon you.*
What does that mean? It means to lift up one's face, or literally, to
look, to see, to be interested, to have one's full attention. God is
saying, "I am watching you. I am looking at you. I am listening to
you, and I like it. I love it when you sing My praises, when you
speak of My name, when you gather together for fellowship."

Fellowship is praying together, serving together, sometimes
weeping together, aging together. These are the strong fibers of
fellowship. And fellowship with God and with His people go
hand in hand. The apostle John tells us, "We proclaim to you
what we ourselves have actually seen and heard so that you may
have fellowship with us. And our fellowship is with the Father
and with his Son, Jesus Christ. We are writing these things so
that you may fully share our joy" (1 John 1:3-4, NLT).

In other words, as I get to know God through His Word, I
will long for fellowship with other believers. That's just the way
it works in the kingdom of God: the stronger your vertical
fellowship, the stronger your horizontal fellowship will be. And
conversely, if you find yourself out of fellowship with God, you
will soon find yourself out of fellowship with other believers
as well.

If your motive, when you step through the doors of a church,
is to be critical and find things that are wrong and out of
balance (as you see it), then you'll probably find exactly what
you're looking for. The church of Jesus Christ is comprised of
imperfect people, led by imperfect leaders, who imperfectly seek
to love and serve God and follow His Word. If that is what
you're looking for, that is what you'll find: imperfection
everywhere.

It's a funny thing: Sometimes the people who are most critical of sin in the lives of others struggle with those same sins
themselves. A person with covered sins in his own life will always
try to uncover sins in others' lives. Sometimes the reason you are
so quick to find fault in others is because you see so much of it
in the mirror. Maybe we shouldn't be so picky, judgmental, and

critical and instead put on a little humility as we come to fellowship with God's people.

Peter said it like this: "All of you serve each other with
humble spirits, for God gives special blessings to those who are
humble, but sets himself against those who are proud."[1]

Caring for one another in practical ways is another part of
true *koinonia*. The book of James says: "Suppose you see a
brother or sister who has no food or clothing, and you say,
'Good-bye and have a good day; stay warm and eat well'—but
then you don't give that person any food or clothing. What good
does that do?" (2:15-17, NLT).

The believers in the early church shared their resources:

> All the believers met together in one place and shared every-
> thing they had. They sold their property and possessions and
> shared the money with those in need. (Acts 2:44-45, NLT)

Let's not misunderstand this verse. The Bible isn't advocating
communism or socialism here because this sharing was strictly
voluntary. It's simply saying that the believers who had the
resources were willingly helping those who did not. Not everyone participated in this. Not everyone sold homes or possessions. The verb forms in verses 45-46 indicate that the selling
and giving were occasional, in response to particular needs, and
not something once and for all. Nonetheless, these people loved
and cared for each other in a way that caught the attention of
the watching world, and we should do the same.

They Were a Worshiping Church

> Continuing daily with one accord in the temple, and
> breaking bread from house to house, they ate their food
> with gladness and simplicity of heart, praising God and
> having favor with all the people. (Acts 2:46-47)

This phrase *gladness and simplicity of heart* simply means that these believers worshiped God and met together with open and unaffected joy. But it was a joy mixed with awe and reverence, as we read in verse 43:

> Fear came upon every soul, and many wonders and signs were done through the apostles.

Fear and *joy*—both are important elements of worship. The Spirit-filled church will be a worshiping church, and the Spirit-filled Christian will be a worshiping Christian. Something very unique happens when believers come together with one heart and one desire in corporate worship. Yes, of course God loves it when you sing to Him in the shower, when you lift a chorus of praise to Him while you're walking on the beach, or when you're having your own private devotional times. That's all part of the "sacrifice of praise" that Hebrews 13:15 speaks of, and God is honored when you do that. But God manifests His presence in a wonderful way when His people approach Him to honor His name *together*. Jesus said, "For where two or three are gathered together in My name, I am there in the midst of them."[2]

The Bible also says that—in some mysterious way beyond our full understanding—the Lord actually inhabits the praises of His people.[3] Our God, of course, is *omnipresent*, which means that He is everywhere at all times. But on the other hand, when you gather together with other believers and lift up His name in praise, God blesses that action with a special sense of His presence and even His glory.

There is nothing in the world like worship.

You and I truly were created to worship the Lord and glorify Him. And when we do, we discover a sense of fulfillment that is like nothing else in life.

The Christian faith is a singing faith—and that isn't necessarily true of other religions. Yes, they may chant. They may recite their petitions. They may have their various forms of

music. But there is no faith that is as full of vibrant, joyful singing as Christianity. We have the best and most joyous songs of
any religion on earth. And the Lord keeps giving us more and
more of them. Why? Because we have more to sing about than
anyone else!

So start singing, my friend. And find someone to sing with
you. The fact is, you will be getting a head start on heaven. In
the book of Revelation, the apostle John gives this eyewitness
account:

> I saw in heaven . . . what looked like a sea of glass glowing
> with fire and, standing beside the sea, those who had been
> victorious over the beast and its image and over the
> number of its name. They held harps given them by God
> and sang the song of God's servant Moses and of the
> Lamb. (15:1-3, NIV)

For sure, we are going to be learning some great new songs,
probably playing instruments we've never played, and singing
with all our hearts when we reach our eternal home. So we may
as well get started now.

"Well," you say. "I don't know about that. I really don't have
a very good voice."

There's nowhere in the Bible that says you could or should
have a professional-quality set of pipes when you praise God.
The truth is, you are God's own child, He made you exactly the
way you are, and He loves to hear you make a joyful noise unto
Him.

"But sometimes," you say, "I just don't feel like worshiping."

I understand that. There are certainly times when we are not
in the mood to sing or express our hearts in thanks and praise.
But let me ask you this: Do you think those first-century believers always *felt* like praising God? They were harassed. They
were beaten. They were threatened. They were mocked,
mimicked, and minimized. And that was all before breakfast!

But they worshiped the Lord nonetheless.

Earlier I mentioned Hebrews 13:15. The passage urges us with these words: "Through Jesus, therefore, let us continually offer to God a sacrifice of praise—the fruit of lips that openly profess his name" (NIV).

Yes, praise and worship sometimes can be a sacrifice because we don't feel like engaging in it. Our flesh resists it, it doesn't seem convenient, or perhaps we feel a bit down and depressed, and things aren't going well for us. Maybe we've experienced a real tragedy in life and just don't want to thank God.

Worship isn't about you; it's about God. It isn't about how you feel in any given moment; it's about the worthiness of the One we honor.

Do you think Job felt like praising God when he lost everything in a matter of moments? He lost his family . . . his home . . . his possessions . . . his health. But what does the Bible say about how this stunned, grieving man responded? Did he complain? Did he curse God? No. Here's what the record tells us:

> Then Job arose, tore his robe, and shaved his head; and he fell to the ground and worshiped. And he said:
>
> "Naked I came from my mother's womb,
> And naked shall I return there.
> The LORD gave, and the LORD has taken away;
> Blessed be the name of the LORD." (Job 1:20-21)

Uttering those words wasn't easy for Job. It *cost* him something, and it was a sacrifice that pleased the Lord. And notice that the Hebrews passage says we should offer the sacrifice of praise, giving thanks with our lips. In other words, this is something we need to verbalize—just as a wife needs to hear her husband say, "I love you," or a husband needs to hear that he is loved and valued by his wife.

We need to verbalize our love one to another, and in the

same way, we need to speak forth our love for God our Father and Jesus, our Lord.

I'm not saying God *needs* praise from us because He doesn't need anything. If He needed anything, He no longer would be God. But He *wants* our praise, He delights in our heartfelt expressions of thanks, and He tells us specifically to verbalize those expressions. When you're in church with God's people, then, lift your voice and really sing out loud—to Him and for Him. Don't worry about what the people around you are doing or thinking. In those moments, you truly have an audience of One: God Himself.

The Bible doesn't say to give thanks to the Lord because you feel good or because you're experiencing some kind of emotional high. The Word of God tells us to "Give thanks to the LORD, for *He is good*! For His mercy endures forever" (Psalm 107:1, emphasis added).

Your worship is also a witness to others. Did you know that?

Acts 2:47 says of these first-century believers that they were "praising God and having favor with all the people. And the Lord added to the church daily those who were being saved."

There is a direct connection between worship and witness. We *are* being watched by the outside world. And when a Christian can praise God through his or her tears, when a believer can hold high the name of the Lord even in a time of hardship or tragedy, it is a powerful testimony to those who observe.

Sometimes that outside world comes into our church building and sits beside us in a chair or pew. And that person (whether you're aware of it or not) takes note what kind of worshiper you are.

"Well," you say, "does that really matter?"

Actually, it does.

It could be they have never been to church before, and this may be the first time they have worked up the nerve to walk through the door and check things out. And that person—though you would never know that he or she is paying attention to you at all—notices how you're chatting with a friend or texting someone when others are worshiping the Lord. Someone looking on can tell whether you are really engaged and if this is actually something that means something more to you than an empty habit or ritual.

So what do they conclude by observing you? Maybe that worship isn't very important to you at all—that it's just another way of playing at church, but it doesn't really touch your heart and soul.

This is an important point to me because I came to faith as a result of worshiping Christians. No one invited me to their meeting. No one broke the gospel down for me and said, "Here's how to come to Jesus Christ." But I saw a group of Christians sitting on the front lawn of my high school campus, singing songs to Jesus, and I stood there watching them for a while. I wanted to walk away, but something (or Someone) wouldn't let me go.

I thought to myself, *Something's different here. These kids mean what they're singing here. They have something I don't have.* Somehow, that created an opening in my heart to hear the message that followed.

There is a connection between our worship and our witnessing. By simply having our heart in the right place with God as we worship, others will be drawn to the Lord.

They Were an Evangelistic Church

The Lord added to the church daily those who were being saved. (Acts 2:47)

What an attractive band of people this was to a lost and watching world! Truly, this was something new; here were people who did everything together—learning, loving, caring, worshiping, praying, and helping each other out in a thousand practical ways. They looked out for each other, and as those around them watched and paid attention, people came to faith.

Witnessing isn't just something we say or do or practice. It is something we *are*. Acts 1:8 says, "But when the Holy Spirit has come upon you, you will receive power to testify about me with great effect" (TLB).

Evangelism for the early church wasn't some occasional, sporadic thing; it was happening all the time. Acts 2:47 says that people were coming to the Lord *daily*.

That is the way it ought to be for every church. Every week we should be giving people an opportunity to respond to the gospel message and come to Christ. Show me a church that doesn't have a constant flow of new believers coming into it, and I will show you a church that is stagnating. The church needs new believers to remind us of what our life here on earth is all about. And new believers need the church to stabilize them, love them, teach them, and be there for them in times of need.

We enjoy taking our grandchildren to Disneyland just as we enjoyed taking our sons. It is so fun to enter that park with a little one. I think they should make a rule that you can't go to Disneyland without having a child along. When you enter Disneyland as an adult in the company of other adults, it's a completely different experience. You can even talk yourself into being miserable.

As adults we start whining right away about how hot it is, how long the lines are, how much the food costs, and on and on. But when you go with a child, you get to see it all through their eyes, and some of that wonder and fun and delight comes back. You begin to remember what it felt like before you became bored and cynical and ho-hum about life.

It is the same when you're around a young believer and watching them encounter so many wonderful truths and experiences for the first time—things you might have perhaps been taking for granted for years.

The early church had new believers constantly coming in.

And we need that. At Harvest Christian Fellowship, I make no apology for the fact that while we emphasize Bible exposition, discipleship, prayer, worship, and helping the needy, we never will get away from preaching the gospel and inviting people to come to Christ.

Outreach was a vital part of the early church's DNA, and we move away from that strong biblical priority at our spiritual peril.

Potlucks and Communion

They worshiped together at the Temple each day, met in homes for the Lord's Supper, and shared their meals with great joy and generosity. (Acts 2:46, NLT)

When the believers in Jerusalem parted company on Sunday, they didn't say, "See you next Sunday."

What they shared together wasn't just a Sunday-morning-go-to-meeting kind of Christianity. It was their very lives, and they met all the time. Something always was going on. They had home Bible studies. They had meals together. In fact, they "shared their meals with great joy and generosity."

In other words, they ate together often, with plenty for all, and there was lots of laughter.

I love that. I love that the Bible's template for the church included *eating.* At some point, they began to be called "love feasts." Like a modern potluck—or, in some parts of the country, a covered dish supper—people would bring food to eat and food to share. For some who were impoverished, this might be the one good meal they would get in a day.

So the believers would gather in different homes, break bread together, have some laughter and fun, maybe do a little singing, and talk about the things of God with one another. Then, before everyone went home, they often would end with communion, or "the Lord's Supper," where they would receive the broken bread and the cup and remember their Lord's broken body and shed blood.

Why do we have communion? Why does the church celebrate the Lord's Supper?

Bottom line: so that we will remember Jesus.

Why do we need to do that?

Because we so easily forget.

"Well," you say, "I would never forget Jesus."

Perhaps not, in the broad sense. But there is something *specific* that He wants us to always bear in mind. He wants us to remember His suffering, His death, and His resurrection.

Sometimes after we have been believers for a period of time, we might forget about how we came to receive our salvation. We might forget our roots.

Perhaps you can't imagine such a thing happening. You love the Lord, you've memorized Bible verses, you're serving in your church, and you're even leading others into the faith. That is all as it should be. But just remember there was a day when you realized you were a poor, helpless sinner, and an offense to a righteous, holy God. But you heard that Jesus Christ, the Son of God, died on the cross and shed His blood for you, and you turned from your sin and put your faith in Him, and you were forgiven.

So it is that Jesus, who knows us so much better than we know ourselves, says, "I want to give you something that will jog your memory. I want to place something into your life that will remind you again and again of how you came to be where you are. I want you to remember Me with broken bread and with the fruit of the vine: broken bread because My body was broken for you, and the fruit of the vine because My blood was shed for you."

The Lord's Supper is a very brief time in our busy lives when we can completely focus on these precious things that literally transformed our lives, changing our eternal destinations from hell to heaven.

Use those times carefully. Don't let other thoughts crowd these truths out. Think about Jesus and what He has done for you. Revisit His cross in your imagination again. Remember the suffering, the sacrifice. Remember the nails in His hands and feet.

Reread the four gospel accounts and, as much as you can, imagine yourself standing at the foot of that crude Roman cross with our beaten, bloodied Lord hanging there in front of you.

Remember what He did.

Remember that He did it for you.

In the original language of the New Testament, however, it is more than just remembering. It is remembering with affection, remembering with love. So Jesus is saying, "Come with an affectionate remembrance of Me."

Sometimes we make communion just a little too somber, a little too much like a funeral. Yes, there is certainly a place for feeling sorrow over what Jesus endured for us and a place for some serious introspection. In 1 Corinthians 11, Paul cautions us with the reminder that "everyone ought to examine themselves before they eat of the bread and drink from the cup. For those who eat and drink without discerning the body of Christ eat and drink judgment on themselves" (verses 28-29, NIV).

So we never want to approach the Lord's Supper in a careless, flippant, or cavalier way.

But on the other hand, this is a time for affection and even joy.

For as much as He had to suffer for us—enduring things beyond what we can begin to imagine in our finite minds—this was something Jesus *wanted* to do for us because of His great love for us. Hebrews 12:2 tells us that it was "for the joy that was set before Him" that Jesus "endured the cross, despising the shame, and has sat down at the right hand of the throne of God."

Isaiah 53, an Old Testament passage that looks forward through the centuries at the suffering of Christ, declares, "And when he sees all that is accomplished by the anguish of his soul, he shall be satisfied; and because of what he has experienced, my righteous Servant shall make many to be counted righteous before God, for he shall bear all their sins" (verse 11, TLB).

At this very moment, there is joy and satisfaction in the heart of God's Son because of what He has accomplished on the cross for each one of us. He anticipates the day when we will be with Him, and He will show us all the wonders of His Father's house (see John 14:1-3; 17:24).

Because of the Cross, because of Calvary, there is joy in my heart too. I have a relationship with God because of Christ's sacrifice for me. My sins have been forgiven, I have a strong purpose for living, and I have the hope of one day being with Jesus and loved ones in Him who have gone on before me. So I rejoice in these things. Yes, I have great reverence in my heart at the Communion table, but my heart also wells up with affection and praise.

The early church, in all their daily activities, meetings, meals, and shared joys and sorrows, made sure they would never forget the most basic truth and the most important fact of all: They were alive because Jesus had died for them.

Part 3

walking the walk

13

The Holy Spirit: Power Beyond Ourselves

A town somewhere in the U.S. was battered one night by hurricane-force winds. In the morning, after the storm had abated, the citizens emerged from their homes and shelters to assess the damage. The power of the storm quickly became clear to one investigator who was dumbfounded by an incredible discovery. Mouths dropped open as people came to check out his report: a common plastic drinking straw had been driven deep into a telephone pole by the night's vicious winds. Obviously, under normal circumstances, a flimsy straw could never penetrate a telephone pole. But the tremendous power of the wind had driven the straw into the wood like a spike.

As believers living in an ungodly world, sometimes we wonder if we can ever make a difference. We wonder if we can effectively penetrate our cynical culture with the good news that God has given us to proclaim. The answer lies in the source of our power. If we rely on our own strength and methods, then no, we cannot make much of a difference. But if we choose to be driven by God's limitless power, we become like that straw in the hurricane where nothing can stop us. We can indeed make a dramatic difference.

Waiting for Power

Where did the early Christians find the power to turn their world right side up for God? The first group had to wait for it. Shortly before His ascension, Jesus told His disciples, "Do not leave Jerusalem, but wait for the gift my Father promised, which you have heard me speak about" (Acts 1:4, NIV). At this point, it was clear that the disciples were not yet fully equipped for the task of world evangelism. Peter had encountered some rough times in recent weeks. The night before Jesus' crucifixion, he denied his Lord three times. If Peter could be demoralized so easily, how could he be expected to stand before thousands and testify of Jesus? Peter and the other disciples needed power beyond themselves. For that reason Jesus told them to wait in Jerusalem until the power He promised them arrived.

Furthermore, the disciples didn't yet understand what Jesus was doing. They asked Him, "Lord, will You at this time restore the kingdom to Israel?" (Acts 1:6). They still thought Jesus was going to establish an earthly kingdom to overthrow the Romans. This was the hope they nurtured all along. When He was cruci-fied, their expectation for a messianic kingdom on earth was dashed. But with His resurrection, their hopes were revived. So they pressed Him on the issue again.

Jesus didn't answer their question directly but instead replied, "It is not for you to know times or seasons which the Father has put in His own authority. But you shall receive power when the Holy Spirit has come upon you; and you shall be witnesses to Me" (verses 7-8). In essence He told them, "Don't be concerned about when My earthly kingdom will be established, but focus your attention on what you should be doing while you await it. That's why you must wait in Jerusalem until you are empowered by the Holy Spirit."

Most of us would probably love to know when Jesus is coming back—but God is not going to give us an exact time or date. His answer to us is the same one He gave to His disciples two thousand years ago: Focus your attention on the task at hand, not the trip ahead.

We have opportunities today that may not remain available and open doors that may soon close. We can't allow ourselves to become so preoccupied with the future that we overlook the present. We need to take hold of the unique opportunities God sets before us each day.

But to do so, we need power beyond ourselves. And that is just what Jesus promised us: "You shall receive power when the Holy Spirit has come upon you." The ineffectiveness of the church today is largely due to our neglect of the power that set the first-century church into motion. Programs have taken the place of power. Gimmicks have taken the place of the gospel. Many years ago, A. W. Tozer said that if the Holy Spirit were taken away from the New Testament church, 95 percent of what they did would come to a halt. But if the Holy Spirit were taken away from today's church, only 5 percent of what it does would cease.[1] We're not seeing the same results as the early believers because we're not relying on the same power they did.

Yet God can still work in the lives of Christians today just as He worked in the first century. Consider the nation of China. Beginning in the nineteenth century, Western missionaries ministered to the people of that country for one hundred years and reaped about eight hundred thousand converts. Then the communist revolution took place and Mao Tse-tung threw out the Westerners. Chinese Christians lost their churches and Bibles. Many believers were tortured and even put to death for their faith. Western Christians wondered whether the church in

China would survive the intense persecution.

So how did these believers fare under forty years of communist rule with almost none of the resources we consider essential? When Western Christians were readmitted into the country and allowed to see how the Chinese church had managed during those turbulent years, they were astonished. The church had not floundered; it had flourished, increasing by as many as 75 million converts!

How did they do it? They got back to the basics, took God at His Word, and laid hold of the same power the early church employed. Vance Havner once said, "We are not going to move this world by criticism of it nor conformity to it, but by the combustion within it of lives ignited by the Spirit of God."[2] The Chinese church, thriving and advancing even under communism, is living proof of his words. This power is still available to the church.

Power to Perform

The word for *power* Jesus used in Acts 1:8 is the Greek word *dunamis*, from which we get the words *dynamite, dynamic,* and *dynamo*. While the word obviously had not yet taken on those meanings when Jesus used it, nevertheless it's clear He was describing something dynamic and potent, something that can turn ordinary Christians into extraordinary Christians.

Because of the nature of *dunamis*, it is important to understand the role of emotions in the outworking of God's power in our lives. Since it is possible to have an emotional response to what God does in us, we must distinguish between emotion and emotionalism. Emotion can be a very good thing. We can feel joy, excitement, or happiness when God answers our prayers or uses us in a special way. The problem comes when we enter the realm of emotionalism, attempting to live constantly on the plane of good feelings.

Let's suppose you are in a worship service and feel God's

powerful presence in a special way. That's wonderful! But if you expect every worship service to replicate that feeling, you have passed from emotion to emotionalism. Sadly, some believers don't believe they are relating to God unless they have a dramatic feeling of His presence. And when they don't feel God's presence, they can't seem to relate to Him.

Or imagine that you are sharing your faith with a non-Christian neighbor and are exhilarated by the sensation of God's power operating in your life at that moment. Great! But if, in the future, you judge whether God is using you by the presence or absence of that sense of exhilaration, you're into emotionalism. God didn't pour out the power of the Holy Spirit to make us *feel* something but to help us *accomplish* something. God's power is practical power. Enjoy the good feelings when they happen, but don't let the lack of feelings prevent you from stepping out in the power of the Spirit to do what God wants you to do.

It's like the difference between dynamite and a dynamo. A stick of dynamite explodes and makes a big impact in only seconds, then it's all over. A dynamo, a machine designed to generate power so work can be accomplished, just keeps running. Sometimes God's power is like dynamite in our lives, blasting us emotionally, jolting us out of our complacency, and motivating us to some great step of growth or feat of ministry. We see a lot of these explosions in the miracles and wonders that highlight the book of Acts.

But in between these explosive moments, God's power is like a strong, steady-running motor inside us that helps us live from day to day at a level we can't achieve in our own strength. This is the power that keeps us operating between emotional highs and mountaintop experiences. Never underestimate the importance of God's explosive, dynamite power in your life. But by the same token, be aware that God's dynamic, dynamo power is available every moment and every day to help you be what God wants you to be and accomplish what He wants you to accomplish.

As the saying goes, it is not how high you jump that counts; it is how straight you walk when you hit the ground. I don't care how loudly you shout hallelujah, how long you sing, or how great you feel emotionally or spiritually. If your dynamite experiences aren't matched by a practical, daily, dynamo lifestyle, your emotional highs don't mean much. God's power is practical and especially designed to affect our daily walk inside and outside the church.

We get a better picture of the kind of power Jesus is talking about when we see how *dunamis* and its verb form *dunamai* are used elsewhere in the New Testament. It should encourage you to know that the power Jesus promises us is the same kind of power God exerted to raise Christ from the dead and seat Him in heaven (see Ephesians 1:19-20). This same, supernatural power is present in you by God's Spirit to:

- Cause you to overflow with hope (Romans 15:13)
- Help you bear up under and escape temptation (1 Corinthians 10:13)
- Equip you to be a servant of God (Ephesians 3:7)
- Give you inner strength (Ephesians 3:16)
- Allow God to do more than you can ask or imagine in and through your life (Ephesians 3:20)
- Equip you to resist Satan (Ephesians 6:11)
- Provide endurance and patience (Colossians 1:11)
- Help you work hard for Him (Colossians 1:29)
- Shield you (1 Peter 1:5)
- Provide everything you need for life and godliness (2 Peter 1:3)

No wonder the early church had such a dramatic impact upon their world. They were power-packed! It's wonderful to know that the very same power that raised Jesus from the dead, gave Peter boldness, saved unbelievers, caused miracles, and much more is just as available to us today.

Power for a Purpose

In Acts 1:8, Jesus tells us the ultimate purpose of God's power in our lives: to be His witnesses. The word "witness" comes from the Greek word *martus*, from which we get our English word "martyr." This doesn't mean that every empowered witness will become a martyr. But in light of the suffering and death of many Christians over the centuries, Jesus seems to be saying, "You shall receive dynamic power to live for Me and, if necessary, even to die for Me."

The word "witness" is used twenty-nine times in the book of Acts as either a verb or a noun. A witness is someone who tells others what he has seen and heard. The apostles had this understanding when they said in Acts 4:20, "We cannot but speak the things which we have seen and heard."

If you were a witness in a court of law and were called to testify, the judge and jury wouldn't be interested in your personal opinion about the guilt or innocence of the person on trial. What they want from you are the facts about what you observed. You might say, "I think the defendant is guilty. Just look at him! He has shifty eyes. He just looks guilty!" But the court isn't interested in your opinion. It only wants you to describe what you saw and heard.

Likewise, we as Christ's witnesses are empowered to proclaim what we have seen and heard about our Savior. Witnessing means telling others what Christ has done for us and what He has shown us in His Word. Our daily witness includes our Spirit-empowered words as well as our Spirit-empowered walk. I frequently hear Christians say, "Let's go witness and share our faith," and that's great. But in reality, a witness is as much what we are as what we say and do. Without God's power in our lives, we are ill-equipped to be the witnesses He has called us to be.

Where are we to be His witnesses? We know that Jesus wants His people to reach out to the entire world with the gospel. He gave us our marching orders after His resurrection and before

His ascension: "Go into all the world and preach the gospel to every creature" (Mark 16:15).

You may say, "But reaching the world is such an enormous task! Where do I start?"

This reminds me of the question, How do you eat an elephant? The answer is one bite at a time. The same is true of the work of world evangelism. It takes place "one bite at a time."

In Acts 1:8, we have God's strategy for world evangelism, "bite by bite" or step by step: "You shall be witnesses to Me in Jerusalem, and in all Judea and Samaria, and to the end of the earth."

Pay special attention to the significance of the order. The first stop was to be Jerusalem. Jerusalem was home base for the church, representing her own backyard. Your Jerusalem is the neighborhood and town where you live.

The second stop was Judea. This area was located all around Jerusalem, representing the disciples' larger community. Your Judea may encompass the county or state where your town is located.

The third stop was Samaria. This province north of Judea was home to a racially mixed segment of people that the Jews despised. It was definitely the other side of the tracks. Your Samaria may be anyplace nearby where people of a different race, culture, or socioeconomic level live.

The fourth stop was the end of the earth. Many of Jesus' disciples left familiar surroundings and traveled great distances as His witnesses. This represents global outreach far beyond our borders.

Sometimes the life of a person on the foreign mission field sounds so glamorous and exciting. You hear veteran missionaries tell of their great travels for Christ and all the people they led to faith. So you begin to daydream, *I sure would like to be a missionary. I want to travel somewhere far away and just tell people about the Lord. That would be so wonderful.*

No matter how sincere your intentions may be, you must

start with home base. You don't need to cross the sea to be a witness; you can start by crossing the street! Your mission field is all around you. If you are not willing to be a witness where you live, don't expect God to give you opportunities elsewhere. Be faithful where you are, and He may open even greater opportunities for you in other places.

The Dynamic Difference

Ten days after Jesus ascended into heaven, the Holy Spirit descended upon the obediently waiting 120 disciples (see Acts 2:1-4). What difference did the empowering of the Holy Spirit make in the lives of these early believers? The same disciples who huddled behind closed doors after Jesus' crucifixion for fear of the Jews could not be kept behind closed doors after they had received this heavenly dynamite. After God's power exploded in their lives, they had the courage to tell the authorities, "We cannot but speak the things which we have seen and heard" (Acts 4:20). And Peter, who had denied Jesus publicly two months earlier, immediately began preaching to a huge crowd in Jerusalem and welcomed three thousand converts. The disciples were transformed into people of power. They were on fire.

God's power still makes a difference in people's lives today. What about you? Do you desire greater boldness in your witness for Christ? Has your prayer life become dry and one-dimensional? Do you fail to see any gifts of the Spirit at work in your life? Do you feel that you're lacking something in your spiritual walk? Is the world turning you upside down instead of you turning your world right side up?

If you've answered yes to these questions, then you are a perfect candidate for the power of God's Spirit to transform your life. What could be hindering your experience of God's power? Perhaps it is unbelief. Unbelief is probably the greatest obstacle to the Spirit's work. Matthew 13:58 records that when Jesus returned to His hometown, "He did not do many mighty works there because of their unbelief." Interestingly, the phrase *mighty works* in this verse is once again the Greek word *dunamis*. Jesus could not display His full power because of the unbelief of the people.

Unbelief is the barrier you erect when you say, "I don't think God can work powerfully in my life." And when you don't believe God can exercise His power through you, that is just what happens. It's your own fault if you are not receiving anything from the Lord or doing anything for the Lord. It's no different than placing your hand over your cup and saying, "No, thank you" when the waitress comes around with more coffee. Through unbelief, you've placed your hand over your life and told God that you're not interested in what He can say to you and do through you.

The promise of God's power is as valid for you as it was for the church in the book of Acts. Peter said during his first sermon, "The promise is to you and to your children, and to all who are afar off, as many as the Lord our God will call" (Acts 2:39). Are you called? If you're a Christian, of course you are! God's promise of power is for you. The first step toward realizing and employing God's power to have an impact on your world is to say, "Lord, I believe Your power is for me. I believe You want to do dynamic things in me and through me by the power of Your Spirit. So fill me, Lord, with Your dynamic power so that I might turn my world right side up for Jesus Christ."

"Okay," you say, "I believe God can empower me with His Holy Spirit. Now what do I do?"

Dunamis is not an impersonal force. *Dunamis* is God's Holy Spirit exercising His power in our lives. People of power are people of the Spirit. If you want God's power flooding your life, you need God's Spirit flooding your life.

Sadly, over the centuries the Scriptures concerning the Holy Spirit and His power have been misinterpreted and twisted. Today there is tremendous confusion regarding the Spirit-filled life. It is vital that we understand what the Bible means when it speaks of the Spirit-filled life so that we don't miss the genuine for the counterfeit. That's what we'll take a look at next.

Embracing the Genuine, Rejecting the Counterfeit

People with a passion for God, who are turning their world right side up for Christ, are people filled and empowered by the Holy Spirit. That is why the infant church made such an impact on its world. On the Day of Pentecost, the Holy Spirit was poured out on the church in Jerusalem in dramatic, never-to-be-repeated fashion (see Acts 2:1-4). The power that energized the early Christians flowed out of the Holy Spirit's infilling. The Acts of the Apostles, as this New Testament book is titled, could just as easily be called the Acts of the Holy Spirit Through the Apostles.

Before Pentecost, godly people were only periodically filled with the Holy Spirit. The Spirit came upon certain people at certain times for certain tasks, and then He left them. As an example, in the Old Testament we find the Holy Spirit coming upon Elijah to work a miracle and upon Samson to accomplish a great physical feat and upon David as he worshiped the Lord on his stringed instrument. The Holy Spirit did not dwell in these people from day to day. But from Pentecost on, He took up permanent residence in the lives of all who come to God through faith in Christ. If you're a Christian, then the Holy Spirit lives within you (see Romans 8:9). And the same power that energized the first-century believers to dramatically impact their world is available today to all who are indwelled by the Holy Spirit.

Sadly, the Holy Spirit's role in the life of the believer has been horribly misrepresented in recent times. Some Christians believe that you must have a great emotional experience with God in order to be genuinely empowered by the Holy Spirit. Others believe that you become a kind of spiritual oddball when you invite the Holy Spirit into your life. Neither is true.

God's Spirit moves powerfully yet *practically*. Paul wrote, "God has not given us a spirit of fear, but of power and of love and of a sound mind" (2 Timothy 1:7). The phrase *of a sound mind* describes a well-balanced, disciplined mind. You don't need to check your brain at the door to be a Spirit-led, Spirit-empowered Christian.

When we see bizarre antics performed in the name of the Holy Spirit, our tendency is to recoil and say, "If that's what it means to live in the power of the Spirit, I don't want anything to do with it." But just because some have misused and twisted the Scriptures, don't conclude that God's Spirit doesn't want to do a genuine, powerful, sound-minded work in the lives of believers today. He does. The key is understanding and following what God's Word says about the ministry of the Holy Spirit.

Finding a Happy Medium

Believers often fall into one of two camps regarding the ministry and gifts of the Holy Spirit. One extreme emphasizes the work of the Holy Spirit in practically everything they say and do. They have conferences on the Spirit, sing songs about the Spirit, and constantly talk about the work and gifts of the Spirit. Often they are so busy seeking direct revelations from the Spirit of God that they overlook the clear, written revelation in the Word of God. Although these believers may have a genuine love for the Lord, their desire to witness power has lead them into unscriptural practices.

At the other end of the spectrum, we have Christians whose focus is on Bible exposition. They study the Word, learn the Word, and memorize the Word (as we all should). Unfortunately, however, sometimes these zealous students of Scripture are close-minded to the working of God's Spirit. They can be very knowledgeable about the Spirit and yet quench the Spirit by not allowing Him to move in their lives outside their time-honored traditions.

The key is balance: knowing the Word of God and implementing the practical power of God's Spirit. God's Word gives us absolutes, guarding us from ill-conceived teachings and self-proclaimed prophets with a false message. Like the Bereans, we should examine every teaching and experience by the Scriptures "to find out whether these things [are] so" (Acts 17:11). This is precisely how the Spirit of God works through the Word of God.

I can't think of a better example of balance between God's Word and God's Spirit than Calvary Chapel of Costa Mesa, in Southern California. Chuck Smith, the senior pastor, began this ministry with twenty-five people in a home Bible study. After twenty-five years, they have a regular attendance (not names on the church roll but people actually attending) of some twenty thousand! Not only that, but there are over eight hundred Calvary Chapel affiliates—many of which have congregations numbering five thousand or more.

What explains the phenomenal success of Calvary Chapel and its branch ministries around the world? Chuck Smith's answer is disarmingly simple: "It is the Spirit of God working through the Word of God in the hearts of the people of God."

The apostle Peter understood this balance. On the Day of Pentecost, he was able to explain from Scripture the incredible experience that caused some to think the disciples were drunk. He said, "This is what was spoken by the prophet Joel" (Acts 2:16). Peter declared the experience valid because it was based in God's Word.

Peter had many wonderful spiritual experiences with Jesus before Pentecost, including the Transfiguration when the Lord's majesty was revealed.[3] Later, when writing about this experience, Peter said, "So we have the prophetic word confirmed, which you do well to heed as a light that shines in a dark place" (2 Peter 1:19). In essence he was saying, "Yes, I have seen many of these things with my own eyes, but I don't base my belief in Jesus on my personal experiences alone. I base my faith on the 'prophetic word,' the Word of God."

Anyone who claims a spiritual experience and yet can't say, "This is what is spoken in the Word of God," should stop deceiving himself. Any so-called spiritual phenomenon or experience that isn't founded solidly on Scripture should be abandoned.

A Profile of the Holy Spirit

People have many misconceptions regarding the work and ministry of the Holy Spirit, undoubtedly because of the many bizarre and unusual exhibitions said to be inspired by Him. Consequently, many Christians recoil from anything that smacks of the Holy Spirit, fearing that they, too, will end up exhibiting the same bizarre behavior.

This, of course, is unfortunate. The Holy Spirit is greatly grieved by many of the antics being blamed on Him these days. He has a distinct and important work in this world, as well as in the life of the believer, and it is a great tragedy to miss out on that work because of misrepresentation and ignorance.

If our spiritual experiences are to line up with the Word of God, then it is vital that we have a basic understanding of who the Holy Spirit is. Some wrongly assume that the Spirit is more of an it than a Him. This may be due in part to a misunderstanding of the portrait we have of Him in Scripture, where He is described as being like the wind or being in the form of a dove, and so forth. Yet we must balance these images with those we find for the rest of the Trinity.

After all, Jesus referred to Himself as the Bread of Life, the Door, and the Vine. Do these images really mean that Jesus is a loaf of bread or an actual door? Of course not! Likewise, God the Father is referred to as a refuge and a consuming fire. Does this mean that He is literally a rock fortress or a blasting furnace? Of course not! These are merely symbols to help our finite minds grasp certain attributes of the Godhead—Father, Son, and Holy Spirit.

Nor is the Holy Spirit an impersonal force or power. When speaking of this member of the Trinity, Jesus said, "When He, the Spirit of truth, has come, He will guide you into all truth. . . . He will glorify Me" (John 16:13-14).

Jesus identified the Holy Spirit as a person, a *He*. Furthermore, personal actions are attributed to the Holy Spirit throughout Scripture. For instance, the Spirit speaks (Acts 13:2), teaches (John 14:26), intercedes (Romans 8:26), gives commands (Acts 13:2), and ordains (Acts 20:28). In addition, as a person, the Holy Spirit can be offended. The New Testament specifically mentions six sins that can be committed against the Holy Spirit. It's only possible to sin against a person; you can't sin against an impersonal force or an inanimate object.

It's great to know that we believers are not influenced by a "force" but by a Person—a Person who is actually God Himself and whose purpose is to conform us to the image of Christ.

The Spirit-Controlled Life

The Spirit-filled, Spirit-empowered life is well-illustrated in the story of Stephen in the book of Acts. Stephen was "a man full of . . . the Holy Spirit" (Acts 6:5). The word *full* in this verse can also be translated, "controlled by." How did Stephen exemplify the Spirit-controlled life? He was full of faith and wisdom, he served widows, preached the gospel boldly, and was martyred for standing up to the unrighteous Jewish leaders. Yet his boldness and death made a major impact on one of those leaders who later became the most influential disciple of the first century, the apostle Paul. Stephen was on fire in the Spirit, and though he didn't live to see it, he changed his world for God.

Ephesians 5:18 exhorts us, "Be filled with the Spirit." Literally translated, this phrase says, "Be constantly filled with the Spirit." In other words, being filled with the Spirit is not just a one-time event; it is absolutely necessary to come back for refills again and again. It is a constant, ongoing process of welcoming the presence and power of the Holy Spirit into your life.

Moreover, the original Greek renders this phrase in the imperative. God is not merely suggesting that you be filled with the Spirit; He is commanding you to be constantly refilled. He wants you to take hold of all the resources He has made available to you.

Note that Stephen's Spirit-controlled life didn't send him into some euphoric state. Acts does specify, however, that he was under the control of the Spirit of God and became a powerful witness for Christ. That is exactly what Jesus said would happen when the Holy Spirit came (see Acts 1:8), and Stephen experienced the full definition of the word *witness (martus)* by giving his life.

Because the Holy Spirit controlled every aspect of Stephen's life, he had the ability to stand up before his accusers and testify to what he believed. You may be thinking, *I could never do what Stephen did.* Yes, you could—not in your own abilities or strengths, but in the power of the Spirit. What was available to Stephen is also available to you. Remember Paul's words to the believers in Philippi: "I can do all things through Christ who strengthens me" (Philippians 4:13).

"The Proof of the Pudding"

We all know that many of the activities attributed to the Holy Spirit have little, if anything, to do with Him. It's been said, "The proof of the pudding is in the eating," or to put it biblically, "By their fruit you will recognize them" (Matthew 7:16, NIV). What is the evidence of infilled believers? Practical results. In the book of Galatians, Paul tells us the natural outgrowth of being filled with the Holy Spirit is "love, joy, peace, longsuffering, kindness, goodness, faithfulness, gentleness, self-control" (5:22-23).

Spirit-filled believers will enjoy great feelings and the use of spiritual gifts. The fruit of joy and peace can't be beat. However, the Spirit-filled life also shows itself practically in longsuffering and self-control. Walking in the Spirit should be seen in the worship service and in the workplace. It should be evident in the church and in the home.

What does it mean to be filled by the Spirit? Three word pictures in the original Greek help us understand what the term *filled* means.

First, it was used of the wind filling a sail and pushing a boat through the water. To be filled with the Spirit is to be moved along by God Himself. He becomes our source of motivation. When we are filled with the Spirit, following His commands becomes a delight instead of a drudgery. That is why the apostle John could write, "This is love for God: to keep his commands. And his commands are not burdensome" (1 John 5:3, NIV).

Second, being filled carries the idea of permeation and was used in reference to salt permeating meat in order to flavor it and preserve it. God wants His Spirit to permeate our lives and influence everything we think, say, and do.

Third, being filled means to be under the control of something or someone. A person who is filled with sorrow is no longer in complete control of himself but is controlled by that emotion. He can't stop weeping. He can't concentrate on his responsibilities. A person who is filled with anger, fear, jealousy, and so forth is also under the control of those overpowering emotions.

Being filled with the Spirit is similar, only in a much more positive sense. It means placing every thought, every decision, and every act under the Spirit's control. Galatians 5:16 promises, "So I say, walk by the Spirit, and you will not gratify the desires of the flesh" (NIV).

When you walk in the Spirit, you have the resources to do what God wants you to do and to not do what God doesn't want you to do.

Are you controlled by the Spirit right now? You must be if you are to be the man or woman God uses to turn your world right side up. Go to Him right now in prayer and ask Him to refill you and give you a heartfelt passion for God.

14 The Power of Prayer

As you read these words, you may find yourself facing a personal crisis.

It might be a lack of employment, a foreclosure on your home, or a deep loss in your investments. Maybe you have a marriage that is falling apart or a prodigal son or daughter who is away from the Lord right now. You could even be facing a life-threatening illness and find yourself paralyzed by fear as you ponder an uncertain future.

So what are you to do?

The Bible says you are to pray.

The apostle Paul gave the church in Philippi these life-transforming words:

Don't worry about anything; instead, pray about everything. Tell God what you need, and thank him for all he has done. Then you will experience God's peace, which exceeds anything we can understand. His peace will guard your hearts and minds as you live in Christ Jesus. (Philippians 4:6-7, NLT)

In the backwash of emotions and mental turmoil following the death of my thirty-three-year-old son, Christopher, I have lived by these words.

In times of deep sadness, when those waves of grief roll over me, I pray. Sometimes my prayers aren't very long—little more than quick cries to God: *God, help me. Lord, give me strength.*

And He does. He gives me the strength that I need for the moment.

God promises that He will give you a peace that *passes* understanding—not necessarily a peace that will always give understanding.

Even so, when you're overwhelmed, that's the time to pray. I don't even want to contemplate what life would be like if I didn't have the privilege of taking my sorrows and cares and worries to the Lord.

In Psalm 61, David wrote,

Hear my cry, O God;
Attend to my prayer.
From the end of the earth I will cry to You,
When my heart is overwhelmed;
Lead me to the rock that is higher than I. (verses 1-2)

In other words, when your heart is overwhelmed, start looking for higher ground. In times of prayer, God lifts us and gives us His strength.

That is what we see the church doing in Acts 12. As the chapter opens, the believers in Jerusalem faced a pretty bleak scenario. They were in one of those situations where, if God didn't come through for them, it would be a complete disaster.

We don't like situations like that. We like to have a backup plan in case things go south. In fact, we would like to have a backup plan for our backup plan. But sometimes the Lord allows us to be caught up in a set of circumstances with no backup plan, no back door, no emergency exit, and no way out except through Him.

In times like that, as David said, our hearts are overwhelmed. And we cry out to God in our distress.

Acts 12 gives an exciting account of the power of prayer, and in this chapter, we'll consider four principles about praying in a way that brings results, about *prayer that prevails.*

Herod's Vendetta

Now about that time Herod the king stretched out his hand to harass some from the church. Then he killed James the brother of John with the sword. And because he saw that it pleased the Jews, he proceeded further to seize Peter also. Now it was during the Days of Unleavened Bread. So when he had arrested him, he put him in prison, and delivered him to four squads of soldiers to keep him, intending to bring him before the people after Passover.

Peter was therefore kept in prison, but constant prayer was offered to God for him by the church. (Acts 12:1-5)

As the story begins, a shocking wave of persecution has shaken the young church to its core. Back in Acts 7, young Stephen had been martyred, and in the attacks that followed, many of the believers had been scattered through out Judea and Samaria. But God continued to work in spite of —and even through—that tragedy.

As we have noted, the comfortable holy huddle the believers had enjoyed in Jerusalem was shattered by that campaign of violence and intimidation, and the believers spread out across the land with the good news about Jesus (which they were supposed to be doing in the first place).

Then things seemed to settle down for a while—until the evil King Herod decided he wanted to boost his poll numbers with certain elements of the Jewish population. The interlude of peace was shattered as "the king stretched out his hand to harass some from the church" (Acts 12:1).

He laid hands on James, the brother of John and one of the men who had been closest to Jesus during his three-year ministry, and had him summarily executed.

Apparently, the king's strategy worked. The enemies of the church were very happy about that move, and Herod's approval numbers soared. In fact, the strategy worked so well that he looked for a way to push his numbers even higher. So he arrested Peter, one of the principal leaders of the church, intending to execute him as well—after a bit of political grandstanding at a show trial.

With Peter behind bars, Herod wanted to make very sure that Peter didn't get out of prison. Something very strange had happened when the high priest had thrown Peter and the apostles into the public jail, as recounted in Acts 5:

During the night an angel of the Lord opened the doors of the jail and brought them out. "Go, stand in the temple courts," he said, "and tell the people all about this new life." (verses 19-20, NIV)

Herod undoubtedly had his own prison and his own security apparatus. But just to be on the safe side, he detailed an extra armed guard to keep Peter under lock and key until he could publicly put him to death.

Acts 12:4 tells us that Herod delivered Peter "to four squads of soldiers to keep him, intending to bring him before the people after Passover."

So Peter was behind two gates, chained to two guards, and guarded by fourteen more. So what did the Jerusalem church do? Flood Herod's switchboard? Call their members of Congress? Organize a protest and picket the palace? No, we have no record of such a thing. There were no petition drives, product boycotts, street demonstrations, bumper stickers, or tearful appeals to the media. (By the way, I am not necessarily critical of any of those expressions in their proper place.)

Verse 5 gives us their entire strategy: "Peter was therefore kept in prison, but constant prayer was offered to God for him by the church."

We have a secret weapon in the church, and it is called prayer. Though all other doors may remain closed, one door is always open: the door into the presence of God through prayer.

So often, however, we save this as our last resort—what we do when all else fails. But this church prayed as a *first* resort, and it was by far the most powerful and effective thing they could have done.

Now let's see if we can identify some principles about the prayer they offered on Peter's behalf.

Four Principles of Effective Prayer

1. They offered their prayer to God.

Constant prayer was offered to God. (Acts 12:5)

Does that seem just a little too obvious? Isn't all prayer offered to God? Not necessarily. Often in prayer there is little thought of God. Our mind can be so taken up with what we need that we actually never think of the Lord Himself. Sometimes in our prayer we pray to impress others. Jesus warned us to not be like the Pharisees, who would stand on the street corners and put on a show when they prayed.

Maybe you're in a prayer meeting, and you're praying out loud. Somehow, the words just come flowing out, and some part of your mind is thinking just how profound you sound. You think to yourself, *Man, this is a great prayer. This is better than anyone else's prayer* . . . as if it was some kind of contest!

Jesus told a story about a Pharisee who got caught up in his own self-congratulating verbiage as he prayed. And the Lord said of him, "The Pharisee stood and prayed thus with himself" (Luke 18:11). In other words, this man's prayers never went any higher than the ceiling; he was praying with himself, and God wasn't even part of the equation. That is possible for you and me, also. We can rattle off or recite some prayer but never really have an encounter with the living God.

We want to truly offer our prayers to Him.

I remember when my little granddaughter Stella was just learning to pray. Before a meal we would say, "Okay, let's pray. Let's fold our hands and close our eyes." So she did that. And sometimes I would look while we were praying, and she would have her eyes open or be eating something! As time went on, we taught her to close her eyes so that she would learn to think about God for a few seconds before she started poking at the food.

But obviously, you don't have to close your eyes when you pray . . . or fold your hands . . . or kneel. Scripture speaks of many postures in prayer, but what really counts isn't posture at all; it is the attitude of the heart. You can be praying when you're walking down the sidewalk, driving on a highway (eyes open, please), or taking a shower.

What God looks for is the movement of your heart toward Him.

Yes, the church's prayer in Acts 12 was offered to God. But here is a corollary to that point: As we present our prayers before God, we must align our wills with His. In other words, if you want to see your prayers answered in the affirmative, your goal should be to pray according to God's will, as you best understand it.

Easier said than done, by the way.

How do we discover God's will? One of the best ways I can think of is to be in the Scriptures every day, seeking His face as you read His Word. That is what the prophet Daniel did in Babylon as he prayed for the return of his captive nation to Israel. He had read in the book of Jeremiah that the captivity was to last seventy years, and as that time reached its conclusion, he "turned to the Lord God and pleaded with him in prayer and fasting" (Daniel 9:3, NLT). He prayed for God's forgiveness and mercy on the nation, knowing he was on firm ground for doing so.

The best way you and I are going to discover the heart and mind of God is through a consistent, diligent study of the Bible. And as you know more and more about God's desires, your prayers will more and more reflect those desires.

Jesus made this amazing promise: "If you abide in Me, and My words abide in you, you will ask what you desire, and it shall be done for you" (John 15:7). Another translation says, "But if you make yourselves at home with me and my words are at home in you, you can be sure that whatever you ask will be listened to and acted upon" (MSG).

We like the sound of that, don't we? Especially the latter part, "whatever you ask." But don't miss the big *if* at the beginning of that sentence: "*If* you make yourselves at home with me and my words are at home in you . . ." In other words, if you are investing daily time in studying His Word and growing in your understanding of the nature and character of God, you will begin praying for what *He* wants. True prayer is not bending God my way; it is bending myself His way.

2. They prayed with passion and persistence.

Look at Acts 12:5 again: "Constant prayer was offered to God for him by the church." What kind of prayer? *Constant* prayer. Another way to translate it would be "earnest prayer." In fact, the word used here to describe their prayer is the same word used to describe the prayer of Jesus in the Garden of Gethsemane. That was a prayer of passion. It was an agonizing prayer. And that is the way this church prayed for their leader, Peter.

Many times our prayers have no power because they have no heart. If we put so little passion in our prayers, we can't expect God to put much passion into answering them.

They didn't pray, "Lord, save Peter . . . or whatever."

Sometimes we can be so wrapped up in our own thoughts and concerns that we really don't give our full attention to prayer. Someone will tell us about a crisis they are facing, and we may send up a quick "Lord help them," but if the truth were known, we don't really care that much. We don't pray with passion, and we don't pray continuously.

Jesus taught, "Ask, and it will be given to you; seek, and you will find; knock, and it will be opened to you."[1] A better translation of the original language, however, would read, "Keep on asking. Keep on seeking. Keep on knocking."

If someone keeps knocking at your door, you might say, "Okay, okay, hold on! I'm coming." And you open the door just to shut them up. But God isn't irritated at all when you keep knocking, knocking, and knocking at His door. He likes it. He likes opening the door to you, His much-loved child. In fact, He tells you to be persistent and to keep at it.

You and I tend to pray for something once or twice and then say, "Well, I guess God isn't going to answer this prayer." No! Keep praying about that matter on your heart. In Luke 18:1, Jesus taught His disciples that "men always ought to pray and not lose heart."

So the church in Jerusalem kept praying with great passion and persistence for Peter, knowing he was in peril for his very life.

Sometimes we will say, "My prayer wasn't answered." But in reality, we just didn't *like* the answer. No is as much of an answer to prayer as yes is. God answers prayer in one of three ways: yes, no, and wait.

But we don't like to wait. In a society of instant gratification in which we get everything on demand, we don't have a lot of patience to spare. Nevertheless, the Lord's timing is perfect, and we have to accommodate ourselves to His schedule, His priorities, and His reading of the seasons of our lives.

You see, sometimes God says go, sometimes God says slow, and sometimes God says grow.

When Paul, for instance, prayed for release from his "thorn in the flesh," God answered that prayer. But it wasn't with a yes. God's answer was, "My grace is sufficient for you" (2 Corinthians 12:7, 9). So effectively God was saying to Paul, "I will use this set of circumstances in your life to cause you to grow."

Moses wanted to deliver the Israelites out of the bondage of Egypt, and it was a great idea—even a God idea. The problem was, his timing was off by about forty years. So through a set of circumstances that came into Moses' life, God was essentially telling him, "Slow."

But sometimes God says go—as in, "Go *now*."

For all the times when God asks us to wait for the answers to our prayers, there are other times when they are answered so fast that it shocks us. The petition is barely out of our mouths when we see the answer walk in through the front door.

3. They prayed together.

The church met together at the home of Mary, mother of John Mark, to plead with God for Peter's release.

There is power in united prayer. Jesus said, "If two of you agree on earth concerning anything that they ask, it will be done for them by My Father in heaven. For where two or three are gathered together in My name, I am there in the midst of them" (Matthew 18:19-20). The term translated "agree" here doesn't just mean agreement in general. It isn't as though three Christians could get together and pray for something stupid and expect to receive it. As I mentioned earlier, your will needs to be in line with God's will, and your prayers need to be in accordance with what He teaches in His Word. So this verse assumes that those who pray together are all in alignment with the will of God and praying with a God-given burden.

So if you have a crisis or a need in your life, you go to your Christian friends and say, "Here's what is going on in my life. Will you pray about this with me? Can we agree together on this?" That is what the church did at John Mark's house. They prayed together.

4. They prayed with doubt, and God heard them anyway.

Yes, these believers prayed to God, prayed with passion, prayed constantly, and prayed together. But Scripture always paints a true picture, and it's obvious that these good, sincere men and women harbored doubts in their hearts about God's answer.

That is the only thing we can conclude when we see them so blown away by the literal answer to their prayers.

You have to love the way Dr. Luke tells the story:

All the time that Peter was under heavy guard in the jail-house, the church prayed for him most strenuously.

Then the time came for Herod to bring him out for the kill. That night, even though shackled to two soldiers, one on either side, Peter slept like a baby. And there were guards at the door keeping their eyes on the place. Herod was taking no chances!

Suddenly there was an angel at his side and light flooding the room. The angel shook Peter and got him up: "Hurry!" The handcuffs fell off his wrists. The angel said, "Get dressed. Put on your shoes." Peter did it. Then, "Grab your coat and let's get out of here." Peter followed him, but didn't believe it was really an angel — he thought he was dreaming.

Past the first guard and then the second, they came to the iron gate that led into the city. It swung open before them on its own, and they were out on the street, free as the breeze. At the first intersection the angel left him, going his own way. That's when Peter realized it was no dream. "I can't believe it — this really happened! The Master sent his angel and rescued me from Herod's vicious little production and the spectacle the Jewish mob was looking forward to."

Still shaking his head, amazed, he went to Mary's

house, the Mary who was John Mark's mother. The house was packed with praying friends. When he knocked on the door to the courtyard, a young woman named Rhoda came to see who it was. But when she recognized his voice—Peter's voice!—she was so excited and eager to tell everyone Peter was there that she forgot to open the door and left him standing in the street.

But they wouldn't believe her, dismissing her, dismissing her report. "You're crazy," they said. She stuck by her story, insisting. They still wouldn't believe her and said, "It must be his angel." All this time poor Peter was standing out in the street, knocking away.

Finally they opened up and saw him—and went wild! (Acts 12:5-16, MSG)

That story gives me hope because I'm not always a man of great faith. There are many times when I will pray for something—even something I truly believe to be in God's will—and yet wonder in my heart (and sometimes worry) if it really will happen. It's encouraging to know that even when we are weak, God can still intervene and answer our prayers. Even though the prayer of the church for Peter that night was weak, it was mightier than Herod. And it was mightier than hell.

Despite their lack of faith, God came through.

In some branches of the contemporary church, we are told that we must have complete faith when we pray, and even if we have a single doubt, it won't happen.

Oh please. Just stop.

I don't care who you are—the truth is we are all going to have times when our faith isn't as strong as it ought to be. But God is faithful and will answer our prayers—even when our faith is shaky and our hearts are gripped with doubt.

I love the story in the book of Mark about the dad with a demon-possessed son who came to Jesus for help. Brokenhearted, knowing his faith wasn't what it ought to be—and yet desperate for help—"the father of the child cried out and said with tears, 'Lord, I believe; help my unbelief!'"[2]

And Jesus immediately healed the boy.

How much faith did Lazarus have when God raised him from the dead? Not much. The weeping people around the tomb weren't exactly overflowing with faith, either. The point is that God can—and will—work, even when we don't have as much faith as we ought to have. That is not to excuse us from having faith. In fact, "without faith it is impossible to please Him" (Hebrews 11:6.) We should pray with faith, and we should pray with persistence. But obviously these believers were shocked when God actually answered their prayer and when they saw the answer standing right before them.

Speaking of faith, you really have to admire the way Peter weathered this storm. There he was, chained up in Herod's maximum-security cell, surrounded by guards, knowing that his fate hung in the balance . . . and he slept like a baby. He was sleeping so deeply that the angel "struck Peter on the side and raised him up" (Acts 12:7). In other words, the angel had to give Peter a little punch and then haul him to his feet.

But even on his feet, Peter still wasn't with it. The angel had to hurry him like a mom hurries a sleepy child with a school bus to catch. *Get your shoes on, Peter. Grab your coat, Peter. Come on, Peter, let's get going.*

Peter had been able to sleep in a crisis, knowing that whatever the outcome, the Lord would be with him. Either he would be rejoining his church family, or he would be joining James, Stephen, and the Lord Jesus on the other side. Psalm 4:8 says, "I will both lie down in peace, and sleep; for You alone, O LORD, make me dwell in safety." Psalm 127:2 says, "He gives His beloved sleep." And that is what He gave to Peter in the middle of a frightening situation.

Once Peter was finally delivered from prison and found himself out on the street, the angel left him. I find that interesting. He needed a miracle to escape the prison, the shackles, and the guards, but he didn't need a miracle to reach Mary's house. He didn't need an angel to guide him through the streets of Jerusalem; he could get there on his own.

Sometimes we get confused and try to do God's part—or expect God to do ours. There is a place for the miraculous and a place for our response to that work of God. For instance, Jesus raised Lazarus from the dead. Only God could do that. But someone else loosed the man from his grave clothes and let him go. Jesus took the five loaves and two fish and fed five thousand men with it, but others distributed the food and picked up the pieces afterward.

Often in our own strength we try to do what only God can do. Only God can convert a soul. I can't, and neither can you. None of us can. But sometimes we imagine that we'll help the Lord out a little with gimmicks or pressure tactics, trying to do what only the Holy Spirit can do.

But on the other hand, there are certain things that God will not do. Only we can do them. Only I can obey God. Only I can choose to apply discipline in my life and do the right thing. Only I can repent of my sins. The Lord will not do those things for me. He wants me to take those steps—for Him.

God will not force me to do His will; He will give me the choice. And then I must decide.

So Peter finds himself delivered and free, and he makes his way over to Mary's house and knocks on the gate. Back at Herod's prison, the iron gate had opened for him automatically—just like at the supermarket. But now, at Mary's house, he can't seem to get past the front door. It's kind of funny—all the doors open for him to get out of prison, but he can't get into a prayer meeting.

The New King James Version says that "when they opened the door and saw him, they were astonished" (Acts 12:16). *They.* In other words, when they finally decided to check out what Rhoda had told them, the whole group went together to open the door.

And there stood Peter. And they went wild. They were so

excited to see the living, breathing, big-as-life answer to their prayers.

Note the way Acts 12 begins and ends. The chapter opens with a seemingly all-powerful, unstoppable King Herod who stretched out his hand "to harass some from the church." He seized James and killed him. He arrested Peter, planning to put him on trial and kill him, too.

Seen from the perspective of those verses, life looked pretty grim. A good man had been murdered. A beloved leader was imprisoned, on death row. On his side Herod had the power of the government, the sword, and the threat of prison. The bad guys won.

Or did they?

The church had on their side the Creator of the universe and the secret weapon He gave them—and us: the mighty power of prayer. Acts 12 continues with Herod giving a speech to the citizens of Tyre and Sidon. And after his speech was done, the people were so taken with it they began to chant in unison, "The voice of a god and not of a man! The voice of a god and not of a man!"

Herod stood there, soaking it up, taking it all in, and reveling in his own self-importance. *Thank you! Thank you very much!* The Jewish historian Josephus points out that at this particular event, Herod was dressed head to toe in silver, so the sun flashed and sparkled from his garments. It apparently was a very impressive sight. The king looked like a god to the people, and he freely accepted their adulation.

But listen to how the story ends:

Immediately an angel of the Lord struck him, because he did not give glory to God. And he was eaten by worms and died.

But the word of God grew and multiplied. (Acts 12:23-24)

What a difference. The chapter opens with James dead, Peter in prison, and Herod triumphing. It closes with Herod dead, Peter free, and the Word of God triumphing.

You see, it isn't over until it's over.

So keep praying.

Never give up.

15 What the Devil Doesn't Want You to Know

What was the greatest day of your life?

It was the day when you put your faith in Jesus Christ. The more we grow in our faith and knowledge of what God actually did for us in that moment, the more we become aware of how significant that day really was.

That was the day when we literally changed our eternal address from hell to heaven. That was the day when we turned from darkness to light and from the power of Satan to God. That was the day when, according to Jesus, there was a party in heaven given in our honor—a victory shout, if you will, from loved ones who have gone before us, as well as the angels.

But it also was the day when you entered into warfare.

The moment you received Christ as your Savior, a spiritual battle was launched against you that continues to this very day. It has been said that conversion has made our hearts a battlefield. And it's true. For just as surely as there is a God who loves you, there is also a devil who hates you and wants to cripple or destroy the work God is doing in your life.

In His parable of the sower and the seed, Jesus spoke about the seed that fell along the roadside and was eaten up by the birds. He explained, "These are the ones by the wayside where the word is sown. When they hear, Satan comes immediately and takes away the word that was sown in their hearts" (Mark 4:15).

It's called an attack, and you'd better get ready for it.

You might say, "Hey, I'm a pacifist. I'm not into fighting."

If so, then you are going down on the battlefield. We all need to buckle on the armor of God because in this spiritual battle, you are either advancing or retreating, winning or losing. There is no neutral ground. You have to fight this battle in order to win it. The good news is, this is a battle that can be won if we march in step with our Lord.

Preparing for Battle

When I first became a Christian at age seventeen, during my junior year of high school, I remember other believers telling me, "Greg, you have to be very careful because the devil is going to tempt you now."

To me that was the craziest thing I had ever heard. In my mind I envisioned this cartoon, caricatured version of Satan with a red suit and a pitchfork. I didn't think of him as a real, living spiritual being. And temptation? I had never really dealt with temptation. Before coming to Christ, I saw temptation as opportunity. For the most part, I didn't have a concept of resisting temptation. I pretty much just did whatever I wanted to do.

So I said to these Christians who were warning me, "How will I know when I am being tempted?"

"You will know," they said.

"Okay, fine."

I wasn't too worried about it. The whole thing just didn't seem real to me.

After one of my classes, either that day or the next, I was stunned when a really attractive girl walked up and began talking to me. I had noticed her many times, of course, but she never had shown any sign that she knew I existed.

"Hi," she said. "How are you?"

I literally was dumbfounded. Why was this beautiful girl speaking to *me*? "What's your name?" she asked.

My name? For a moment, I couldn't even remember it. (I knew it started with a G.)

"I'm Greg."

You have to understand something here: Girls usually ignored me. What was happening just then never had been part of my universe. Suddenly it flashed into my mind that this might be the "temptation" the other Christians had warned me about.

As it turned out, that is exactly what it was.

"Hey, you know what?" she said. "My parents have a cabin up in the mountains. I was thinking of going up there this weekend. Why don't you come with me?"

I thought to myself, *Okay, this is it.* This girl didn't have horns or a pitchfork or a red suit, but could there be any doubt? This was temptation.

It was so attractive, so enticing! And in that moment, it was no longer a theory. This was the real deal.

Because I had been warned, I resisted this temptation and told her no. But when my heart finally stopped pounding so hard in my chest, I remember thinking, *Okay, so this is how it works.*

Our enemy, you see, is very clever; he knows how to package his wares in an attractive way. Don't ever underestimate him. In a classic hymn, Martin Luther put it like this:

For still our ancient foe
Doth seek to work us woe—
His craft and power are great,

And, armed with cruel hate,
On earth is not his equal.

Satan is a sly and skillful adversary with thousands of years of experience in dealing with mankind. But he can be overcome!

God did not create the devil as we know him today. God created a high-ranking angel known as Lucifer, son of the morning. When Lucifer became proud in his heart and rebelled against God, he took one-third of the angelic host along with him. They became his compatriots, his minions, his soldiers, his fallen angels.

In short, they became demons. And to this very day, they help the evil one in his war against God and God's people. (See Isaiah 14:12-21; Ezekiel 28:11-19; Revelation 12:4.)

Even though Satan no longer has the exalted position he once had, he still has access to heaven. The Bible gives him many names. He is called Satan, Lucifer, Beelzebub, the devil, the father of lies, the god of this world, and the prince of the power of the air. Sometimes he (or his demons) comes to us in all of his wicked depravity and shows his true colors as the evil one. At other times he is much more subtle, coming to us in an attractive way—perhaps in the form of an attractive guy, a gorgeous woman, or something else that is very enticing to us.

One of his best tactics is imitation; he pretends to be something he is not. I read a newspaper article that described a strange phenomenon in a city in Denmark. According to this article, many of the birds in this city have changed the way they sing and have begun to imitate the sound of cell phones ringing. Can you imagine how obnoxious that would be? Maybe you want to get away from the office and enjoy some peace and quiet in some outdoor café. And the birds in the trees all around you are imitating cell phones! One guy told about a little bird that comes to his garden that sounds just like his cell phone. "We've named him Nokia," he said.

The greatest imitator of all, however, is Satan himself.

The apostle Paul noted that "Satan himself masquerades as an angel of light. It is not surprising, then, if his servants also masquerade as servants of righteousness" (2 Corinthians 11:14-15, NIV). He also said, "We are not unaware of his schemes" (2:11, NIV).

With those truths in mind, let's take a closer look at a number of things the devil doesn't want you to know.

What the Devil Doesn't Want You to Know

Satan is nowhere near being equal to God.

Earlier in this book, we discovered that God is all-powerful, all-knowing, and everywhere-present.

Satan has none of these attributes.

Yes, our enemy has great power—more than any man and most angels. But his power is clearly limited. His power—as that of a created being—doesn't come close to the power of God. Satan also knows many things, but he doesn't know all things. Finally, he is not in all places at once as our God is; he can only be in one place at a time. When someone says, "The devil has been hassling me lately," what they are probably talking about is one of his many demons.

Satan can do nothing in the life of a Christian without God's permission.

As we noted earlier, even though Satan has fallen, he still has access to heaven. How do we know this? Because we read in the book of Job how the angels came to present themselves before the Lord, and Satan was among them. God directed His remarks to the devil himself.

One day the members of the heavenly court came to present themselves before the LORD, and the Accuser, Satan, came with them. "Where have you come from?" the LORD asked Satan.

Satan answered the LORD, "I have been patrolling the earth, watching everything that's going on."

Then the LORD asked Satan, "Have you noticed my servant Job? He is the finest man in all the earth. He is blameless—a man of complete integrity. He fears God and stays away from evil."

Satan replied to the LORD, "Yes, but Job has good reason to fear God. You have always put a wall of protection around him and his home and his property. You have made him prosper in everything he does. Look how rich he is! But reach out and take away everything he has, and he will surely curse you to your face!" (Job 1:6-11, NLT)

A number of truths strike us from this text. First of all, we see that Satan still has access to the throne of God. We also see that even though he has a wicked agenda, he has to ask permission to attack the children of God because of the hedge of protection that is around us.

As believers, you and I have an impenetrable wall that God has placed around us that Satan cannot penetrate. Now, that doesn't mean we can't be tempted, harassed, or attacked. But it does mean that God never will give you more than you can handle.

Here is what I would suggest: When the devil comes knocking at your door to tempt you, just say, "Jesus, would You mind getting that?" He will be happy to go to that door and turn the evil one away. And we need Him to do that because you and I are no match for the devil. In the Lord's Prayer, Jesus even taught us to pray, "And do not lead us into temptation, but deliver us from the evil one" (Matthew 6:13).

In 1 Corinthians 10:13, Paul gives us these encouraging words:

No temptation has overtaken you except such as is common to man; but God is faithful, who will not allow you to be tempted beyond what you are able, but with the temptation will also make the way of escape, that you may be able to bear it.

That is certainly good news, but here is the problem: Sometimes we unnecessarily put ourselves in the way of temptation. We dip our hands into the fire, so to speak, and then act surprised when they get burned.

One person put it this way: "Lead me not into temptation. I can find it myself!" And that is the problem. Instead of hearing what the Lord is saying and taking practical steps to stay away from the things that could drag us down, we unnecessarily step out into oncoming traffic and place ourselves directly in the path of temptation.

We live in the real world, not a convent or a monastery, and we are surrounded by any number of things that could entice us, distract us, and ultimately lead us astray.

That's bad enough. But it's much worse when we help the temptation along by putting ourselves into situations and places where we already know that we are weak and vulnerable.

For instance, maybe you have a problem with drinking. You may have been an alcoholic at one time, and it almost ruined your life.

So I run into you one Monday morning, and you tell me, "Greg, I am really struggling with the temptation to drink. It seems like the temptation is always right there."

"That's tough," I say. "It's really difficult. I'll be praying for you. Oh, by the way, where were you last night at church?"

"I wasn't at church. I was at a sports bar."

"What in the world were you doing at a sports bar?"

"Well, I went in there to watch the big game and eat some of the peanuts. They really have great peanuts there. But boy, I really get tempted to drink when I see everybody else drinking."

No kidding!

You are putting yourself unnecessarily in the way of

temptation. You say to the Lord, "Lead me not into temptation," but then you go there on your own!

Maybe a young man says to me, "Greg, I'm always getting tempted to have sex with my girlfriend. I don't know why this temptation comes."

"So where were you last night?"

"Um . . . lying on the bed with my girlfriend with the lights out."

Temptation will come when you do stuff like that.

If there is a door, you need to walk—or run—through that door and get out of the way of temptation. Sometimes we ask the Lord for a surge of power to deal with our temptation when the Lord says to us, "Do you see that door? Use it! Get out of there!"

The story of Joseph in Genesis 39 is a great case in point. He was a young, red-blooded man with a normal, healthy sex drive. And his boss's wife kept throwing herself at him, day after day after day. Finally, she cast aside all subtlety and tried to pull him down onto the bed with her. What did he do? He did what any clear-thinking young man would do under such circumstances. *He ran like crazy.*

We need to walk very carefully through life, but we also need to remember that God never will give us more than we can handle. As the Scripture says, He will always give us a way out of the temptation.

Remember, the devil does not work alone; he has a well-organized network of fallen angels that do his bidding.

One of the key Scriptures in all the Bible for dealing with this evil spiritual empire is in Ephesians 6:10-13:

Finally, my brethren, be strong in the Lord and in the power of His might. Put on the whole armor of God, that you may be able to stand against the wiles of the devil. For we do not wrestle against flesh and blood, but against principalities, against powers, against the rulers of the

darkness of this age, against spiritual hosts of wickedness
in the heavenly places. Therefore take up the whole armor
of God, that you may be able to withstand in the evil day,
and having done all, to stand.

Paul uses an interesting phrase: *we do not wrestle.* It's a term
describing a life-and-death conflict. It is mortal hand-to-hand
combat, not shadowboxing or even boxing with padded gloves.
This is a fight to the death.

Another translation puts it this way: "For our fight is not
against any physical enemy: it is against organisations and
powers that are spiritual. We are up against the unseen power
that controls this dark world, and spiritual agents from the very
headquarters of evil" (verse 12, PH).

Just as God has His holy angels, secret agents who do His
bidding in the heavens and on earth, so the devil has his unholy
angels doing his dirty work from the headquarters of evil.

What is the agenda of demons? They want to hinder the
purposes of God and extend the power of Satan. Whenever we
engage in the work of the Lord in any form, we should expect,
anticipate, and brace ourselves for demonic attack. We should
be aware that God will allow demons to tempt us, bother us,
and harass us at times.

Even the great apostle Paul had to deal with this. In his
second letter to the church in Corinth, he spoke about a certain
"thorn in the flesh" that was giving him great difficulty and
causing distress. We don't know what that "thorn" was, though
most commentators believe it was some kind of a physical
disability—possibly as a result of one of his many beatings.
Here is what Paul said in 2 Corinthians 12:7-10:

I was given a thorn in my flesh, a messenger of Satan, to
torment me. Three times I pleaded with the Lord to take
it away from me. But he said to me, "My grace is sufficient
for you, for my power is made perfect in weakness."

Therefore I will boast all the more gladly about my weaknesses, so that Christ's power may rest on me. That is why, for Christ's sake, I delight in weaknesses, in insults, in hardships, in persecutions, in difficulties. For when I am weak, then I am strong. (NIV)

The word Paul uses in this passage for torment (*buffet* in the New King James Version) means "to strike with a fist." So this was no minor nuisance. These were more like violent, crushing blows. This was the real thing.

But why? Why would God allow this—in Paul's life or our own? Why does God permit the attacks? Why does He allow the hardships and illnesses and tragedies?

We could go on and on asking, "Why? Why? Why?"

We can't always answer these questions. But listen to what Paul said as he explained why the painful "thorn" was allowed in his life in particular. This is from *The Message*:

Because of the extravagance of those revelations, and so I wouldn't get a big head, I was given the gift of a handicap to keep me in constant touch with my limitations. Satan's angel did his best to get me down; what he in fact did was push me to my knees. No danger then of walking around high and mighty! (verse 7)

The devil wanted to get him down, and it worked. But not in the way Satan had hoped. Instead of Paul getting down on himself, down on his situation, or down on God, *he got down on his knees.*

Satan's plan backfired. The evil one had wanted to drive Paul away from God, but he succeeded in causing Paul to cling to Jesus that much tighter.

These times of suffering and hardship can be terribly difficult. I know; I've been through them, too. And yet the fellowship I have had with God in those times has never been sweeter, and I

have never been more dependent on Him. There are times I
don't think I can handle it, and that is when the Lord steps in
and gives me the strength that I need. In the process, He has
taught me things I could not have learned in any other way.

Satan cannot control you.

He would love you to think that you are powerless against his
attacks, that you have no recourse, and that you are no match.
He wants you to imagine that you will always be a victim or an
addict—a puppet for him to control.

That is a lie, from the one rightly called "the father of lies."

Though it is true that a believer can be hassled like Paul was
or tempted and oppressed, the devil *cannot* control us.

Now certainly, if we deliberately yield to his power, he will
have sway in our lives. But if we resist him, we can be free from
that. God is greater than Satan! As the apostle John tells us, "He
who is in you is greater than he who is in the world" (1 John 4:4).

When Christ comes into the life of a man or a woman, He
becomes the sole occupant. Some people have suggested that
Christians can be demon possessed—that you can have both
Christ and demons living inside of you. That is a ridiculous
notion. Jesus is not into a timeshare program with your heart.
The Bible says, "What harmony can there be between Christ
and the devil?" (2 Corinthians 6:15, NLT). In 1 John 5:18 we
read, "We know that God's children do not make a practice of
sinning, for God's Son holds them securely, and the evil one
cannot touch them" (NLT). Literally, this passage is saying that
the evil one cannot attach himself to the one whom God holds
securely.

Some churches speak of exorcising or casting out demons
from believers who are struggling with various vices and issues.

I think they are using the wrong term. Believers don't need to
have demons cast out of them; they need to deny and resist
demons. You can't "cast out" temptation or attacks. But you can
put on your armor and resist those attacks. The Bible says,

"Therefore submit to God. Resist the devil and he will flee from you" (James 4:7). The key is to stay as close to God as you possibly can.

Going back to Ephesians 6:10, we read, "Finally, my brethren, be strong in the Lord and in the power of His might." Or literally, "Strengthen yourselves in the Lord."

This is another reminder that we don't want to face Satan or his demons in our own strength. We don't want to engage these dark forces on our own. We all know what police officers do when they find themselves in a difficult situation where they might need help: They call for backup. And that is what we need to do in the spiritual realm as well.

Years ago, when I was a little boy, I remember walking down the street with my newly acquired six-shooter cap guns, a little holster around my middle, and a boy-sized cowboy hat. I was feeling very good about myself.

Then some hoodlum types standing on a street corner saw me, started pushing me around, knocked the cowboy hat off my head, took my cap guns, pushed me to the ground, and walked off, laughing.

As you might imagine, I was devastated. So I ran home and told my brother Doug about it, who was five years older than I was. "Come with me, Doug," I said. "I want my guns back."

We found the kids who had roughed me up, standing on the same corner. This time I was feeling courageous because I had my brother behind me—and he was bigger than them and me. He walked over to them, pushed them around a little, and got my guns back. That felt really good. But from then on, I didn't want to leave the house without my big brother.

What we need to remember is that we can be bold in our spiritual battles, knowing that the Lord is with us, walking beside us. And He is bigger and stronger than any devil or demon in the universe. We're not alone. We stand in the Lord and in the power.

Satan knows this fact very well, and that is why he wants to separate you from your power base. His chief aim is to get between you and God.

Just remember that Jesus Christ Himself is in your corner. Our defense against the accusations of the devil lies in the personal intercession of the Son of God Himself:

My little children, these things I write to you, so that you may not sin. And if anyone sins, we have an Advocate with the Father, Jesus Christ the righteous. (1 John 2:1)

Who will bring any charge against those whom God has chosen? It is God who justifies. Who then is the one who condemns? No one. Christ Jesus who died — more than that, who was raised to life — is at the right hand of God and is also interceding for us. (Romans 8:33-34, NIV)

Picture it this way. I'm on trial in a courtroom, with God the Father as the judge. Behind Him on the bench are the commandments engraved in stone that I have broken. The prosecuting attorney, Lu Cipher by name, is slick and effective. He is seasoned, articulate, and knows how to win a case. But my defense attorney is none other than Jesus Christ.

So here's how it goes. The prosecutor stands up and says, "Today we have in our courtroom Greg Laurie, who is on trial for breaking the commandments of God, Your Honor. We all know very well that Greg has broken these commandments. In fact, I'm going to now review every one of Greg's offenses and all the wrong he has done in his life."

As he begins, I'm thinking, *This is not good.*

A month later the prosecutor is still talking, still detailing all of my sins and transgressions. By now I'm thinking, *This is getting worse and worse! I'm in big trouble.* Then I glance over at my defense attorney, Jesus. But He doesn't seem too stressed at all. He is very calm. In fact, He's just doodling a little on the yellow tablet before Him. Seeing the fear on my face, He looks over and smiles.

"It's okay, Greg," He says. "Don't worry."

And I am thinking, *Easy for Him to say,* "*Don't worry.*" *He's not on trial.* So the prosecution—the case against me—goes on and on and on. Lu Cipher seems to be enjoying himself. As for me, I don't even want to look up at the judge. I don't want to make eye contact with Him. I am so embarrassed. Finally, Lu Cipher completes his attack against me and says, "And so Your Honor, Your own law says, 'The soul who sins shall die.' Therefore, this man is worthy of death. I rest my case."

The prosecutor sits down, well-pleased with himself and with a smile on his face. I look over at Jesus and whisper, "He's got me! What in the world can You say now?"

"It's all right, Greg," He says again. "Just be calm."

Then He says, "Permission to approach the bench?"

"Permission granted," the judge replies.

Jesus walks right up to the front of the courtroom, faces the judge eye to eye, and says, "Father, we both know Greg Laurie is guilty of everything Lu Cipher accused him of. But we also both know that I died on the cross and shed my blood in payment for every sin he has ever committed."

The judge says, "That's right, Son." And He pounds down the gavel and says, "All is dismissed and forgiven. The price already has been paid."

That is how it works when the enemy attacks you.

But the devil doesn't want you to know that. He wants you to think that you will rise or fall on your own worthiness and merit. Not a chance! The only place you or I or anyone can rest is in the finished work of Jesus Christ.

Satan was defeated soundly at the cross.

Looking ahead to the cross that loomed just a few hours away, Jesus said, "Now is the time for judgment on this world; now the prince of this world will be driven out" (John 12:31, NIV). Referring to that same event on Calvary, Jesus spoke of the coming Holy Spirit, who would convict the world of judgment "because the prince of this world now stands condemned" (16:11, NIV).

Through His death on the cross, Jesus destroyed "him who had the power of death, that is, the devil" (Hebrews 2:14).

Jesus didn't just say His last words on the cross; the Bible says that He cried them out with a loud voice. What were those words? "It is finished!" But the statement was actually the Greek term *tetélestai*, which was a common word at the time that meant "completed," "accomplished," "finished." It was used by people after a job was done. If you were a carpenter and just finished work on a table you had been laboring over for days, you would say, *Tetélestai!* It's completed. No more work needs to be done.

That was the word Jesus used on the cross.

DONE!

FINISHED!

ACCOMPLISHED!

TRANSACTION COMPLETE!

The stranglehold of Satan has been broken when a person puts his or her life in Jesus Christ.

You don't fight *for* victory, you fight *from* it. You don't fight to gain victory, you fight because it already has been obtained. You don't need to say, "Lord, give me victory." You need to say, "Lord, I *have* victory, and I will live accordingly. Because You have told me in Scripture that I am more than a conqueror in Jesus Christ."

We can win the spiritual battle against Satan.

We can overcome the enemy if we put on the armor of God. I'm not saying that you will win every skirmish and every conflict, but I am saying that you will win the war. I'm not saying that you will never sin or stumble again, because you will . . . I will . . . we all will. And in case we had forgotten that fact, the apostle James reminds us that "we all stumble in many ways" (James 3:2, NIV).

Certainly we will stumble. But as David said in the Psalms,

"The steps of a good man are ordered by the LORD, and He delights in his way. Though he fall, he shall not be utterly cast down; for the LORD upholds him with His hand" (37:23-24).

As we wrap up this chapter, let's delve a little more deeply into that incredibly encouraging "armor" chapter, Ephesians 6:

> Take up the whole armor of God, that you may be able to withstand in the evil day, and having done all, to stand.
>
> Stand therefore, having girded your waist with truth, having put on the breastplate of righteousness, and having shod your feet with the preparation of the gospel of peace; above all, taking the shield of faith with which you will be able to quench all the fiery darts of the wicked one. And take the helmet of salvation, and the sword of the Spirit, which is the word of God. (verses 13-17)

The Bible is saying, "Armor up! Get ready to do battle."

And just like any soldier who wants to live through the war, make sure you check your equipment.

The belt of truth. When you think of a belt here, don't think of a fashion statement. Think instead of a utility belt—the kind of belt police officers would wear. It is not to hold their pants up, but it's to keep all of their gear in reach. For instance, a police officer might have a holster and gun, handcuffs, a Taser, chemical spray, a radio, a flashlight, and maybe another place to hold extra magazines of ammunition. Every officer on duty needs such a belt. They call it a Sam Browne, and it keeps all their equipment within easy reach. A Roman soldier also would wear such a belt going into combat. It was an essential for survival.

Was the belt such a crucial piece of armor, compared with the shield or sword or other pieces? Yes, it was. In fact, without it, the other pieces wouldn't work. The breastplate for the Roman soldier was attached to the belt. The sheath for the sword attached to the belt. Also, with the belt you cinched up your garment that would sometimes hang below your knees, giving you freedom of movement.

What does this belt of truth stand for in our lives? It represents a life and mind that are pulled together and ready to serve for the glory of God. It talks about a man or a woman who is living in truth before God. If I am living a lie, if I am saying that I am a Christian when I am living in a way that is contrary to that, then nothing else is really going to matter. I will be quickly cut down on the battlefield of life—one of the first to fall. The strong message here is, don't be a hypocrite! Put on the belt of truth and stay ready for battle.

The breastplate of righteousness. This piece of armor protected the vital organs of the Roman soldier. This is the kill zone, not unlike where you would aim a gun. Police officers are trained to shoot for the chest, not the head. Why? Because you might miss the head, and you may only get one shot. When a police officer shoots someone, he isn't trying to wound or maim them. If he has to draw his gun on someone, he wants to take that person down permanently. A breastplate would be like a bulletproof vest, protecting the heart and the chest.

What does the breastplate of righteousness represent in our lives? It is talking about the imputed righteousness of Christ. When I became a Christian, God justified me, forgiving me of all my sins. Then He deposited the very righteousness of Jesus Christ into my spiritual bank account. As a result, I stand positionally as a righteous person. Do I always live as one? No. Am I technically one? Yes. Why? Because Jesus gave me His own righteousness.

Here's how that works. The devil will accuse us, saying, "You are not a worthy person. You are always failing. You continually fall short." And it's true. We do fall short of God's desires and standards all the time. *But we also stand in the righteousness of God's Son.* As the book of Ephesians says, God the Father has "made us accepted in the Beloved" (1:6).

If you are in Christ, you *are*—right now, present tense—

accepted by God. Again, this is not based on what you have done, but on what *He* has done. So when the devil tries to strike that fatal blow against you, it is repelled by the breastplate because you stand right with God, and you know it.

Feet shod with the preparation of the gospel of peace. The Romans wore interesting shoes, wearing different kinds of footwear—everything from boots to sandals—for different needs. When they were going into battle, however, their shoes had to have three qualities. First, they had to grip the ground. This was accomplished with spikes on the soles. Second, they had to be tough to protect from the blow of a sword. And thirdly, they had to be light. A Roman soldier could cross one hundred yards of open field in one minute.

The right shoes enable us to continue on when everyone else is quitting, to keep our footing when others are failing, and to move when others are weighed down.

What does the shoe represent? Paul describes it as "the preparation of the gospel of peace." The Bible says, "How beautiful are the feet of those who preach the gospel of peace, who bring glad tidings of good things!" (Romans 10:15).

Look down at your own feet for a moment. They are probably covered in socks and shoes, and you may or may not like the appearance of those feet. But if those feet carry you to bring the message of Jesus to others, in the sight of God they are beautiful, you see.

Shoes also help us to gain ground in the spiritual battle. With the right shoes, I am moving forward, gaining traction, and covering ground. In the same way, the church gains ground—in a community, in a city, in the kingdom of Christ—through evangelism and the presentation of the gospel.

The shield of faith. Paul said, "Above all, taking the shield of faith with which you will be able to quench all the fiery darts [or flaming arrows] of the wicked one." The words *above all* mean this is of great importance.

Roman soldiers used two types of shields. They had a small,

round shield for close hand-to-hand combat, in company with their shorter sword. But they also had the shields with which they marched into battle. This shield was basically like a big door. In combat, the soldiers could even advance by locking their shields together. And then when they came under a barrage of flaming arrows, the soldiers would lift those shields on all sides and over the top, creating a big wooden box. They would do this because one of the tactics of ancient warfare was to barrage your opponent with arrows that were on fire. If the arrow hit you, obviously you could catch on fire. This was a tactic used to disorient the enemy; you would be marching into battle, look up, and see thousands of flaming arrows raining down on you. So the soldiers used their shields to absorb such attacks.

Our enemy, Satan, has flaming arrows too. We might even call them guided missiles. Sometimes they are just inappropriate, out-of-place thoughts. You might be engaged in doing something and suddenly an evil thought comes into your mind. You think to yourself, *Where did that come from?* I will tell you where it came from: the devil. It might be a blasphemous thought. It might be a thought of doubt. It might be a thought of lust or hatred or envy. Whatever it is, it is ungodly and doesn't belong in your mind.

As I said earlier, we don't have to take this stuff. You and I can say, "I know where this thought came from, and I am not owning it. I refuse to engage it at all, and I resist it right now, standing in my faith."

I am not saying it is always easy to defy such thoughts and emotions, taking our stand on the Word of God. That is one reason I think it is important for believers to be together whenever possible, worshiping, learning, praying, and fellowshiping together. When we do, it is like those Roman soldiers who locked their shields to resist attack. It's good to realize that you are not alone and that you don't fight the battle alone. There are others who are fighting the battle with you.

The helmet of salvation. The helmet protects the mind (the brain), guarding us from impure thoughts and dark emotions. Strapping on that helmet means "bringing every thought into captivity to the obedience of Christ" (2 Corinthians 10:5).

It also means filling up your mind with right things. Remember the way Paul put it to the Philippians?

> Fix your thoughts on what is true and good and right.
> Think about things that are pure and lovely, and dwell on
> the fine, good things in others. Think about all you can
> praise God for and be glad about. (Philippians 4:8, TLB)

The sword of the Spirit. This is the only offensive piece of weaponry God has given to us. With the sword, the Roman soldier *attacked.* And what is our sword? It is the Word of God.

The devil doesn't want you to read your Bible. Did you know that? Have you ever noticed how often you can read the newspaper with no disturbances or interruptions at all, but then when you say, "I'm going to spend some time reading the Bible," all chaos breaks out? The phone starts ringing. The kids start screaming. The dog starts barking. And a thousand distracting thoughts begin to pour into your mind. The devil is saying to us, "Oh no! Don't unsheathe that sword. Don't get that sword out. Keep that thing put away."

What shape is your sword in? Is it polished from daily use? Do you study the Scriptures on a regular basis? Do you sharpen what you learn from the Bible on the anvil of experience as you obey its truth and apply its principles in your life? One thing you don't want is a sword that is dulled from disobedience — or rusty from lack of preparation.

I love to see Bibles that are so well-used, they're falling apart at the binding. Good! Go out and buy another one and wear out that one, too. As it has been said, "A Bible that is falling apart usually belongs to someone who isn't." Use your Bible, write in your Bible. Learn your Bible. Quote your Bible. Be familiar with your Bible, backward and forward. Know the Word of God.

Remember, the devil is still a powerful enemy, but he is also a defeated enemy. He was defeated at the cross of Calvary two thousand years ago.

And you and I can live out our lives within that circle of victory.

But the devil doesn't want you to know that.

16 How to Resist Temptation

G oing on a diet is a fine idea . . . until you get hungry.

Anyone can fast . . . on a full stomach.

But when you are hungry—really ravenous—the whole idea of that diet book you bought at the bookstore seems absurd. You walk through a grocery store to pick up a bunch of celery and a carton of tofu and you make the mistake of walking by the deli. Man, does that stuff look good! *Mac and cheese. Swedish meatballs. Barbeque ribs.* Then you happen to stroll by the bakery, where they have just put out fresh doughnuts, and nothing in all the world smells like a fresh doughnut. Suddenly your desire for food puts a move on you like a champion wrestler.

In the same way, Satan, the enemy of our souls, knows how to package his temptations in ways that appeal to us. He knows how to market his wares in a way that makes bad things look not so bad at all.

Forbidden things, after all, have a certain charm, don't they? Someone says, "This thing is really bad. Stay away from it. Don't even look at it." And something inside of us says, *I want to have a little look at that. I want to see what's so bad about it.* And we are drawn to the very thing we know we ought to shun.

It happened to Eve in the Garden of Eden. God had given her and her husband complete freedom over the entire garden—and presumably, the place must have been vast. But He had given only one small restriction: Don't eat the fruit from one particular tree. And what happened? She was drawn to *that* tree like a magnet. With all the thousands and tens of thousands of beautiful trees in Eden, why did she find herself standing next to that particular tree, talking to the serpent? It was the wrong place at the wrong time with the wrong one.

Temptation, however, isn't sin. Everyone will be tempted. In fact, if you *aren't* being tempted, there is something wrong with you. It was Matthew Henry who said, "The best of saints may be tempted to the worst of sins.[1]

So there is no sin in being tempted. It isn't the bait that constitutes sin, it's the *bite*. It is giving in to that impulse. The fact is, if you find yourself being barraged by temptations lately, that could be an indication that you are doing something right rather than doing something wrong. When the enemy sees you as a threat to his kingdom, he will try to bring you down. If you are no threat to him and he knows it, he probably will leave you alone.

In this chapter, we will consider six questions about temptation and where it comes from.

Where Does Temptation Come From?

Then Jesus, being filled with the Holy Spirit, returned from the Jordan and was led by the Spirit into the wilderness, being tempted for forty days by the devil. And in those days He ate nothing, and afterward, when they had ended, He was hungry.

And the devil said to Him, "If You are the Son of God, command this stone to become bread."

But Jesus answered him, saying, "It is written, 'Man shall not live by bread alone, but by every word of God.'"

Then the devil, taking Him up on a high mountain, showed Him all the kingdoms of the world in a moment of time. And the devil said to Him, "All this authority I will give You, and their glory; for this has been delivered to me, and I give it to whomever I wish. Therefore, if You will worship before me, all will be Yours."

And Jesus answered and said to him, "Get behind Me, Satan! For it is written, 'You shall worship the LORD your God, and Him only you shall serve.'"

Then he brought Him to Jerusalem, set Him on the pinnacle of the temple, and said to Him, "If You are the Son of God, throw Yourself down from here. For it is written: 'He shall give His angels charge over you, to keep you,' and, 'In their hands they shall bear you up, lest you dash your foot against a stone.'"

And Jesus answered and said to him, "It has been said, 'You shall not tempt the LORD your God.'"

Now when the devil had ended every temptation, he departed from Him until an opportune time. (Luke 4:1-13)

Where does temptation come from? In a broad sense, it clearly comes from the devil. But the fact is, we play a key role in our own temptation. Satan needs our cooperation in this area for us to give in. The enemy works within the context of our own desires.

Have you ever noticed how telemarketers always seem to call at dinner? Is that intentional? I guess they figure that is when we're at home. Sometimes when we get one of those calls, my wife will answer, and she will be very polite to them.

I will say to her, "Cathe, just hang up! Don't talk to telemarketers."

Not long ago the phone rang and I picked it up. Cathe looked at me and saw me nodding, and she heard me say, "Oh really?"

She said, "Greg, who are you talking to?"

"A telemarketer."

"Hang up the phone!"

"You're right," I said, and I hung up.

"Why were you talking to that person? You always tell me to hang up on those calls."

"Well, yes," I explained, "but this time they were offering something that was interesting to me. A better deal on cable TV!"

That is how it is with Satan and temptation. He sizes you up, figures out your vulnerabilities, and then brings a temptation across your path that will be attractive to you. It takes two to make a successful temptation—and you are one of the two.

The apostle James explains how it works:

> Each one is tempted when he is drawn away by his own desires and enticed. Then, when desire has conceived, it gives birth to sin; and sin, when it is full-grown, brings forth death.
>
> Do not be deceived, my beloved brethren. (James 1:14-16)

Step 1. "Each one is tempted."

So the temptation comes to you. That evil thought knocks on the door of your imagination. (It may be true that opportunity only knocks once, but temptation beats on the door every single day, doesn't it?) So each person is tempted. That's a given.

What do we do with that temptation? The best thing to do is close the door to it immediately. We get into trouble when we . . . think about it.

Step 2. "He is drawn away by his own desires."

In other words, the temptation comes, and you're checking it out a little, trying it on for size, thinking about it, and taking it for a little test drive. People who slide into this second step say to themselves, *Of course I would never actually DO this, but just for the sake of research, I need to know a little bit more. . . .*

Frankly, the whole battle can be won or lost in those first few seconds. What makes temptation so difficult for so many people is they don't want to discourage it completely. They don't immediately embrace the temptation, but they do let it hang around, thinking they can toy with it a little.

Step 3. "And enticed."

By this time, it's almost too late. You're almost hooked.

Now you have moved from toying with the temptation to really giving it your attention. You've almost fallen into sin, but there is still a way out. There is still time to make a quick retreat. You can hang up the phone. You can walk out the door. You can shut down your computer. You can push that red off button on the remote. Those are the steps we need to take, and we may save ourselves from getting tangled up in sin and grieving the heart of God.

Step 4. "When desire has conceived, it gives birth to sin."

At this point the hook is set. The temptation has come, and you have looked at it, you have thought about it, and you have pursued it a little. And then suddenly you say, "I'm going for it." *Chomp!* You bite down, the hook is in, and you experience a very temporary euphoria.

But all too soon, however, the repercussions of sin start to kick in.

Step 5. "And sin, when it is full-grown, brings forth death."

Death comes in a thousand little ways. Guilt and remorse flood in after the euphoria vanishes. You feel dead inside. And you begin dealing with the consequences or repercussions of your act.

That is when you need to go immediately to the Lord and say, "Lord, I fell. I am sorry. I repent." And you get right with

Him as quickly as you can. You *run* back to Jesus.

We have three enemies to contend with as Christians: the world, the flesh, and the devil. The world, with its allure, is the external foe. The flesh, with its evil desires, is the internal foe. And the devil, with his enticements, is the infernal foe. These are our opponents, and this is the warfare that never stops until we step through the gate of heaven.

"Frenemy" with the World?

I think the problem is that we become *frenemies* with the world. What is that, you ask? A frenemy is a person whom you normally wouldn't get along with, but you patch things up with them temporarily if it serves both of your purposes. In other words, you have developed a love-hate relationship. Sometimes you're on, and sometimes you're off, depending on the circumstances.

It might also describe a relationship that is essentially poisonous and that drags you down spiritually, but you have allowed it to continue anyway. The person is not a friend and is really more like an enemy. Some of us have become frenemies with this world.

You say, "What do you mean by 'the world'?"

The Bible says in 1 John 2:15-16,

Do not love the world or the things in the world. If anyone loves the world, the love of the Father is not in him. For all that is in the world—the lust of the flesh, the lust of the eyes, and the pride of life—is not of the Father but is of the world.

If you are a friend of the world, you are God's enemy. When the Bible speaks of "world" here, that is not a synonym for *the earth*. It's okay to love the earth. It's okay to get excited about sunsets and rainbows and crashing surf and snowcapped mountains. The Bible isn't speaking about God's creation here; it is referring to a system, a mentality, a pervasive philosophy that infects everything everywhere.

Listen to another translation of 1 John 2:15-17:

Don't love the world's ways. Don't love the world's goods. Love of the world squeezes out love for the Father. Practically everything that goes on in the world—wanting your own way, wanting everything for yourself, wanting to appear important—has nothing to do with the Father. It just isolates you from him. The world and all its wanting, wanting, wanting is on the way out—but whoever does what God wants is set for eternity. (MSG)

Yes, the world—with all its glitter, sparkle, and glamour—can appear very enticing at times. But for its pull to work, we must desire what it is offering. Jesus said, "For out of the heart proceed evil thoughts, murders, adulteries, fornications, thefts, false witness, blasphemies. These are the things which defile a man . . ." (Matthew 15:19-20). The problem is within. We have ourselves to thank when we give in to temptation. It is just our nature.

I'm reminded of the classic story of the scorpion and the tortoise. One day there was a tortoise sitting by a pond, sunning himself. A scorpion walked up to him and said, "Hello, Mr. Tortoise. I was wondering if you would give me a lift across the pond?"

The tortoise replied, "I don't think I should do that. You would sting me, and then I would drown."

The scorpion replied, "My dear tortoise, if I were to sting you, I would go down with you. Now where is the logic in that?"

"That is true," said the tortoise. "All right. Hop on." And as they were making their way across the pond, the scorpion sticks his stinger into the tortoise's neck, and they both begin to sink.

Before he goes under, the tortoise says, "Do you mind if I ask you something?"

"Ask away," said the scorpion.

"You said there was no logic in stinging me. Now we're both going to drown. Why did you do it?"

The scorpion replied, "It has nothing to do with logic, tortoise. It's just my nature."

That is how it works with us, too. Why do we do the stupid stuff we sometimes do? It's just our sinful human nature, which we inherited from our parents, which they inherited from their parents, all the way back to Adam.

I'm thinking right now of a family. God had blessed them, and both husband and wife were raising their children to love the Lord. Why did that husband betray his wife and his family and his Lord to commit adultery? Why did he do such an insane, damaging, hurtful, suicidal thing as that? Why did he destroy his marriage and his family? Why did that guy go out and commit that act of adultery against his wife and destroy that family? But that is the point. It had nothing to do with sense or logic. *It's just our nature.*

So we have to be aware of that. We have to be cognizant of the unruly, combustible, evil sinful nature that makes its home inside every one of us, with no exceptions.

Sometimes we blame God. We say, "It's God's fault. He gave me more than I could handle." No, He didn't. As James 1:13 says, "Let no one say when he is tempted, 'I am tempted by God'; for God cannot be tempted by evil, nor does He Himself tempt anyone."

Or someone else will say, "The devil made me do it."

No, he didn't make you do it. You cooperated. You willfully engaged in the temptation that landed in front of you.

When Does Temptation Come?

The broad answer to that question is simple: It comes all the time. We are never truly free from it.

But there are certainly times when it becomes more intense.

I believe one of the times when we have to be most on our guard against temptation is after a time of great blessing.

When did Satan hit Jesus with his first recorded barrage of temptation? It was immediately after Jesus' baptism in the Jordan River. It was such a glorious moment in the life of Christ—and I'm sure it meant more to Him than we can begin to comprehend.

> Just as Jesus was coming up out of the water, he saw heaven being torn open and the Spirit descending on him like a dove. And a voice came from heaven: "You are my Son, whom I love; with you I am well pleased." (Mark 1:10-11, NIV)

The sky was "torn open"? Yes, Mark used a term in the original language that means "to split, sever, or tear open." Something *very* dramatic happened in that moment.

And then Jesus heard those incredibly affirming words from His Father as the Holy Spirit, in the form of a dove, descended on Him. It was a Trinity moment, and how can we calculate how joyful that must have been for Jesus?

That is why the very next verses in Mark are so significant: "At once the Spirit sent him out into the wilderness, and he was in the wilderness forty days, being tempted by Satan" (verses 12-13, NIV).

Immediately after the dove came the devil.

Immediately after the affirmation came the testing.

That is often the way it happens in our lives as well. After a time of blessing, after we have had the strong sense that the Lord has used us in a positive way, we get hit with a drone strike from hell.

It might be right after church or a Bible study or a significant spiritual conversation. I have seen the pattern repeated over and over in my life, and many others would say the same thing.

Remember the story in Scripture of the Transfiguration of Jesus? The Lord and His three closest disciples were up on a mountaintop when the disciples suddenly saw Jesus transformed before their very eyes: "His face shone like the sun, and His clothes became as white as the light. And behold, Moses and Elijah appeared to them, talking with Him" (Matthew 17:2-3).

Wow, talk about a mountaintop moment! Moses and Elijah? For a Jew it doesn't get much better than that. But then they come back down from that mountain of blessing, and the first thing they encountered was a child possessed by a powerful demon.

That is how it so often is; after the blessing comes the attack.

But mark this: temptation also will come *when think you are the strongest.* Sometimes you will hear someone say, "I could potentially fall in areas A, B, and C, but I *never* would fall in area D."

Don't say stuff like that.

The fact is, you don't know what you are capable of doing in your sinful nature. You could do the worst thing imaginable. *Anyone* could. As the old hymn says, "Prone to wander—Lord, I feel it—prone to leave the God I love."

That is all of us. We are prone to wander. Never doubt it! In the book of Jeremiah, the Lord describes the human heart as "deceitful above all things, and desperately wicked; who can know it?" (17:9).

Remember that it was immediately after Simon Peter began boasting about his great devotion to the Lord that he stumbled badly and fell. As Solomon wrote, "Pride goes before destruction, and a haughty spirit before a fall" (Proverbs 16:18).

To Whom Does Temptation Come?

As we have noted, temptation comes to everyone; we are all susceptible. Even so, the enemy often focuses his attention on those who are young in the faith and those who are making a difference in the kingdom.

Young believers are particularly vulnerable to Satan's

deceptions and attacks. I think of my little granddaughters. When they were babies, they would grab things without any idea of what they were grabbing. They would try to stuff random things into their mouths that had no business being in their mouths. They didn't know any better. In their innocence, they would wave to and chatter at any stranger who walked by. The fact is, young children need to be nurtured, loved, and protected because the world can be a hostile, hurtful place.

Newborn Christians need the same kind of care. Here at our church, we give out copies of *The New Believer's Bible* to everyone who receives the Lord. We tell our people, "If you see someone carrying that Bible, it's a good indication they have recently come to Christ. Take time to introduce yourself to them. Ask them how they're doing. Ask them when they committed their lives to Jesus, and how it's been going. Offer to pray with them and for them. Remind them that God will be faithful to them and help them, even when the inevitable attacks come."

We need to help and encourage new believers whenever and however we can.

But there is another target group on Satan's hit list, and it is those who are truly making a difference for the kingdom of God. Would you imagine that if you were to stand up and say, "Lord, I will do what You want me to do, and go where You want me to go," that you would get a standing ovation in hell?

Hardly. It is more likely that you would acquire a target on your back. So you had better stay very alert and keep your guard up. As Vance Havner once wrote, "If you have not been through the devil's sifter, you're probably not worth sifting!"[2]

Someone says, "Greg, I can't even remember the last time I was tempted."

That may not be good news. You don't kick a dead horse. The devil looks at such people and says, "Why should I bother attacking them? They're no threat to me. I'm going to save my attacks for this person over here who keeps being used by God. She's really getting on my nerves!"

How Does Temptation Come?

Temptation comes primarily through the doorway of our minds.

Paul wrote, "I am afraid that just as Eve was deceived by the serpent's cunning, your minds may somehow be led astray from your sincere and pure devotion to Christ" (2 Corinthians 11:3, NIV).

Beware of those flaming arrows aimed at your mind. Beware of allowing ungodly thoughts to gain any traction. You can't stop them from coming, but you can dispose of them as soon as they arrive!

In 2 Corinthians 10:5-6, Paul tells us,

We use our powerful God-tools for smashing warped philosophies, tearing down barriers erected against the truth of God, fitting every loose thought and emotion and impulse into the structure of life shaped by Christ. Our tools are ready at hand for clearing the ground of every obstruction and building lives of obedience into maturity. (MSG)

Fill your mind with God's Word!

I recently filled up the hard drive on my computer, mostly with photographs. It wouldn't let me load even one more picture. So I had the drive replaced and a larger hard drive installed. Until I did, my hard drive was too full to absorb any new information.

Wouldn't it be great if the devil couldn't fit any evil thoughts into your mind because it was already filled up with the Word of God?

Philippians 4:8 says, "Summing it all up, friends, I'd say you'll do best by filling your minds and meditating on things true, noble, reputable, authentic, compelling, gracious—the best, not the worst; the beautiful, not the ugly; things to praise, not things to curse" (MSG).

Temptation comes to us because we're not strict with ourselves about shutting evil thoughts out of our minds. Someone says, "Yes, I agree with you that sin would hurt me, but I don't really intend to buy anything. I just want to do a little window shopping and see what's out there." So we allow ourselves to do a little browsing, and the next thing we know, we're hanging out with the wrong people at the wrong places and end up doing the wrong things.

Satan has an amazing marketing strategy for sin. You think all of those ad agencies on Madison Avenue are clever? They can't hold a candle to Satan's marketing. The key is, don't listen to even the first words of his pitch. Shut him down. As James 4:7 says, "Resist the devil and you'll find he'll run away from you" (PH).

Where Is the Best Place to Be When Temptation Comes?

The best place to be is in God's will.

In other words, don't put yourself in places where you don't belong. Don't hang out with people who aren't good for you and who lead you into doing things you shouldn't.

Let's imagine that you had a severe coffee allergy and had to give up coffee altogether. But you have always loved coffee. Every time you smell it brewing, you want to get a cup of it, even though you know you'll pay a heavy price. So don't go anywhere near a coffee shop. Don't tell yourself that you'll order tea or just get a cookie and a juice. Stay away from coffee as best you can in this coffee-crazy culture of ours.

The best place to be when temptation comes is smack-dab in the middle of God's will, doing the things He has asked you to do, and being with people who will build you up and encourage you in your faith.

Yes, Jesus faced intense temptation in the wilderness. But the Spirit of God led Him there. And when it was over, angels came and ministered to Him. Jesus was in the very center of His Father's will when He went one-on-one with Satan and turned back every one of the enemy's attacks with Bible verses that He quoted from memory.

To sum up, being in God's will and being in God's Word won't keep you from temptations or Satan's attacks. In fact, Satan might quote some Scripture right back at you—out of context.

In one of Satan's last temptations of Jesus, we read that he transported Him to Jerusalem, set Him on the pinnacle of the temple, and said,

> If You are the Son of God, throw Yourself down. For it is written: "He shall give His angels charge over you," and, "In their hands they shall bear you up, lest you dash your foot against a stone." (Matthew 4:6)

Now check this out. Satan was quoting the Bible. He was quoting from Psalm 91:11-12:

> He shall give His angels charge over you,
> To keep you in all your ways.
> In their hands they shall bear you up,
> Lest you dash your foot against a stone.

Yes, the devil apparently knows the Scriptures well and may quote from them when it serves his purposes. But he quoted them out of context. God certainly will protect us with His angels, but He doesn't promise to shield us from deliberate self-destruction.

Satan was using Scripture, but not in the way it was intended.

I heard a story not long ago about the comedian W. C. Fields, whose whole shtick was playing an inebriated man. Sadly, his real personal life seemed to reflect his public image because Fields was an alcoholic. According to the story, someone actually saw W. C. Fields leafing through the pages of a Bible once.

"W. C. Fields reading the Bible?" the person asked. "Why on earth would you be reading the Bible?"

"Looking for loopholes!" Fields deadpanned.

That is the way Satan reads the Bible: looking for loopholes, looking for ways to misuse it, misquote it, or rip it out of its proper context. Our best defense, of course, is to know its context and to be conversant with its content so we can defend ourselves when we're hit with someone who twists and misuses the Bible.

The book of Acts tells us about a group of believers who pursued that very course. We read, "Now the Berean Jews were of more noble character than those in Thessalonica, for they received the message with great eagerness and examined the Scriptures every day to see if what Paul said was true" (17:11, NIV).

Which brings us to our final point . . .

What Is the Primary Weapon We Should Use to Resist Temptation?

The Word of God. It's great to carry a Bible in your briefcase or purse or have it loaded on your smartphone or tablet. But the best place to carry the Word of God is in your heart. You need to know the Word of God and memorize it. Psalm 119:9 says, "How can a young man cleanse his way? By taking heed according to Your word." Verse 11 says, "Your word I have hidden in my heart, that I might not sin against You."

Are you memorizing the Bible?

"I just can't memorize," you say. "It's just too hard. I'm not very good at remembering things."

Really? The truth is, we all have so much information in our brains—much of it totally useless. It is astounding what the brain can retain. I talk to some guys who know the scores of their favorite sports teams going back twenty years. Many of us can quote mindless jingles of ads we heard on TV decades ago. Some people know the codes for certain video games so they can gain an advantage. Others know all kinds of trivia about the entertainment world or minutiae about people we admire.

But you can't memorize the Word of God?

Yes, it takes some time and some discipline. But when you find yourself under attack by the evil one and his minions, you will be glad you equipped yourself to come out victorious.

For instance, when the devil whispers in your ear, "You've really blown it this time. God is so disgusted with you that He might not forgive you for a long time!"

Instead of panicking or falling into depression, you quickly say back to him, "No, that is a lie! First John 1:9 says, 'If we confess our sins, He is faithful and just to forgive us our sins and to cleanse us from all unrighteousness.'"

Or maybe Satan says, "God condemns you for what you have done. You're under His condemnation!"

Again, you say, "Not so! Romans 8:1 tells me, 'There is therefore now no condemnation to those who are in Christ Jesus. . . .'"

Satan might say, "You'll never make it as a Christian. You're going to fall away and God will give up on you."

And you reply, "Get out of here, Satan. That isn't true. Philippians 1:6 tells me, 'Being confident of this very thing, that He who has begun a good work in [me] will complete it until the day of Jesus Christ.'"

When tragedy hits your life, as it inevitably will, the devil may say, "That's it. Your life is over. It's ruined. God has abandoned you."

"Oh no, He hasn't!" you reply. "Because Romans 8:28 says that 'all things work together for good to those who love God, to those who are the called according to His purpose.'"

When a Christian loved one dies, Satan may whisper, "That's it. They're gone. You'll never see them again."

Again, you reply, "That's a lie, and you are a liar, Satan. Jesus said in John 11:25-26, 'I am the resurrection and the life. He who believes in Me, though he may die, he shall live. And whoever lives and believes in Me shall never die.'" And then you quote 2 Corinthians 5:8, which says that to be absent from the body is to be present with the Lord.

Temptation will be part of our lives until we finally arrive home in heaven. Even so, it can be effectively resisted while we're on earth as we memorize Scripture, stay close to God and His people, and stay away from the ungodly influences that hurt us and drag us down.

Paul summed it up well in his words to his young friend Timothy, "Run from anything that stimulates youthful lusts. Instead, pursue righteous living, faithfulness, love, and peace. Enjoy the companionship of those who call on the Lord with pure hearts" (2 Timothy 2:22, NLT).

Run and *pursue.* Run from temptation, and pursue the Lord. And don't leave a forwarding address.

17 Why Does God Allow Suffering? Part 1

Looking back, I've probably spoken about this topic on and off throughout my thirty-five years of being a pastor. But as you know, our perspective and views on major life issues change with the passing of time. Hopefully, your understanding deepens as you get older, and you see a bit more of the picture than you saw as a young person.

In my case, I'm sure my views on suffering have changed with additional suffering in my life. Yes, I went through some very difficult times in my turbulent childhood, moving from place to place as I did and going through such a succession of "fathers."

I've had some hard times through the years. But when our oldest son went to heaven in July of 2008, I went through some of the deepest suffering I have ever experienced.

As a result, I approach this subject a little bit differently now. You might say that this has become very, very personal to me. Nothing has really changed with the content of my teaching, but because I have had such an encounter with grief and pain in my own life, I probably don't approach it in the same way.

All I know is that when I search the Word of God for truth on this subject, I am also looking for myself as well because it's so personal to me.

No one escapes suffering.

Everyone has to navigate this fact of life at some point—or probably several points—on their earthly journey. Some years ago, a Barna poll asked the question, "If you could ask God any question you wanted and get a response, what would you ask?" And the number one question people wanted to ask God was, "Why is there pain and suffering in the world?"

Whenever you share the gospel with someone, it won't be long until the question will pop up: "Well, if God is all-loving and so good, why does He allow innocent people to suffer?"

It was C. S. Lewis who said that the problem of pain is atheism's most potent weapon against the Christian faith.

More than any other reason, people point to the problem of evil and suffering as their reason for not believing in God. It is not merely *a* problem; it is *the* problem with men and women coming to faith.

It's only natural, isn't it? We look around at this world we live in, read the headlines, hear all the sad stories of cruelty, pain, disease, hunger, war, and brutality, and we wonder, *Why does this happen? Why was there an earthquake in Japan? Why was there a hurricane on the Gulf Coast? Why was there a tsunami that took so many lives? Why did so many people die in the World Trade Center towers or in the Pentagon or in the hijacked planes on 9/11? Why did my friend just get cancer? Why was that child born with a disability? Why? Why? Why?* The questions go on and on.

Why does God allow tragedy? Why does He allow wars to rage? Why does He allow injustice in the world? Why do these things take place?

Maybe for you, it's "all those other poor people" who suffer. But it will come to you, too, as it comes to all of us. It is not a matter of *if;* it is a matter of *when.* So what we need to do is prepare ourselves for suffering so that we will be ready ahead of time.

Is it a pessimistic view of life, to suggest that all of us will face hardship and suffering? No, I think it is a realistic view of life. Job 5:7 says, "People are born for trouble as readily as sparks fly up from a fire" (NLT).

Randy Alcorn wrote,

"Most of us don't give focused thought to evil and suffering until we experience them. This forces us to formulate perspective on the fly, at a time when our thinking is muddled and we're exhausted and consumed by pressing issues. If you've been there, you'll attest to the fact that it's far better to think through suffering in advance."[1]

That is one of the purposes of this book on essentials. In Colossians 3:16 we read, "Let the word of Christ dwell in you richly in all wisdom. . . ." The idea is to help lay a biblical foundation in your life so that you will have something to draw on when the storm comes and when the crisis hits.

I know we would rather avoid these things. If you are out at sea and notice a rough patch of water, you try to sail in another direction. If you are flying and find yourself approaching a storm front, you attempt to go over it or around it. But there is no escaping tragedy in our lives. It is mind-boggling how quickly it can burst into our lives. It is startling to realize that within a one- or two-minute period, your entire life can be altered.

As ours was.

And in that moment, everything changes. The way you view so many things changes. There are also a thousand surprises. Some people whom you expected to be there for you are nowhere to be found—or inexplicably try to hurt you in the moment when you're down. Other people whom you barely know find amazing ways to show you understanding, compassion, and love.

Back to the Big Question

Here is the way you will often hear the question worded: If God is a good and loving God, then why does He allow evil?

And here is the implication behind that question: Either God is all-powerful but not all good, and therefore He doesn't stop evil, or, He is all good but not all-powerful, and therefore He *can't* stop evil.

The problem with this question is that it is based on a false premise. The premise is that I am the one who determines what is good and what is not good. And by the very nature of that question, I am already suggesting that I don't believe God *is* good.

Here is my rather blunt response to that question: When did you become the moral center of the universe? Who are you, and who am I, to say what is good or not good? The fact is, God isn't good because you or I think Him to be good. Nor is He good because someone took a poll and determined that 98 percent of us believe He is good.

No, God is good because He *said* He is good. And there is no higher authority than God Himself. In Luke 18:19, Jesus said, "No one is good—except God alone" (NIV). God is good whether I believe it or not. God, and God alone, is the final court of arbitration. As Paul said in Romans 3:4, "Let God be true but every man a liar."

But what is "good"?

In Romans 8:28 we read, "And we know that all things work together for good to those who love God, to those who are the called according to His purpose."

He works for our good? Yes, He does. But we need to make sure that our definition of good and God's definition of good line up.

Good is whatever God approves. If God says it is good, then it is good. You protest, "But that is circular reasoning. You are quoting God to prove God."

Yes, I am. I call that biblical reasoning. It starts with God and ends with God because that is how life works.

God wants us to think these things through. In Isaiah 1:18, He says, "Come now, and let us reason together." But a better rendering of that verse would be, "Come, let's sit down and argue this out."

The Bible says that God's thoughts are above my thoughts, and that God's ways are above my ways.[2] There is no higher standard of goodness than God's own character, and His approval of whatever is good is consistent with that character.

So God is good. Period.

But Why Does He Allow Evil?

First of all, we have to understand that God did not *create* evil. He created man uniquely in His image and placed him in a paradise called the Garden of Eden. He gave Adam and Eve free will, the ability to choose.

Within this paradise, God gave only one restriction.

Just one.

He said, "You are free to eat from any tree in the garden; but you must not eat from the tree of the knowledge of good and evil, for when you eat from it you will certainly die" (Genesis 2:16-17, NIV).

So there they were in this incredible paradise with presumably hundreds or even thousands of trees to admire and pick fruit from. But where do our first parents choose to hang out? Right in front of the one tree that God told them to stay away from.

So Adam and Eve sinned, breaking God's command (and probably His heart) by eating the fruit He had told them not to eat. But why did God create human beings who weren't even capable of sin? Wouldn't that have saved a lot of future grief?

You probably know the answer to that as well as I do. God wanted us to love because we chose to, not because we had to.

Let's say you go to the toy store and buy a little doll that has a computer chip in its little body. If you squeeze the doll, she says, "I love you!"

That's nice. But do you really find fulfillment from that? Of course you don't.

Or imagine that you, as a parent, were to go up to your little son or daughter and say, "Tell me that you love me right now, or I will spank you."

"Okay, I love you."

What kind of a love is that? The child is afraid of the repercussions and will say anything you order him to say.

God wants us to love Him because we *choose* to. Nothing warms the hearts of parents more than having their child voluntarily come up to them and say, "I love you, Daddy. I love you, Mommy." God wants the same thing from all of us. He gave us the freedom to choose to love Him . . . or not love Him.

So much of what we call evil in our world happens because we choose to disregard God's Word, choose to break His commandments, or choose to deliberately hurt one another.

To a certain degree, I think we can understand why bad things happen to bad people. In fact, there are times when we look upon it as poetic justice. "What goes around comes around! He got what was coming to him!" As Solomon wrote, "Whoever digs a pit will fall into it; if someone rolls a stone, it will roll back on them" (Proverbs 26:27, NIV). The person building a bomb to hurt innocent people has it blow up in his own face. It's hard to waste much emotional energy worrying about such events.

The question that really bothers us is, "Why does God allow bad things to happen to good people — or to *godly* people?" We can accept the idea of suffering in general, especially when it happens as a consequence of bad behavior. But when bad things happen to good people, we don't get it.

Here is something I want to establish right out of the gate: Being a Christian does not exempt us from suffering. Christians will fall and break their legs. Christians will have miscarriages. Christians will get cancer. Christians will get in car accidents and plane crashes. In fact, Christians face the same tragedies the world faces.

We are surprised by that—shocked by that. Nevertheless, it happens. Tragedy comes into our lives as well. In his first New Testament letter, Peter wrote, "Dear friends, do not be surprised at the fiery ordeal that has come on you to test you, as though something strange were happening to you" (1 Peter 4:12, NIV).

In other words, don't be shocked that such things could happen to you. They can. They will. After Christopher's accident, I actually had people come up to me and say, "Greg, why did this happen to you *of all people*?"

Do they imagine that I somehow get a free pass because I'm a pastor? No, I suffer along with everyone else out there. As Jesus said in John 16:33, "I have told you all this so that you may have peace in me. Here on earth you will have many trials and sorrows. But take heart, because I have overcome the world" (NLT).

Why do bad things happen to good or godly people?

I don't know.

You should have asked me when I was twenty-one, and I would have had an answer for you. I had an answer for everything when I was twenty-one. But in the intervening years, *life* has happened to me, and I don't know as much as I used to think I knew. These days, I'm not afraid or reluctant to say, "I just don't know. I can't explain that."

Am I evading the question, then? No, I am simply acknowledging there are things—many things—I never will know this side of heaven.

In his commentary on Job, Charles Swindoll wrote,

I don't care if you have a PhD you earned at Yale or in Scotland. Just stand in front of the mirror, all alone, nobody around, shrug, and say, "I don't know . . . I really don't know." You can also add, "I can't tell you why that happened. I just don't know." Repeat the words several times. . . . God never promised He would inform us ahead of time all about His plan. He's just promised He has one. Ultimately, it's for our good and His glory. He knows—we don't. That's why we shrug and admit, "I don't know."[3]

That isn't to say there aren't answers to some of these thornier questions of life. It is just to say that I don't know all of them—or even very many of them—at this point in my life.

But I do know this: I know that God is good.

And I do know this: I know that God is in control.

What's more, I know that (somehow) He works all things together for good in my life. I also know that He allows sometimes terrible, heartbreaking things to happen to good men and women.

I can think of no better illustration of these truths than the story of Job.

Job's Story

Job was an amazing man, a godly man of great integrity—so much so that God Himself bragged on him in heaven. But Job faced some of the worst calamities that we have ever heard of.

Job was a real man living in a real place in real history. He experienced real pain, turned to God, and found real answers. This is the same God who will help you in your hour of need. Many believe the book of Job to be the oldest in the Bible. Let's zero in for a moment on his story:

There once was a man named Job who lived in the land of Uz. He was blameless—a man of complete integrity. He feared God and stayed away from evil. He had seven sons and three daughters. He owned 7,000 sheep, 3,000 camels, 500 teams of oxen, and 500 female donkeys. He also had many servants. He was, in fact, the richest person in that entire area.

Job's sons would take turns preparing feasts in their homes, and they would also invite their three sisters to celebrate with them. When these celebrations ended—sometimes after several days—Job would purify his children. He would get up early in the morning and offer a burnt offering for each of them. For Job said to himself, "Perhaps my children have sinned and have cursed God in their hearts." This was Job's regular practice. (1:1-5, NLT)

Four points jump out about Job that I think are worth noting.

Job was a man of integrity and character.

Here was a man who practiced what he preached. No matter what all the voices in our contemporary culture might say, character really does count. In fact, it may be the most important thing in a person's life. I'm not talking here about what a person says, but about what a person *does* and who that person *is* in their essence.

The real you isn't necessarily the person who sits in church on Sunday. The real you is who you are in private, when there is no one to impress, and when you know that no one is watching. As D. L. Moody put it, character is what you are in the dark. Job was a man of supreme character.

Job was a wealthy man.

He was the wealthiest man in all the region. And yet the wealth did not go to his head or change his righteous character. He seemed to keep it all in perspective.

Obviously, that isn't true of everyone. Wealth has turned many a head and heart away from God. In fact, we are warned in Psalm 62:10, "If riches increase, do not set your heart on them."

Here is the funny thing about wealth and affluence. You may have a lot of it and not necessarily be affected by it. Conversely, you may have very little of it and be obsessed with it. We often think that it is the wealthy people who are materialistic and live out of balance, but sometimes the most materialistic people around are the ones who *want* to be rich.

Sometimes it is said, "The Bible teaches that money is the root of all evil." But that is not what Scripture says. The Bible teaches, "For the *love of money* is the root of all kinds of evil. And some people, craving money, have wandered from the true faith and pierced themselves with many sorrows" (1 Timothy 6:10, NLT, emphasis added).

It isn't necessarily those who have money who are in danger, but it is those who are obsessed with money.

Job had a great deal of money and it didn't control his life. He was a wealthy man and remained a man of integrity.

Job was a family man.

He clearly loved his ten children and sought to raise them in the way of the Lord. From the verses we read in Job 1, it sounds like Job even was concerned about his adult children's whereabouts and what they were up to. He was a godly father.

Job was a prayerful man.

Job 1:5 tells us that he would offer up burnt offerings for his children, which is an Old Testament way of saying that he prayed for them—not sporadically but regularly. Do you pray for your children? Do you set a godly example for them to follow? Sometimes when we find ourselves with trouble in our home or trouble with our children, it is because we have trouble in our hearts.

Job, however, had it together. He was a man who loved God and loved his family. He was man of faith and prayer and lived with real integrity.

But let's go on a little further with the story.

In Heaven, Behind the Scenes

One day the members of the heavenly court came to present themselves before the LORD, and the Accuser, Satan, came with them. "Where have you come from?" the LORD asked Satan.

Satan answered the LORD, "I have been patrolling the earth, watching everything that's going on."

Then the LORD asked Satan, "Have you noticed my servant Job? He is the finest man in all the earth. He is blameless—a man of complete integrity. He fears God and stays away from evil."

Satan replied to the LORD, "Yes, but Job has good reason to fear God. You have always put a wall of protection around him and his home and his property. You have made him prosper in everything he does. Look how rich he is! But reach out and take away everything he has, and he will surely curse you to your face!"

"All right, you may test him," the LORD said to Satan. "Do whatever you want with everything he possesses, but don't harm him physically." So Satan left the LORD's presence. (Job 1:6-12, NLT)

Wow. Talk about having friends in high places! God actually was bragging on Job in front of Satan and the angels. But know this: When God is your friend, the devil will be your enemy. But then again, if the devil is your friend, then God will be your enemy. So you ought to choose who you want your friends and enemies to be.

Nevertheless, the very fact that Job was the friend of God and that the Lord was bragging on him caused the devil to want to wreak havoc in his life.

Notice how active Satan is:

The Accuser, Satan, came with them. (1:6)
Satan answered. (1:7)
I have been patrolling the earth, watching everything. (1:7)
Satan left the LORD's presence. (1:12)

He never stops. He never slows down. Wouldn't it be nice if he took a year off? But he doesn't take a year off — or a month, a week, a day, an hour, or a minute. He is always working. As Peter tells us, "The devil walks about like a roaring lion, seeking whom he may devour" (1 Peter 5:8).

And what is his ultimate agenda?

There is no mystery there! Jesus Himself told us that "the thief comes only to steal and kill and destroy" (John 10:10, NIV).

Satan's end game, if you will, is to take you out of God's protection and to ruin your life. In contrast, Jesus also said in the same verse, "I have come that they may have life, and that they may have it more abundantly."

In the presence of many heavenly witnesses, Satan made this accusation before the Lord, saying, in essence, "Do you know why Job fears You? It's because You give him lots of stuff. He has a really good life because You have sheltered him and put a hedge of protection around him. I can't penetrate that wall of Yours to get at him, but if You were to take it away, then You'd get the real picture on whether this man loves You or not!"

Do you know that God has the same hedge of protection around you? It's an impenetrable fortress, and no one can get through it to lay a glove on you without His divine permission.

But in this case, the Lord gave the devil permission to bring a series of tragedies into the life of Job. And that is where we continue the story.

Job's Difficult, Wise Choice

One day when Job's sons and daughters were feasting at the oldest brother's house, a messenger arrived at Job's home with this news: "Your oxen were plowing, with the donkeys feeding beside them, when the Sabeans raided us. They stole all the animals and killed all the farmhands. I am the only one who escaped to tell you."

While he was still speaking, another messenger arrived with this news: "The fire of God has fallen from heaven and burned up your sheep and all the shepherds. I am the only one who escaped to tell you."

While he was still speaking, a third messenger arrived with this news: "Three bands of Chaldean raiders have stolen your camels and killed your servants. I am the only one who escaped to tell you."

While he was still speaking, another messenger arrived with this news: "Your sons and daughters were feasting in their oldest brother's home. Suddenly, a powerful wind swept in from the wilderness and hit the house on all sides. The house collapsed, and all your children are dead. I am the only one who escaped to tell you."

Job stood up and tore his robe in grief. Then he shaved his head and fell to the ground to worship. He said,

"I came naked from my mother's womb,
    and I will be naked when I leave.
The LORD gave me what I had,
    and the LORD has taken it away.
Praise the name of the LORD!"

In all of this, Job did not sin by blaming God. (Job 1:13-22, NLT)

In one day, Job was completely bankrupt. Everything he had acquired through his lifetime was gone in a moment. But worst of all, his children were taken as well: seven sons and three daughters gone, just like that. For a parent to lose a child is a fate worse than death. When David's son Absalom died, even though he was an ungrateful, wicked young man, David wept uncontrollably and said he wished it would have been him instead of Absalom.[4] And any parent would say the same thing and gladly trade places with his or her child.

But I want you to notice what else Job did.

He worshiped the Lord.

As I have said, tragedy will come to all of us in life, and it will have one of two effects. It either will strengthen our faith, and we will turn to God for comfort, or we will become angry at God and turn away from Him. It's your choice. Hardships in life will make you either better or bitter, and you will decide which it will be.

Character is not made in crisis; it is *revealed*.

It is when the crisis hits and the veil is torn away that we see what that man or woman really was. In the case of Job, we see him being exactly what he was in his essence: a man of faith, a man of character, and a man of prayer.

Some people have said to me, "Oh, you have so much faith the way that you have trusted in God through your hard time."

Faith? Yes, you can call it that. I call it common sense. Where else could I turn in my crisis, in my sorrow? To the bottle? To drugs? To illicit pleasures? No thank you! I turn to the One who can actually support me and uphold me at such a time, the One who has promised to give me what I need.

I'm reminded of the time when many of Jesus' followers turned away from Him and walked away. And the Lord said to the Twelve, "Are you guys going away, too?"

Peter replied: "Lord, to whom shall we go? You have the words of eternal life" (John 6:68).

Allow me to loosely paraphrase that: "Lord, we don't always get You. We don't always understand why You do what You do or why You say what You say. But this much we know: You are the One, You are the Messiah, You are the Lord, and we will keep following You."

This is one of the good things that can come out of crisis and suffering. You turn to God with a dependence like you never have had before. Instead of praying proper, polite, orderly prayers, you become like a child who runs to his dad for comfort and just buries his face on his shoulder. A friend who lost his wife to cancer told me that he had learned to pray with his face in the carpet, his arms outstretched. He never had prayed that way before, in complete dependence.

God can be an incomparable comfort to us, even when we still don't have all the answers.

He is there.

And He deeply cares.

As Peter wrote, "You can throw the whole weight of your anxieties upon him, for you are his personal concern" (1 Peter 5:7, PH).

As much as we would like to believe otherwise, our faith will not grow very much in times of ease and peace. Faith grows best through challenges and difficulty. Sometimes you hear people say, "This tragedy has shaken my faith."

Really? Maybe you didn't have very much faith to begin with. As Randy Alcorn has written, "The faith that can't be shaken is the faith that has been shaken."[5] In other words, when your faith has been shaken and is revealed to be real, that faith will see you though in your times of difficulty.

Feelings and Faith

On Job's worst-of-all-nightmares day, He worshiped the Lord and prayed these words right out loud: "I came naked from my mother's womb, and I will be naked when I leave. The LORD gave me what I had, and the LORD has taken it away. Praise the name of the LORD!" (Job 1:21, NLT).

Job worshiped, though his emotions were in rags and tatters. He worshiped because honoring the name of the Lord was the right thing to do, not because he felt like it.

If you and I only worshiped God when we felt like it, we wouldn't be worshiping Him very often. Worship is always the right thing to do, no matter what our physical or emotional state.

Maybe you have sat in church, neglecting to worship God because you "weren't in the mood," or "didn't feel at the top of your game." Maybe you held back from worship because of problems in your marriage or with your kids. The truth is, you should praise the Lord regardless of how you feel. The Bible doesn't say, "Give thanks to the LORD when you feel good." No, it says, "Give thanks to the LORD, for He is good! For His mercy endures forever" (Psalm 107:1).

Worship God because He is worthy of your worship—regardless of your circumstances. That is what Job did, and that is what we need to do.

You might say, "If something like that ever happened to me—even if it was on a much smaller scale—I just couldn't handle it."

Yes, you could.

"How do you know? You don't know me."

No, I don't. But I know God. And He promised that He would never give you more than you could handle. You see, the One who allowed the storm is also your Hiding Place in that storm. Whatever comes into your life has been allowed by God, and it has been allowed for a reason.

What is that reason? We may or may not learn the reason in this life. As I said, Job never did.

In 2 Corinthians 1, the apostle Paul tells us that one of the reasons for our suffering is to enable us to help others who are going through the same things we have gone through.

When you are suffering, you want to go to someone who has suffered and found God's comfort. I never asked to have a ministry to suffering people, and frankly, I didn't want such a ministry.

But I have one now—more than I've ever had before.

I have never put a sign on my door that says, "Come to me when tragedy hits."

But people do.

Knowing that I have endured the loss of my son, they come to me for prayer, for advice, and for some kind of perspective on their pain.

Mostly, I just listen. I'm not as quick on the draw with Bible verses as I used to be, though I still quote certain passages. But I have found that the best thing I can do for someone who has endured a tragedy is to simply be there and weep with them.

But here is the bottom line. There is only so much that I can do for you or that you can do for me. If you want to go to the ultimate source of comfort for your times of difficulty, then go to Jesus Himself. Who suffered more than Jesus? The Bible calls Him "a man of sorrows, acquainted with deepest grief" (Isaiah 53:3, NLT). In Hebrews 2:18 we read, "Since he himself has gone through suffering and testing, he is able to help us when we are being tested" (NLT).

Someone will say, "Yes, I know, Greg. And Jesus has been with me and has been a comfort to me. But I just miss my loved one."

I know what you're talking about. And I also miss Christopher. But I need to step back and try to see the whole event from a heavenly perspective, remembering that my son is still alive in another place, in the best place of all.

Imagine yourself standing in line in the hot sun, waiting to get into Disneyland. Suddenly the CEO of Disney walks up to you and says, "I see that you are having a difficult time getting into our park. I want you to come with me." So you follow the CEO, and he walks with you right through the gate while the other people in line just shake their heads.

In the same way, when someone is called to heaven, it is a promotion. An earthly death means an early crown. It is a privilege, not a punishment.

When this happens, we often will speak of our loved one as being "gone." And in one sense, that is true. But I think a more accurate way to say it would be, "They are gone *for now.*" To say that person is gone implies that he or she no longer exists. But to say that person is gone for now speaks of reunion.

The Bible tells us that when a believer dies in the Lord, he or she departs to be with Christ, which is far better.[6]

I can't control this world that I live in, although time and

314 | essentials 2

again I have wished that I could. Ultimately, God is in control and all I can do is respond. On the darkest day of his life, Job responded by getting down on his knees and worshiping.

He said, in effect, "I don't get this, and I don't begin to understand why these things have happened. But I choose in this moment to glorify God."

It wasn't an easy thing for him to do, and it won't be an easy thing for us to do, either.

But it will be the first step toward healing, restoration, and future blessing.

18 Why Does God Allow Suffering? Part 2

S atan was pretty sure he had it all figured out. He had been watching the way men and women responded to crises since the beginning of time, and he was ready to lay heavy odds on what was going to happen.

If God took away all that Job owned, all that was precious to him, Job would fold like a cheap road map and end up cursing God to His face. Of course he would! If you hit a man in his pocketbook, and on the same day destroy his family, there would be nothing left for him, and he would cash in his faith.

But it hadn't worked out that way.

Instead, on the darkest, most terrible day of Job's life, the broken man "fell to the ground and worshiped" the Lord. Furthermore, "In all this Job did not sin nor charge God with wrong" (Job 1:22).

So, Satan had to admit that he had miscalculated a little. But he still wasn't willing to yield the point and still thought he knew best. That set up round two in the presence of God.

One day the members of the heavenly court came again to present themselves before the LORD, and the Accuser, Satan, came with them. "Where have you come from?" the LORD asked Satan.

Satan answered the LORD, "I have been patrolling the earth, watching everything that's going on."

Then the LORD asked Satan, "Have you noticed my servant Job? He is the finest man in all the earth. He is blameless—a man of complete integrity. He fears God and stays away from evil. And he has maintained his integrity, even though you urged me to harm him without cause."

Satan replied to the LORD, "Skin for skin! A man will give up everything he has to save his life. But reach out and take away his health, and he will surely curse you to your face!"

"All right, do with him as you please," the LORD said to Satan. "But spare his life." So Satan left the LORD's presence, and he struck Job with terrible boils from head to foot.

Job scraped his skin with a piece of broken pottery as he sat among the ashes. His wife said to him, "Are you still trying to maintain your integrity? Curse God and die."

But Job replied, "You talk like a foolish woman. Should we accept only good things from the hand of God and never anything bad?" So in all this, Job said nothing wrong. (Job 2:1-10, NLT)

In the previous chapter, I raised the question "Why does God allow suffering?" To this day, that is a question hurting people ask on all sides. As I mentioned, since the early departure of our son to heaven, I hear from people all the time who are struggling, in pain, and have lost children to death. They write me honest letters and e-mails and come talk to me about what they're dealing with.

The following, for instance, is a letter I received from a lady named Patricia:

Hello, Pastor Greg,

I learned about your tragedy about a year ago, and though I wanted to write several times, I have never felt such an overwhelming urge like I do now. Several years ago after living for only two days, my daughter died. I am ashamed to say it is six years later, and I am still baffled and confused about why God chose to take my firstborn child. Though taught oftentimes that God is sovereign and does what He wants to do, the question still lingers in my mind: Why? I know that all things work together for good to those that love the Lord, but I fail to see any good that has or will come out of this disastrous life experience. How did you or how are you coping with your loss? What Scripture has been a comfort to you?

It is a very honest letter, and she raises some difficult questions. I so appreciate that she is completely candid about where she stands.

Patricia had her life collapse around her, and perhaps you have had that same crushing experience. Most of us, on at least some level, can identify with Job's situation in this passage of Scripture. There were so many questions in his heart and so few answers.

It is easy for us to read Job's story and even critique him at certain points. But we need to keep this one thing in mind: Job had never read the book of Job. He didn't know how it would all turn out in the end. He didn't know about the conversations between God and Satan in some other dimension he couldn't see. He didn't know why all of those heartbreaking things had happened to him. All he knew was that one day everything was going along so beautifully. He was walking with God and praying for his family, just as he always did. And then, in a matter of just a few, terrible minutes, the bottom dropped out of his life.

I'm reminded of the recent news story of the man in Florida who was resting comfortably in his bed when the earth suddenly opened up and swallowed his bedroom in a gigantic sinkhole. That must have been how Job felt on that disastrous moment in his life.

But even so, he held onto his faith in God. James 5:11 says, "We give great honor to those who endure under suffering. For instance, you know about Job, a man of great endurance. You can see how the Lord was kind to him at the end, for the Lord is full of tenderness and mercy" (NLT).

The Lord's plan for Job finally ended in good?

Yes, it did.

Before his life was over, Job would again be blessed with God's great favor, kindness, and blessing.

But Job couldn't see any of that in his crisis. He was still in the storm. He was still midstream. He was still reeling from a succession of events that had flattened him like a dump truck.

Did he have questions? You bet he had questions! And so do we at times. Why does God allow this tragedy? Why does God even allow evil in our world? Why does He allow someone as wicked and depraved as Satan to exist, since God could vaporize him in a millionth of a second?

Believe it or not, even Satan at times serves the purposes of God. God didn't create the being we know today as Satan as a wicked spiritual power. He created him as a glorious, magnificent angel who ultimately rebelled against God and became the devil. But even the devil's hateful attacks can serve the purposes of God. God can take the greatest tragedies and turn them into the greatest of victories.

Bringing Good Out of Satan's Attacks

What, for instance, was more inexplicable, tragic, and heartbreaking than the crucifixion of Jesus Christ, the Son of God?

Imagine if you had been one of His disciples. Suddenly Jesus appears in your life—the long-awaited Messiah of Israel—and He chooses you to be one of His handpicked followers. What a privilege that would be! Through the coming weeks and months, you hear His profound words, witness His astounding miracles, and see the lives of thousands in your country impacted by His teaching. You see Him walk on water, feed a multitude from a few loaves of bread, confound the arrogant religious leaders of the day, give hope to the hopeless, and even raise the dead to life. Your heart swims with visions of Him establishing His earthly kingdom, where you will rule and reign at His side, freeing Israel from Roman oppression and bringing a new golden age into the world.

But then He starts talking crazy.

He starts saying things like, "The Son of Man is being betrayed into the hands of men, and they will kill Him. And after He is killed, He will rise on the third day."

What? Was He speaking metaphorically? Could He really mean what He was saying? It made no sense!

But then it began to happen—terrible things. Judas Iscariot (of all people!) betrays your Lord to His enemies. Jesus is arrested in Gethsemane and led away in chains. He's given a phony trial and treated despicably by the authorities. You keep thinking, *He's going to get out of this. There will be a last-minute miracle that will set Him free.*

But there are no miracles. Jesus is scourged and then sent to the cross. But even as He hangs there, His face hardly recognizable from the abuse, you find yourself thinking, *He will come down from that cross. Somehow, He will escape. This can't be happening!*

And then He dies.

What happens to your hopes, your expectations, your dreams? What happened to this One who became more valuable and precious to you than your own family?

He is dead!

How could that be a good thing? It's the worst tragedy imaginable.

Who was behind the Crucifixion? It was Satan, of course. He filled the heart of Judas Iscariot to betray the Lord for thirty pieces of silver. The evil one worked through the Roman governor, Pilate. He worked through the cruel, sadistic soldiers. He worked through the vengeful religious leaders, and he worked through the fickle, bloodthirsty crowds.

Satan was behind all of that.

But someone else was behind Satan.

For one rare moment in human history, God the Father and the devil were working toward the same goal—although not for the same objective. Satan's goal was to kill Jesus and stop Him. God's goal was to see the Son of God die on the cross for the sins of the world and then to rise again from the dead. Why? Because there was no other way to atone for the sins of humanity.

It was all the plan of God, and He pursued it for you and me.

Isaiah 53:10 tells us that "it was the LORD's will to crush him and cause him to suffer" (NIV). So God took the greatest tragedy imaginable and turned it into the greatest victory imaginable.

On a much smaller scale, the same thing can happen in our lives. God can use Satan's evil, hateful attacks to accomplish His own good purposes. God can use our trials and even our temptations to make us stronger and help us grow spiritually. He can bring good out of the bad.

It doesn't mean that bad *becomes* good because bad is bad, period. But it does mean that God can bring good *despite* bad. And our tribulations can bring forth good things. We are told in Hebrews 12:11, "No discipline is enjoyable while it is happening—it's painful! But afterward there will be a peaceful harvest of right living for those who are trained in this way" (NLT).

Sometimes before a parent disciplines a child, that dad or mom will sometimes say, "Sweetheart, this is going to hurt me more than it is going to hurt you."

And the child is saying, "Yeah, right."

That is how we feel when we are being disciplined by the Lord or going through some painful hardship. It hurts! But the Bible tells us that, for God's children, it brings forth something good.

Randy Alcorn writes, "If God brought eternal joy through the suffering of Jesus, can he bring eternal joy through my present suffering and yours? If Jesus endured his suffering through anticipating the reward of unending joy, can he empower you and me to do the same?"[1]

"With Friends Like These . . ."

So there was Job, sitting on a heap of ashes, scraping at his painful boils with a piece of broken pottery and still reeling from multiple heartbreaks.

Enter "his friends."

You have to put those words in quotation marks because they certainly didn't live up to the title. Here is how it's captured in the Bible record:

> When three of Job's friends heard of the tragedy he had suffered, they got together and traveled from their homes to comfort and console him. Their names were Eliphaz the Temanite, Bildad the Shuhite, and Zophar the Naamathite. When they saw Job from a distance, they scarcely recognized him. Wailing loudly, they tore their robes and threw dust into the air over their heads to show their grief. Then they sat on the ground with him for seven days and nights. No one said a word to Job, for they saw that his suffering was too great for words. (Job 2:11-13, NLT)

There are times when someone is suffering so deeply, there simply aren't any words. Sometimes we feel as though we have to say something. But we don't. We've already said something by our presence alone. Sometimes the best thing you can do for someone who is hurting is to just be with them. Please don't try to explain anything to them, because (let's face it) you don't know what you are talking about. Nor do I.

If you say anything, just say, "I'm here for you. I love you. I care about you." Sometimes I think we feel obligated to try to explain things for God — or at least fill up the silence with meaningless words.

No, there are times when you just need to *be there*. And hold your peace.

When the Lord was going through His terrible trial in the Garden of Gethsemane, torn apart by anguish and literally sweating blood, He had asked His three closest disciples to just be with Him during that time. He didn't ask for a sermon, a poem, or a book recommendation. No, in His humanity and grief, He just asked for a little companionship. Sadly, His friends all fell asleep.

In the beginning, Job's friends had it right. When they saw him, they said, "There is nothing we can say." And they sat with him in silence for seven days. It's easy to criticize these guys for their later shenanigans, but at least give them credit for their comfort on that first week. When have we ever sat with someone to comfort them for an entire week?

The problem began, of course, when they finally opened their mouths. These three so-called friends offered the same lame explanations people offer today for suffering.

Eliphaz: "You are reaping what you have sown."

Eliphaz saw God as One who is inflexible, hard, and gives us what we deserve.

In Job 4:7-8 he said to his suffering friend, "Stop and think! Do the innocent die? When have the upright been destroyed? My experience shows that those who plant trouble and cultivate evil will harvest the same" (NLT).

He was effectively saying to Job, "You are clearly reaping what you have sown. You've done something wrong, and this is why this evil has come upon you."

Now, there is a law of sowing and reaping in Scripture that is valid. But in this particular instance, Job was not reaping the repercussions of godless living. Yes, there are times when that happens—when people do indeed reap the results of foolish or selfish choices. At the same time, there are others who reap the good and pleasant results of wise choices. Life often makes sense in that regard. But there are other times when the law doesn't apply at all. This was one of those situations in which God, for His own purposes, had allowed these tragedies to happen.

This is a matter between an individual and his or her God, and we dare not draw hasty conclusions.

In Job 8:20 Eliphaz says, "But look, God will not reject a person of integrity, nor will he lend a hand to the wicked" (NLT). In so many words, he is saying to his friend, "Obviously you are a different person in private than you are in public. If you were a man of integrity, these tragedies would never have happened to you."

But Eliphaz was dead wrong, wasn't he? In fact, Job was such a man of integrity that God had been bragging about him in heaven.

Zophar: "You actually deserve worse."

This guy was the worst egg in a bad omelet. He coldheartedly suggests that Job lost his possessions and children because of his obvious sinfulness, and he went on to say, "I think you got off easy, Job. Frankly, you deserve worse."

In Job 11:6, he makes this statement: "Listen! God is doubtless punishing you far less than you deserve!" (NLT). Then in chapter 20, verses 7-8, he says of Job and any person who lives like Job, "They will vanish forever, thrown away like their own dung. Those who knew them will ask, 'Where are they?' They will fade like a dream and not be found. They will vanish like a vision in the night" (NLT).

Wow. I could never recommend these guys for writing

sympathy cards for Hallmark. Can you imagine? If Eliphaz wrote a sympathy card, on the cover it would say, "Sorry you are sick." Then you would open it up and read the words, "But you got what you deserved."

Bildad's card would say on the cover, "Hope you get well soon." Then you would open up the card, and it would say, "But if you were really as godly as you claim, this would not have happened."

But Zophar's card would have been really brutal. On the cover it would have said, "I hope you get worse." Then you would open it up, and it would say, "You will die, no one will ever remember you, and you will be thrown away like poop."

That is what he really did say!

So these friends, after initially doing the right thing and sitting quietly with Job, proceeded to undo all the good they had done by judging him and making ignorant and false accusations.

For his part, Job went before the Lord and asked the question, "Why?"

It's a question I have asked many times. There is really nothing wrong with asking God the question, as long as you don't get the idea that He owes you an answer. Even Jesus, hanging on the cross of Calvary, said, "My God, My God, why have You forsaken Me?"

The truth is, however, that we may never know why. But God won't discipline us for asking anyway. I don't even think there is anything wrong with saying to the Lord, "I don't *like* this plan. I don't even agree with this plan."

Even Jesus, in the Garden of Gethsemane, said, "If it is possible, let this cup pass from Me." In other words, "Father, this is so hard. Father, I don't really want to do this. If there is another way, I would rather we find that way." But then He added these words, "Nevertheless, not as I will, but as You will."

That is what it comes down to.

Go to God with your whys. Go to God with your doubts and

struggles. But ultimately we need to say to the Lord, "Nevertheless, not as I will, but as You will."

Job asked a lot of questions and then began giving his own opinion on what had happened to him, trying to make some kind of sense of something that seemed so senseless. That went on for chapter after chapter.

Finally the Lord replied, "Brace yourself like a man, because I have some questions for you, and you must answer them. Where were you when I laid the foundations of the earth? Tell me, if you know so much" (Job 38:3-4, NLT).

Effectively God was saying, "Okay, Job, if you're such an expert on how things ought to be run, why don't *you* tell *Me* what's going on? Come to think of it, I don't remember seeing you around when I was creating the planets."

As we have said, God never gave Job an answer to all his why questions. He simply revealed more of Himself to Job. I think what we really need in life isn't so much an explanation but an encounter with God. We need a fresh revelation of Him. Why? Because when we see God for who He is, we see our problems for what they are.

Small God . . . big problems.

Big God . . . small problems.

Six Reasons God Allows Suffering

To wrap up this chapter, let me suggest six reasons God allows human suffering in our world.

1. Suffering reveals the true condition of our hearts.

The devil can do nothing in the life of the believer without the express permission of God. But why would God give Satan that permission? Because Satan's attacks will show what you are made of — and whether you truly are a believer in Christ or not a believer at all.

I've heard people say, "Well, when such and such happened

to me, that shattered my faith. I don't believe in God anymore."

But honestly, did that person *ever* believe in God?

If your faith is genuine, it will endure even terrible trials. Temptations, crises, and severe testings separate the wheat from the chaff, the true from the false, the genuine from the counterfeit.

2. Suffering makes us stronger in our faith.

This is a strong New Testament theme. The apostle James writes,

> When all kinds of trials and temptations crowd into your
> lives my brothers, don't resent them as intruders, but
> welcome them as friends! Realise that they come to test
> your faith and to produce in you the quality of endurance.
> But let the process go on until that endurance is fully
> developed, and you will find you have become men of
> mature character with the right sort of independence.
> (James 1:2-4, PH)

Suffering takes our faith from the realm of theory to reality.

3. Suffering can bring glory to God.

How so? Listen, any fool can be happy when the sky is blue and the sun is shining. But when the big storm hits, that is a different matter. Satan was essentially saying to God, "Job only worships You because You bless him. Let calamity come his way, and he'll be whistling a different tune. In fact, he will curse You."

But this proved to be just one more lie from the father of lies. Job worshiped the Lord before, during, and after the crisis. He had his questions, but he never stopped honoring the Lord. To prove Satan wrong and strengthen Job's faith, God allowed the pleasant things of life to be stripped away from Job—including his children, possessions, and health—and Job passed the test with flying colors. What a rebuke to the enemy that was. And what a powerful witness Job's story has been to generations of

Bible readers. Here we are talking about it thousands of years after it took place.

People around us every day have to learn to deal with severe challenges that come into their lives: a disability, a handicap, an illness, a painful accident. It's difficult for any of us to adjust to a new reality in life.

The apostle Paul wrestled with some kind of painful infirmity that he referred to as a "thorn in the flesh." Here was a man whom God had used to heal many people and even to pray over a young man and raise him from the dead. This is the same man who gave us such a large portion of our New Testament. Yet even this great apostle had to learn to live with some physical challenge or affliction. On three separate occasions, he had asked the Lord to take it away. Each time, the Lord gave him this answer: "My grace is all you need. My power works best in weakness" (2 Corinthians 12:9, NLT).

Now listen to Paul's response:

> Once I heard that, I was glad to let it happen. I quit focusing on the handicap and began appreciating the gift. It was a case of Christ's strength moving in on my weakness. Now I take limitations in stride, and with good cheer, these limitations that cut me down to size—abuse, accidents, opposition, bad breaks. I just let Christ take over! And so the weaker I get, the stronger I become. (verses 9-10, MSG)

Sometimes God will remove the thorns that hurt us. Sometimes God will step in and change our circumstances, just because we asked Him to. Sometimes you get the bad news from the doctor, you're told there is no hope, you cry out to God in prayer, and He heals you. Sometimes God provides in the situation where you have no resources. Sometimes God unravels the knot you have made in your life.

There are times when God will intervene in your life and do just what you have asked. But there are other times when He won't take that painful challenge away from you, urging you instead to draw on His strength, help, and supernatural encouragement to get you through.

4. God may allow suffering and sickness to get our attention.

Sometimes the Lord will allow something to come into our lives to wake us up to important realities. In Psalm 23:1-3, David writes, "The LORD is my shepherd; I shall not want. He makes me to lie down in green pastures; He leads me beside the still waters. He restores my soul." A little later he says, "Your rod and Your staff, they comfort me" (verse 4).

Have you ever wondered what that means? First of all, we are being compared to sheep, which isn't really much of a compliment. Sheep are pretty low on the intelligence scale in the animal kingdom. They also have a tendency to go astray, so the shepherd uses two tools—a rod and a staff—to deal with that. The staff is a long piece of wood with a crook in the end that he uses to pull the wayward sheep back into line. When the sheep refuses to respond to the staff and keeps going astray and endangering its own life again and again, the shepherd uses his rod to break the animal's leg. After the shepherd binds up that leg, the sheep isn't as inclined to wander anymore.

Sometimes God will use something dramatic in our lives to get our attention and bring us where we need to be spiritually. The psalmist wrote, "Before I was afflicted I went astray, but now I keep Your word" (Psalm 119:67).

Could God even use the death of a child to bring a person to faith?

According to one person who wrote to me, the answer would have to be yes. She wrote, "A person expects to lose a parent. Maybe even a brother, sister, aunt, or uncle, but never a child. My son would have been sixteen years old today. It has been fifteen years since his death, but he was the person who brought me to the Lord. . . . Because of his death I received my salvation. God knows my pain. He lost a Son, too." She concludes,

"I found salvation through God's Son because of the loss of mine."

God knows how to bring great good out of deep pain.

5. Our suffering won't last forever.

It might seem like it at times. But in the bigger scheme of things, it is only for a brief time. Paul expresses it like this in 2 Corinthians 4:17-18,

> "These troubles and sufferings of ours are, after all, quite small and won't last very long. Yet this short time of distress will result in God's richest blessing upon us forever and ever! So we do not look at what we can see right now, the troubles all around us, but we look forward to the joys in heaven which we have not yet seen. The troubles will soon be over, but the joys to come will last forever" (TLB).

6. God can use our suffering to prepare us for a special task.

The greatest example of this is Joseph in the book of Genesis, who was mistreated by his brothers. They eventually sold him into slavery for twenty pieces of silver. It was a devastating thing to happen to a young teenager, but Joseph believed and trusted in God. Even though he didn't have Romans 8:28 at that point in time, he lived out its truth: "And we know that all things work together for good to those who love God, to those who are the called according to His purpose."

How so? Joseph's brothers had obviously thought they would never see him again. But in the providence of God, Joseph came into the favor of Pharaoh and was promoted to be second in command of all Egypt. He also was placed in charge of Egypt's vast grain reserves at a time when a famine gripped the world. Hearing there was grain in Egypt, Joseph's brothers went to obtain provision for their starving families, never realizing they would be standing in front of their long-lost brother whom they had betrayed.

When they came before Joseph, they didn't recognize him —and certainly didn't expect to see him in such a position. Joseph, however, recognized them, and finally revealed himself to them, saying, "I am Joseph!"

Understandably, they all thought, *Oh no! We're really toast now. He'll have us killed!*

But then Joseph made this amazing statement: "Don't be afraid. Am I in the place of God? You intended to harm me, but God intended it for good to accomplish what is now being done, the saving of many lives. So then, don't be afraid. I will provide for you and your children" (Genesis 50:19-21, NIV).

In other words, "Listen, brothers, I know your motives were wrong, but God has used it despite what you did to me. God has brought great good out of an old injury."

The same is true for us. Even when difficulty and heartache come into our lives, God, in His wisdom and sovereignty, can bring good out of the bad.

We often isolate Romans 8:28 and don't consider the highly significant verse that follows the more familiar one. Here they are together:

> We know that all things work together for good to those
> who love God, to those who are the called according to
> His purpose. For whom He foreknew, He also predestined
> to be conformed to the image of His Son, that He might
> be the firstborn among many brethren.

God's end game, God's master plan for you, is not merely to make you happy; it is to make you *holy*. God's desire is that you and I, during the course of our lives, will become more and more like Jesus. For that reason, He causes all things to work together for good to those who love Him—that we might be conformed into the image of His own dear Son.

As Randy Alcorn puts it, "Everything that comes into your life—yes, even evil and suffering—is Father-filtered. Whether suffering brings us to Christlikeness depends, to some degree, upon our willingness to submit to God and trust him and draw our strength from him."[2]

The experiences of your life can be used to help others. And when you have gone through suffering, you can offer a special measure of help to someone else who has suffered.

If you are a cancer survivor and find yourself in a conversation with someone who has just learned they have the disease, you can speak comfort and hope and compassion into their life like no one else. Why? Because you have been there. It isn't just theory for you. You know the emotions. You know what it's like. You know what the treatments are like. And yet you are able to say, "Here is what the Lord has done for me, and here is how the Word of God has spoken to me."

If you have lost a child, you can minister to someone else who has lost a child like no one else can. If you have some physical affliction, you speak to other people who suffer something similar like no one else because you are in those circumstances. God can use your experiences in life. He never will waste your pain.

Brian Birdwell was a lieutenant colonel serving our country on 9/11 when a passenger jet slammed into the Pentagon where Brian had his office. As a result of that attack, Brian suffered burns on 60 percent of his body, and his lungs were seared. After that, he went through ninety-two days of grueling surgery. To this day, he is somewhat disfigured from those burns.

Not long ago he spoke at our church, and he was so witty and fun and full of life that he delighted everyone. After the third service, I invited him to go out to lunch with me.

"I would love to, Greg," he told me, "but I have an appointment."

"Oh really," I said. "After preaching three times, you have an appointment?"

"I'm going to the local burn unit at the hospital here in town."

"Why are you doing that?"

"Well," he said, "when the patients see a guy like me walking in, and they hear my story, it gives them hope. You comfort others with the comfort you've been comforted with."

He went on to tell me that when he was in the hospital himself, receiving one of his many treatments, his pastor had said to him, "Brian, don't waste your pain."

Pain will come into our lives—just as it came for Brian, for Job, and for our family. But as time goes on, you can use even pain in your life to comfort others and bring glory to the name of God.

The hardships of today are preparing us for great opportunities tomorrow.

19 Knowing the Will of God

D oes God still speak to humanity today?
Is He interested in what happens to us as individuals?

Does He truly have a master plan for our lives?

If so, how do I discover it? How do I hear His voice? How can I know the will of God?

These are all important questions, and the answer to the first one sets us on an exciting journey of discovery: Yes, God does speak to humanity today—and especially to His own sons and daughters. We as Christians are not simply victims of chance in a random world, hoping against hope that our luck won't run out on us. Just as God led men and women in the pages of Scripture, so He wants to lead us. There are, however, no foolproof formulas or easy one-two-three steps we can follow that will instantaneously reveal God's will to us at our every whim.

But let there be no doubt: God guides His own. The gospel of John tells us that Jesus "calls his own sheep by name and leads them out. And when he brings out his own sheep, he goes before them; and the sheep follow him, for they know his voice" (10:3-4).

God speaks to us and shows us His will—in terms both general and specific—and in the next few pages, we will examine some of the foundational principles of His guidance in our daily lives.

The good news is that God does not play hide-and-seek with us. *He wants to lead you even more than you want to be led.* God is more concerned about keeping us in His will than we are about being kept in it!

His Will Is Best

Far too often we can make knowing God's will into something misty, mystical, and other-worldly. And yet through my years of walking with God, I have found there are concrete, practical steps that we as believers can take to more easily grasp and understand His will.

God's way becomes plain when we start walking in it. But sometimes we fear or don't like His plan and don't want to follow it. A story made the rounds a number of years ago, purportedly giving an account of an actual conversation between the captain of a U.S. Navy ship and Canadian authorities off the coast of Newfoundland. It has since been proved to be apocryphal. But it still makes a point:

Canadians: Please divert your course fifteen degrees to the south to avoid a collision.

Americans: Recommend you divert your course fifteen degrees to the north to avoid a collision.

Canadians: Negative. You will have to divert your course fifteen degrees to the south to avoid a collision.

Americans: This is the captain of a U.S. Navy ship. I say again, divert your course!

Canadians: No, I say again, you divert your course.

Americans: This is the aircraft carrier USS Lincoln, the second largest ship in the United States Atlantic fleet. We are accompanied by three destroyers, three cruisers, and numerous support vessels. I demand that you change your course fifteen degrees north. I say again, that's one five degrees north, or counter measures will be undertaken to ensure the safety of this ship.

Canadians: This is a lighthouse. Your call!

Often we're just like that Navy captain when it comes to the will of God. We want Him to divert His course when we're in desperate need of diverting our own. Above all else, however, we should keep one important fact in mind: In the long run, God's will is always better than our will.

In the long run?

The reality is, at certain times in our lives we may not understand or even like God's will. If you were to interview young Joseph, deep in the bowels of an Egyptian prison on a trumped-up rape charge (see Genesis 39–40), he may not have been all that excited about the will of God for his life. But if you were to talk to him just a short time later, after he came into power as the second-in-command of Egypt, he might have preached a sermon to you about the value of waiting for God's will.

Keep this in mind: God is always looking out for your spiritual and eternal welfare. We tend to look out for our physical and immediate welfare. But what is good *now* may not be for eternity. And what is difficult now may be the best thing for the endless ages to come.

Paul wrote these encouraging words to the church in Corinth:

Our present troubles are small and won't last very long. Yet they produce for us a glory that vastly outweighs them and will last forever! So we don't look at the troubles we can see now; rather, we fix our gaze on things that cannot be seen. For the things we see now will soon be gone, but the things we cannot see will last forever." (2 Corinthians 4:17-18, NLT)

The story before us in this chapter uncovers several essential principles for knowing the will of God in our lives. It also happens to be a beautiful love story—on two levels. First, it's the story of a man and woman who come together against almost impossible odds, all because of the providence of God. Second, it's a picture or type of God's love for each of us, how He sought us out and graciously brought us to Himself.

Matchmaker, Matchmaker

When the patriarch Abraham was an old man, at this point pushing one hundred and forty years, his miracle son, Isaac, was about forty. Sarah, Isaac's mother, had died, and Isaac was lonely and heartsick.

Abraham may have been old, but there was nothing wrong with his memory. It didn't take him long to figure out what his son needed. Isaac needed a wife. Hard as it might be to imagine, there weren't any Internet matchmaking sites in those days, so Abraham called his most trusted servant and gave him some specific instructions.

Abraham said to the oldest servant of his house, who ruled over all that he had, "Please, put your hand under my thigh, and I will make you swear by the LORD, the God of heaven and the God of the earth, that you will not take a wife for my son from the daughters of the Canaanites, among whom I dwell; but you shall go to my country and to my family, and take a wife for my son Isaac."

The servant said to him, "Perhaps the woman will not be willing to follow me to this land. Must I take your son back to the land from which you came?"

But Abraham said to him, "Beware that you do not take my son back there. The LORD God of heaven, who took me from my father's house and from the land of my family, and who spoke to me and swore to me, saying, 'To your descendants I give this land,' He will send His angel before you, and you shall take a wife for my son from there. And if the woman is not willing to follow you, then you will be released from this oath; only do not take my son back there." So the servant put his hand under the thigh of Abraham his master, and swore to him concerning this matter.

Then the servant took ten of his master's camels and departed, for all his master's goods were in his hand. And he arose and went to Mesopotamia, to the city of Nahor. (Genesis 24:2-10)

As the servant, Eliezer, arrived at his destination, he shot a quick prayer heavenward and asked God for direction and success in his mission. This is the privilege of a man or woman who enjoys a moment-by-moment walk with God. Scripture tells us to "pray without ceasing" (1 Thessalonians 5:17). That doesn't mean we are to be on our knees 24/7, but it does mean staying tuned in to heaven's frequency every waking hour of our day. Then, when the road forks in front of us, when a sudden need arises in our lives, we can launch a swift arrow prayer toward heaven, confident that God is watching and that He will hear us.

That is what Eliezer did. When he saw some young women approaching the well where he stood with his minicaravan, he prayed that the one whom God had chosen for Isaac would not only offer him a drink of water (a common courtesy), but also offer to water his camels (a great inconvenience).

Before he had finished his prayer, a beautiful young woman named Rebekah approached the well. *Lord, let her be the one! Let her be the one!* As she was drawing water, Eliezer asked her for a drink. She graciously complied and then offered to get water for his camels until they were no longer thirsty.

Don't minimize that act of courtesy. Watering the camels was no small feat when you consider the fact that an average camel drinks more than twenty gallons of water—especially after a long day's journey through the desert. And Eliezer had ten camels with him. You do the math. That's a lot of water to be hauled up from a well with a bucket.

In fact, if Rebekah's pitcher held a gallon, that meant she would have had to make two hundred trips from the spring to the watering trough. At the least, it would have involved several hours of labor. And remember, at that point Rebekah had no idea who this stranger was. She had no clue about a wealthy and godly eligible bachelor named Isaac waiting many miles away. She simply saw a stranger in need and took it upon herself to help him.

Eliezer was overjoyed and immediately pulled out a ring and some bracelets from his bag, asking the surprised Rebekah who her family was and if he could meet them. When Rebekah arrived at the family tent, bedecked with beautiful jewelry, followed by a distinguished stranger, and with ten camels in tow, she definitely had her brother Laban's attention.

When the young woman told Laban the story, he was all smiles. Opening his arms in welcome, he declared, "Come in, O blessed of the LORD! Why do you stand outside? For I have prepared the house, and a place for the camels" (Genesis 24:31). Laban must have been expecting company.

Eliezer, however, wasted no time in declaring his mission. At the request of Abraham, he had come seeking a bride for his master Isaac. Then he related the story of his prayer at the well and what Rebekah had done. Rebekah's family couldn't deny the evident hand of God in these developments, and they agreed to her going back with Eliezer to be the bride of Isaac. Realizing they probably would never see her again, they asked if she could wait awhile, allowing them to say a long good-bye. But Eliezer knew he was on God's business and said no, she must leave immediately.

Search the Scriptures for God's General Will

The first principle of laying hold of God's will is that you must look for it. And the best and primary place to begin your search is in the pages of Scripture. When this story unfolded, nothing approaching Scripture as we have it today existed. But the principles of biblical truth already existed, being passed on orally from generation to generation. In this situation, God's Word came through the lips of Abraham:

> The LORD God of heaven, who took me from my father's house and from the land of my family, and who spoke to me and swore to me, saying, 'To your descendants I give this land,' He will send His angel before you, and you shall take a wife for my son from there. (Genesis 24:7)

Abraham also added that this wife for Isaac was not to come from the pagan Canaanites. She was to be of his extended family, which was the equivalent of being a believer at this time.

Today, God speaks to us through His Word. That is the bedrock of truth by which we measure all other truth, the clear revelation by which we measure all other so-called revelations. It is the rock of stability by which we measure our fickle human emotions. The way we know something is true or right is by comparing it to what Scripture teaches.

Everything you need to know about God is found in the pages of Scripture. Paul told his young disciple Timothy that "All Scripture is inspired by God and is useful to teach us what is true and to make us realize what is wrong in our lives. It corrects us when we are wrong and teaches us to do what is right. God uses it to prepare and equip his people to do every good work" (2 Timothy 3:16-17, NLT).

From this—and others like it—we know that God would never lead us contrary to the plain teachings of Scripture. This truth seems obvious (and it is), but it's amazing how many seem to miss it. They're busy seeking some mystical word from God when He has plainly spoken to them in the Bible that is sitting on their nightstand.

It would be like wanting desperately to hear from someone that you deeply loved. Then one day you looked in your mailbox and found a letter from him or her. (Or an e-mail on your computer.) But instead of opening that piece of correspondence, you simply continue to whine about how this person never communicates with you.

Don't be ridiculous. Open the letter!

In the same way we must open The Book! Jesus said, "Behold, I have come—in the volume of the book it is written of Me—to do Your will, O God" (Hebrews 10:7).

Whenever you begin to imagine that the will of God is mysterious, mystical, or out of reach, remember that Scripture plainly states God's specific will for you—again and again. Are you looking for God's will but don't know where to begin? Start with what God has already told you. If you're not ready to obey His clearly written instructions, what makes you think you will follow special revelation out of the blue?

Check out the following verses. I have added italics for emphasis:

This is the will of God, your sanctification: that you should abstain from sexual immorality. (1 Thessalonians 4:3)

Rejoice always, pray without ceasing, in everything give thanks; *for this is the will of God in Christ Jesus for you.* (1 Thessalonians 5:16-18)

Do not be unwise, *but understand what the will of the Lord is.* And do not be drunk with wine, in which is dissipation; but be filled with the Spirit, speaking to one another in psalms and hymns and spiritual songs, singing and making melody in your heart to the Lord, giving thanks always for all things to God the Father in the name of our Lord Jesus

Christ, submitting to one another in the fear of God.
(Ephesians 5:17-21)

Ask for God's Specific Will

When I was a young man, I never found any specific passage in Scripture that told me I must marry a girl named Cathe. What do I do, then? I take God's principles, keeping them in the fore-front of my mind and heart, and then ask Him for His specific will in my life. From the Scriptures, I understand that it is not good for a man to be alone, that an excellent wife is the crown of her husband, and that he who finds a wife finds a good thing and obtains favor from the Lord—not to mention the verse that says it's better to marry than to burn with passion.[1]

Having understood God's general will for my life through the Scriptures, I seek His specific will for individual situations as they arise. That is what Eliezer did:

Then he said, "O Lord God of my master Abraham, please give me success this day, and show kindness to my master Abraham." (Genesis 24:12)

Nothing is too insignificant, too minute, to take to the Lord in prayer. There's an old Jewish proverb that says it is better to ask the way ten times than to take the wrong road once. The apostle James reminds us, "If you need wisdom, ask our gener-ous God, and he will give it to you. He will not rebuke you for asking" (James 1:5, NLT).

Wait for God's Timing

The timing of God is just as important as the will of God. And it is clear that God has both His perfect will and perfect time to do what He wants. Ecclesiastes 3:11 tells us that "He has made everything beautiful in its time."

Eliezer waited for the right moment to act. He saw the beautiful Rebekah and hoped she might be the one.

> The man, wondering at her, remained silent so as to know whether the LORD had made his journey prosperous or not. (Genesis 24:21)

The problem with so many of us is that having found God's will, we want to act quickly. Eliezer waited to see if she was indeed the one. The Lord answered his prayer, Rebekah responded, and Eliezer knew it was time to move.

We're so prone to rush things, aren't we? In our culture of instant gratification, it's hard for us to be still and know that He is God.[2] But if God says no—or even slow down—it is for your own good.

If the request is wrong, God says no.

If the timing is wrong, God says slow.

If *you* are wrong, God says grow.

But if the request is right, the timing is right, and you are right, God says go!

Act on God's Will

> He said to them, "Do not detain me, now that the LORD has granted success to my journey. Send me on my way so I may go to my master." (Genesis 24:56, NIV)

Obedience to revealed truth guarantees guidance in matters unrevealed. The wind of God is always blowing, but you must hoist your sail! In the book of Acts, when God spoke to the apostle Philip with orders to go to the desert, he went—even though it made no logical sense at the time.[3] We must do the same. God won't necessarily give you a detailed blueprint. He will reveal to you as much as you need to know—nothing more, nothing less.

God leads us step by step, from event to event. It only will be afterward, when we look back with the luxury of hindsight, that we will discover how God led us more than we ever realized. Important moments of our lives, even times of crisis, or situations we may have balked at or complained about at the time, were all used to lead us in His will through life.

God Confirms His Will

How did Isaac deal with being a forty-year-old single guy? Here's a little snapshot from the Bible:

> He went out to the field one evening to meditate, and as he looked up, he saw camels approaching. Rebekah also looked up and saw Isaac. She got down from her camel and asked the servant, "Who is that man in the field coming to meet us?"
>
> "He is my master," the servant answered. So she took her veil and covered herself.
>
> Then the servant told Isaac all he had done. Isaac brought her into the tent of his mother Sarah, and he married Rebekah. So she became his wife, and he loved her; and Isaac was comforted after his mother's death. (Genesis 24:63-67, NIV)

So many single people I have known work themselves up into a mad rush-rush to find that right person. And there is certainly nothing wrong with wondering and praying about such a deep, God-given desire. In Genesis 2:18 God said of Adam, literally, "It is not good that man should be alone." It was God Himself who brought Eve to Adam's side. And if He sees that aloneness is ultimately not good for you, He will bring your mate to you, in His perfect timing. But there is nothing wrong with bringing your desire before Him in prayer. You can start praying for that future husband or wife right now.

While you're still single, however, you need to take advantage of your mobility and availability. Paul had these things in mind when he penned these words to the single men and women in the church at Corinth:

> I want you to be free from the concerns of this life. An unmarried man can spend his time doing the Lord's work and thinking how to please him. But a married man has to think about his earthly responsibilities and how to please his wife. His interests are divided. In the same way, a woman who is no longer married or has never been married can be devoted to the Lord and holy in body and in spirit. But a married woman has to think about her earthly responsibilities and how to please her husband. I am saying this for your benefit, not to place restrictions on you. I want you to do whatever will help you serve the Lord best, with as few distractions as possible. (1 Corinthians 7:32-35 NLT)

Sometimes we think of single adults as second-class citizens. *What? You're not married yet?* But many of the great movers and shakers of Scripture were unmarried. Elijah had no wife, and he shook a nation. The apostle Paul turned his world upside down. Jesus never had a wife. And the list goes on.

The bottom line? While you're single, serve the Lord with all your heart. But at the same time, don't feel guilt about your desire for companionship. Wait on the Lord. Jesus said, "Your heavenly Father already knows all your needs. Seek the Kingdom of God above all else, and live righteously, and he will give you everything you need" (Matthew 6:32-33, NLT).

Isaac wasn't running around like a chicken with its head cut off; he was meditating in the field. And then . . . in the very place of meditation and prayer, the beautiful Rebekah appeared on the horizon.

Seeing him, Rebekah said, "Who is this man walking in the field to meet us?" Or, as it says in the Greg Translation, "Who is that *fox* out there in the field?"

Eliezer replied, "It is my master."

Rebekah wrapped a veil around her face. Could it have concealed a big smile? *Yes, Lord!*

God's plans for you are always better than your plans for yourself. God provided Abraham's son with a beautiful bride who also had a beautiful heart. And Isaac loved her.

It's a nice love story, but it's more than that. It's also a picture of God's love and call upon our lives. He will reveal His general will to us in the Bible, He will give us wisdom on specific matters as we wait on Him, and once we feel we have the sense of His direction, He will confirm that in our lives in multiple ways.

He may cause a verse from Scripture to leap out at you from the page, speaking exactly to your situation. He may move obstacles and shift circumstances in such a way that you can recognize His hand clearing the way for you. He may speak to you through a trusted friend, family member, or pastor. God's creativity is endless, and He knows how to move you into the main current of His will if you're ready to wade out into the water with a humble, obedient heart.

Beyond showing us how to seek and find God's will, the story of Isaac and Rebekah is also a picture of God's love and His call upon our lives.

Chosen and Treasured

Rebekah was thought of before she herself even knew it. Abraham had told his servant:

> You shall go to my country and to my family, and take a wife for my son Isaac. (Genesis 24:4)

In the same way, God thought of and chose us, the bride of Christ, before we were ever aware of it. Paul reminds us of this in his letter to the church of Ephesus:

He chose us in him before the creation of the world to be holy and blameless in his sight. (Ephesians 1:4, NIV)

Jesus said, "You did not choose Me, but I chose you" (John 15:16). Before you were even aware of His presence, He was thinking of you, loving you, and getting ready in His timing, to reveal His unique and wonderful plan for your life.

Proclaiming the Message

Abraham didn't just sit back and wait for Rebekah to come to his son; he sent his servant to seek her out. The one objective of the servant was to announce Abraham's purpose, which was to find a bride for his son.

It is the same with the Lord. He not only has chosen us, but He also has sought us out. Make no mistake about it: the Bible clearly teaches predestination. *And it also teaches the free will of humanity.* It teaches that God has chosen me, but it also teaches that I must choose Him.

Choose for yourselves this day whom you will serve. (Joshua 24:15)

I have set before you life and death, blessing and cursing; therefore choose life, that both you and your descendants may live. (Deuteronomy 30:19)

Whoever believes in Him should not perish but have everlasting life. (John 3:16)

How, then, do I reconcile those two contradictory ideas? I don't.

I don't *have* to reconcile the two. That is God's affair, and His thoughts are a great deal higher than my thoughts. I just concentrate on what He has told me to do and leave the choosing part up to Him. He has told me to know Him and make Him known, to believe and then to proclaim. He has asked me to simply trust Him and obey Him, not try to unravel the mysteries of the universe. What a relief!

The Bible says, "We are therefore Christ's ambassadors, as though God were making his appeal through us. We implore you on Christ's behalf: Be reconciled to God. God made him who had no sin to be sin for us, so that in him we might become the righteousness of God" (2 Corinthians 5:20-21, NIV).

Notice the words here: God makes His appeal through us. Christ implores nonbelievers through us. In other words, the almighty God of the universe pleads with fallen man through you and me. If this doesn't inspire us, then I don't know what will.

The Power of the Message

There was power in the message Eliezer brought. As a servant, his objective was to simply declare the facts. He was not to add to them or take away from them—just proclaim what was true.

The same is true for each of us. We are to proclaim the gospel. Paul wrote, "For Christ didn't send me to baptize, but to preach the Good News—and not with clever speech, for fear that the cross of Christ would lose its power" (1 Corinthians 1:17, NLT).

He is reminding us there is a distinct power in the simple message of the life, words, death, and resurrection of Jesus Christ. We often underestimate the raw power the gospel message has in reaching even the most hardened heart.

Don't underestimate its appeal.

Don't be ashamed of its simplicity.

Don't add to it or take away from it.

Just proclaim it, then stand back and watch what God will do.

I have been amazed time and time again how God so power-fully uses this simple yet incredibly profound message to radi-cally change lives—from outright Satanists to moral yet lost people, from broken families and people addicted to drugs to those deceived by the cults, from the hardened atheist to the deceived cultist. The words of the gospel, driven home to hearts by the Holy Spirit, is the most powerful message in all the world.

The Down Payment

Upon accepting the offer of marriage, Rebekah received the down payment of things to come.

> Then the servant brought out jewelry of silver, jewelry of gold, and clothing, and gave them to Rebekah. He also gave precious things to her brother and to her mother. (Genesis 24:53)

In the same way, God sent His Holy Spirit into our lives as a down payment of things to come.

> You also were included in Christ when you heard the message of truth, the gospel of your salvation. When you believed, you were marked in him with a seal, the promised Holy Spirit, who is a deposit guaranteeing our inheritance until the redemption of those who are God's possession— to the praise of his glory. (Ephesians 1:13-14, NIV)

We have received a down payment on heaven, and it is the most amazing deposit that could ever be made. The Holy Spirit, God Himself, the Third Person of the Trinity, takes up residence in our own inner being.

But what does that part about "marked in him with a seal" mean? Back in the first century, when goods were shipped from one place to another, they would be stamped with a wax seal, imprinted with a signet ring bearing a unique mark of ownership. It was the same with important documents. If a king sent an important letter to one of his officials, it would be sealed with wax and imprinted with the royal seal.

If anybody messed with that seal, they would be messing with the king himself. And that was big, big trouble. No one would dare break that seal unless they were the person to whom the document was addressed. In the same way, God has put His royal seal of ownership on us. He has made the down payment, and He will follow through with our full inheritance in Christ.

Making the Break

Rebekah had to make a break with all that would slow her down or hinder her progress.

> Then they ate their meal, and the servant and the men with him stayed there overnight.
>
> But early the next morning, Abraham's servant said, "Send me back to my master."
>
> "But we want Rebekah to stay with us at least ten days," her brother and mother said. "Then she can go."
>
> But he said, "Don't delay me. The LORD has made my mission successful; now send me back so I can return to my master."
>
> "Well," they said, "we'll call Rebekah and ask her what she thinks." So they called Rebekah. "Are you willing to go with this man?" they asked her.
>
> And she replied, "Yes, I will go." (Genesis 24:54-58, NLT)

When the work of the Holy Spirit has begun in our lives, Satan tries to stop us. Even close friends and family can be a real snare. Jesus said, "If anyone comes to Me and does not hate his father and mother, wife and children, brothers and sisters, yes, and his own life also, he cannot be My disciple" (Luke 14:26).

In response to a man who wanted to wait until his mother and father died before he followed the Lord, Jesus said, "Let the dead bury their own dead, but you go and preach the kingdom of God" (9:60).

Rebekah's family took her aside and said, "Are you willing to go with this man?" (Translation: "Are you *sure*, honey?")

And she said, "Yes, I will go."

If you deal with one excuse to keep you from completely following Christ, another invariably will take its place. And though God will do what is necessary to bring an awareness of our need for Him, He will not force the issue. He will convict us, speak to us, and most importantly, love us, but the ultimate decision lies with us.

Eliezer used no high-pressure appeals. He presented the simple facts of the case. But Rebekah said, "I will go."

She had made up her mind to leave everything she had ever known behind and travel to a far country to meet a stranger. And the first step of that journey probably was the hardest of all.

But it probably was all forgotten when she looked up one evening and saw her bridegroom walking toward her through the field.

She was home.

Immortality

Have you ever had one of those seemingly perfect moments in life when everything just came together? It may have been that stunning sunset, that beautiful, star-filled night, or that special moment with someone you love. You thought to yourself, *I always want it to be this way.*

But it isn't.

Maybe you thought when you reached certain goals you had set in life, then that would bring complete fulfillment to you.

But they haven't.

Or when that right person came into your life, the man or woman of your dreams, then that would satisfy the sense of longing deep within you.

But it didn't.

Why is that? From the day you were born, you have been on a quest. You have been searching for that something more, because deep down inside, there is a sense in you that life must have some kind of meaning and purpose beyond mere existence. Maybe you have even wondered whether you are the only person who feels this way.

You aren't.

Deep down inside, we are all searching. Even Madonna. She once told an interviewer,

I think a few years ago, I wasn't sure what I was on this earth for. I think I was mostly concerned with getting things for myself.

More clothes, more money, more popularity, and more boyfriends. I wasn't really thinking, I was just doing.

Then I woke up and said, "What am I on this earth for?"[1]

Maybe you are wondering, *What am I on this earth for?*

When you are young, you think, "If only I were older, say, eighteen! The big kids have all the fun!"

When you're eighteen you say, "Twenty-one! That's the age I need to be!"

Then when you're twenty-one, you think to yourself, "No one takes me seriously yet. I can't wait until I'm in my thirties."

Then you hit thirty. You say, "When I'm in my forties, then I will have arrived! Those are the earning years!"

Then the forties come, and you find yourself wistfully wishing you were young again: "I wish I were in my teen years again. Man, we had some fun times back then!"

Then ages fifty and sixty arrive. And before you know it, you have more of your life behind you than ahead of you.

It's even funny how we describe the aging process. The terms change with the passing of time. When you are really young, you are "four-and-a-half." (You are never "thirty-six-and-a-half.") You want everyone to know you are "four-and-a-half, going on five!"

When you hit those teen years, you're "going to be sixteen." Of course, you might be twelve at the time, but you're "going to be sixteen."

Then adulthood finally arrives. You *become* twenty-one. Even the words sound like a ceremony: "I've become twenty-one!"

But suddenly things start going downhill. Yes, you've become twenty-one, but then you *turn* thirty. What's going on here?

You *become* twenty-one, you *turn* thirty, you're *pushing* forty, you *reach* fifty, and your dreams are gone. Then you *make it to* sixty.

So you *become* twenty-one, you *turn* thirty, you're *pushing* forty, you *reach* fifty, and you *make it to* sixty. Then you build up so much speed that you *hit* seventy.

After that, it's a day-by-day thing. You *hit* Wednesday. And when you get into your eighties, you *hit* lunch. And it doesn't end there.

Into your nineties, you actually start going backward. You're "just ninety-two years young."

Then a strange thing happens. If you make it to one hundred or more, you become a child again. You're "one hundred and a half"!

Yes, life passes by much too quickly. And sooner or later, every thinking person gets around to asking the questions "What is the meaning of life?" "Why am I here on this earth?" "Why do I exist?" and "What should be my purpose in life?"

We all have built into us as humans the desire to achieve something, to make a mark, to distinguish ourselves. We all want our lives to count for something bigger and greater than ourselves. This desire for greatness is not in itself wrong. In Romans 2:6-8 we are told that God "will judge everyone according to what they have done. He will give eternal life to those who keep on doing good, seeking after the glory and honor and immortality that God offers. But he will pour out his anger and wrath on those who live for themselves, who refuse to obey the truth and instead live lives of wickedness" (NLT).

Paul is speaking approvingly of those who seek "the glory and honor and immortality that God offers." God essentially wired us this way. It's built into us. The Bible tells us that God "has put eternity in [our] hearts" (Ecclesiastes 3:11). This verse tells us why we find, deep within our souls, a yearning to rise above the commonplace, the ordinary.

But why this desire to make our mark? Because, as humans, we were uniquely created in the very image of God Himself. We are the highest of all created beings. We don't want to think that our lives don't matter, that existence is somehow meaningless. We want to live life to its fullest. We want immortality, an endless existence, and enduring fame.

For instance, some people find a certain type of immortality through fame. Everyone knows their name, such as Tom Cruise, Madonna, Britney Spears, and Brad Pitt. Still others are famous for just being famous, like Paris Hilton.

Others find a kind of immortality through becoming infamous—people like Charles Manson, Lee Harvey Oswald, Osama bin Laden, and Adolf Hitler.

Others hope they can prolong their lives by way of all the latest potions and lotions. They are looking for that eternal Fountain of Youth.

I read about a well-known movie star who was once dubbed by *People* magazine as the sexiest man alive. He had lived a hard life of drinking, smoking, and partying. Now in his sixties, he is determined to push back the ravages of time by devoting himself to a so-called anti-aging regimen. He uses a microscope to study his blood every day. He spends tens of thousands of dollars per year on vitamins and raw food and takes sixty pills daily. But he doesn't just stop with pills. He also uses a syringe to inject himself with other vitamins. He says, "I suppose [that] deep down, there's a passion to live forever. Rationally, I know that's impossible. I know that we all die. I accept the dying process. I would just like to be as healthy as I possibly can at each step and phase along the way."

He is typical of my generation. We baby boomers want to be "Forever Young."

My generation has to update a lot of our songs, by the way. Here are some new title suggestions for a few of them:

The Who: "Talkin' 'bout My Medication"

ABBA: "Denture Queen"

Herman's Hermits: "Mrs. Brown, You've Got a Lovely Walker"

The Beatles: "I Get By with a Little Help from Depends"

The Bee Gees: "How Can You Mend a Broken Hip?"

Crystal Gayle: "Don't It Make My Brown Hair Blue?"

The Eagles: "Heartburn Tonight"

Jerry Lee Lewis: "Whole Lotta Achin' Goin' On"

Lynyrd Skynyrd: "Rest Home Alabama"

Nancy Sinatra: "These Boots Give Me Arthritis"

The Troggs: "Bald Thing"

Yes, life is passing by more quickly than we may like. We all want immortality. But let me say something that may surprise you: Immortality is not something you achieve; it is something you already have. You will live forever.

"That is good news!" you may say.

That all depends. Let's say, for example, that I said to you, "I just bought you a plane ticket to go on vacation for five years, all expenses paid!"

You probably would say, "That's great!"

But first you should ask, "Where is this plane ticket to?"

"It is to outer Siberia—in the dead of winter."

You probably wouldn't be too eager to take me up on my offer. But if I were to say the plane ticket was to Hawaii or Tahiti, it would be a different matter.

So our question should not so much be, "*How* can I live forever and be immortal?"

Rather, it should be, "*Where* will I live forever because I am immortal?"

The Bible has a lot to say about this topic. According to Scripture, you never will die—in a spiritual sense, that is. Man has inside of him a soul, and that soul is eternal. But the body in which we live will indeed die. And all the vitamins, lotions, and potions will not postpone the inevitable.

The question is often asked, "What happens when we die?"

If you have put your faith in Jesus Christ, you will go immediately to heaven. The moment you take your last breath on

Earth, you will take your first breath in heaven. It's that fast.
Paul said that "to be absent from the body [is] to be present
with the Lord" (2 Corinthians 5:8). He also said,

> This corruptible must put on incorruption, and this mortal
> must put on immortality. So when this corruptible has put
> on incorruption, and this mortal has put on immortality,
> then shall be brought to pass the saying that is written:
> "Death is swallowed up in victory."

> "O Death, where is your sting?
> O Hades, where is your victory?" (1 Corinthians 15:53-55)

That is why the believer does not need to fear death itself.
This doesn't mean that we Christians have a death wish. As
Paul said, "To live is Christ, and to die is gain" (Philippians
1:21). Nor does it mean that we don't grieve when we lose a
loved one who is a believer (though a person isn't "lost" if you
know where he or she is). But death no longer has to terrify us.

However, it is a different matter altogether for unbelievers.
What happens to them when they die? They, too, are immortal.
They, too, live forever. But where? We find the answer in
Revelation:

> I saw the dead, small and great, standing before God, and
> books were opened. And another book was opened, which
> is the Book of Life. And the dead were judged according
> to their works, by the things which were written in the
> books. The sea gave up the dead who were in it, and
> Death and Hades delivered up the dead who were in
> them. And they were judged, each one according to his
> works. Then Death and Hades were cast into the lake of
> fire. This is the second death. And anyone not found writ-
> ten in the Book of Life was cast into the lake of fire.
> (20:12-15)

Note that again and again in this passage, the phrase *the dead* is used. Back in the Garden of Eden, God gave the word: "Of every tree of the garden you may freely eat; but of the tree of the knowledge of good and evil you shall not eat, for in the day that you eat of it you shall surely die" (Genesis 2:16-17). There is no getting around it. Death is coming.

I read of a tombstone in England with this inscription:

Pause now stranger, as you pass by.
As you are now, so once was I.
As I am now, so you will be,
So prepare for death, and follow me.

Someone reading that inscription was overheard to say, "To follow you is not my intent, until I know which way you went!"

Which way are you going in life—and beyond? According to the Bible, there are only two options after death: heaven or hell. Most of us are afraid to die. The Bible speaks of those "who through fear of death were all their lifetime subject to bondage" (Hebrews 2:15). It is the fear of the unknown.

Also note that death is no respecter of persons: "I saw the dead, small and great, standing before God" (Revelation 20:12). Everyone will stand before God one day. Not only will we die, but we will face a judgment.

The teaching of a final judgment is clearly taught in Scripture. In Acts 17:30-31, we read, "Truly, these times of ignorance God overlooked, but now commands all men everywhere to repent, because He has appointed a day on which He will judge the world in righteousness by the Man whom He has ordained. He has given assurance of this to all by raising Him from the dead."

And 2 Peter 2:9 tells us, "The Lord knows how to rescue the godly from trials and to hold the unrighteous for punishment on the day of judgment" (NIV).

Jesus said, "But I say to you that for every idle word men may speak, they will give account of it in the day of judgment" (Matthew 12:36).

The fact there is a future judgment assures us that ultimately, God is fair. This teaching of future judgment should satisfy our inward sense of a need for justice in the world. We have all seen things that seem so unjust: horrible crimes, wicked actions. We say to God, "How can they get away with that?"

But know this: God is in control. And He keeps very accurate records: "But he who does wrong will be repaid for what he has done, and there is no partiality" (Colossians 3:25). Listen, every wrong in the universe ultimately will be paid for. Either it will turn out to have been paid for by Jesus Christ when He died on the cross (if the offender repents of his or her sins and trusts in Him), or it will be paid for at the final judgment (by those who do not put their faith in Jesus for salvation).

Only unbelievers will be at the Great White Throne Judgment: "He who believes in Him is not condemned; but he who does not believe is condemned already, because he has not believed in the name of the only begotten Son of God" (John 3:18). Yet if the unbeliever is already condemned, then what is the purpose of the last judgment? The purpose of this final confrontation between God and humanity is to clearly demonstrate to the unbeliever *why* he or she is already condemned.

The Bible tells us what will happen at this judgment: "And the books were opened, including the Book of Life. And the dead were judged according to what they had done, as recorded in the books" (Revelation 20:12, NLT).

One of these books surely will be the book of God's law. Anyone who has been exposed to the truth of God's law is held responsible, "that every mouth may be stopped, and all the world may become guilty before God" (Romans 3:19). For those who may say, "I lived by the Ten Commandments," it will be clearly shown they did not. We all have fallen short of God's standard for us, which is absolute perfection. "For the person who keeps all of the laws except one is as guilty as a person who has broken all of God's laws" (James 2:10, NLT).

Perhaps another book will be a record of everything we have said or done. The Bible says, "God will judge us for everything we do, including every secret thing, whether good or bad" (Ecclesiastes 12:14, NLT). And Jesus said, "For every idle word men may speak, they will give account of it in the day of judgment" (Matthew 12:36).

Another book might show how man fails to live up to his own standards. Many years ago, my son Jonathan asked me, "What about the person on a desert island who has never heard about Christ? What will happen to someone like that?"

The apostle Paul pointed out that deep down inside, we all have a sense of right and wrong:

Even Gentiles, who do not have God's written law, show that they know his law when they instinctively obey it, even without having heard it. They demonstrate that God's law is written in their hearts, for their own conscience and thoughts either accuse them or tell them they are doing right. And this is the message I proclaim —that the day is coming when God, through Christ Jesus, will judge everyone's secret life. (Romans 2:14-16, NLT)

Some people say, "I have my own religion, my own beliefs. I'll live by those." But the fact of the matter is that we don't even live up to our own standards we have set for ourselves, much less God's standards.

Still another book might have a record of all the times you have heard the gospel. And know this: knowledge brings responsibility. I watched a TV program celebrating the tenth anniversary of *Inside the Actor's Studio*, hosted by James Lipton. On each program, Lipton would ask his guests, "If heaven exists, what would you like to hear God say when you arrive at the Pearly Gates?" Here were some of the actors' answers:

"Your friends are in the back. They're expecting you." (Ben Affleck)

"Come in, have a drink, sit down, smoke a cigarette." (Ellen Barkin)

"Welcome." (Carol Burnett)

"You see, I *do* exist!" (Kevin Kline)

"Nice to meet you." (James Caan)

"Everybody you love and all your friends are here! We already got you a table." (Kevin Costner)

"You're much better-looking in person." (Harrison Ford)

"Come on in! It's not as boring as you might have thought." (Richard Dreyfus)

"Fabulous, darling." (Hugh Grant)

"What were you doing down there?" (Anthony Hopkins)

"I love you." (Val Kilmer)

"You've tortured yourself enough! Those two hookers and the eight ball are inside. Come on in!" (Sean Penn)

"Good work, dawg!" (Will Smith)

"*She* will say, 'Let's party!'" (Susan Sarandon)

"If heaven exists, He has a lot of explaining to do!" (Robert De Niro)

Hmmm. I think Robert De Niro will have a lot explaining to do—not God. Many of these answers are quite flippant. I'm sure that will all change when they face God in all His glory. The main issue on that day will be what you did with Jesus. People will offer various excuses as to why they rejected Him. But Jesus put it this way: "Many will say to Me in that day, 'Lord, Lord, have we not prophesied in Your name, cast out demons in Your name, and done many wonders in Your name?' And then I will declare to them, 'I never knew you; depart from Me, you who practice lawlessness!'" (Matthew 7:22-23).

I'm sure that some will say, "But Lord, I went to church every week, received communion, was baptized, gave my confession, . . ." and so on. But you can do all those things and never have known Jesus. Notice Jesus will say, "I never knew you; depart from Me. . . ."

If you know Him now, He will know you then.

If you walk with Him now, you will walk with Him then.

If you say, "Come in!" now, He will say, "Enter in!" then.

But if you say "no time" or "too busy" or "maybe later" now, He will say, "I never knew you; depart from Me" then.

The Bible says, "Then Death and Hades were cast into the lake of fire. This is the second death. And anyone not found written in the Book of Life was cast into the lake of fire" (Revelation 20:14-15). As it's been said, "Born once, die twice. Born twice, die once." There are no second chances at the second death.

You may ask, "How can a God of love send people to hell? Is this an inconsistency on God's part?"

The fact is, because He is a God of love and justice, He invented hell. But hell was not made for people; it was created for Satan and his fallen angels. God took radical measures to keep us out of hell. Being just and holy, the sin issue had to be settled because the Bible says, "The soul who sins shall die" (Ezekiel 18:20).

God wants you in heaven. Jesus prayed, "Father, I desire that they also whom You gave Me may be with Me where I am, that they may behold My glory which You have given Me" (John 17:24). When you're in love with someone, you want them with you. So God poured out His wrath on His own dear Son so that we wouldn't have to face it.

Let's say you were driving on the freeway and were on your way to cross a large bridge spanning a raging river. Suddenly you saw a big sign that read, "WARNING: Bridge out. Use alternate exit."

But you were determined, so you sped up toward that bridge. As you got closer, you saw more signs: "Do not enter"; "DANGER"; and "Bridge out." Still, you sped on. As you got even closer, you saw police cars with lights flashing and officers waving and yelling for you to turn back. Yet you sped on until you broke through those barriers and went off the top of that bridge into a watery grave. Now, whose fault was it that you died? Was it the fault of the construction crew? Was it the fault of the police officers? No, it was your own fault because you ignored the warnings.

In the same way, those who end up in hell on that final day will have no one to blame but themselves. God has clearly placed the warning signs. He has told us, "For the wages of sin is death, but the gift of God is eternal life in Christ Jesus our Lord" (Romans 6:23). As C. S. Lewis said, no one ever goes to heaven deservingly—and no one ever goes to hell unwillingly.

Every one of us has sinned and will face hell if we do not turn to Jesus Christ. Don't put it off. The road to hell is paved with excuses. Yes, we are all immortal. But the big question is, *Where* will we live out that immortality? Heaven? Or hell?

Jesus died on the cross for your sins so that you don't have to be afraid to die. He died and rose again. Because Jesus rose, we as Christians will rise, too. Jesus said, "I will not leave you orphans; I will come to you. A little while longer and the world will see Me no more, but you will see Me. Because I live, you will live also" (John 14:18-19).

God will change your eternal address today if you will turn from your sin.

So what do you need to do to go to heaven?

Admit you are a sinner.

Repent of your sin.

Realize that Christ died for your sin.

Receive Him as your Savior.

Do it now.

Notes

Chapter 1: Who Is God? Part 1

1. See Genesis 1:26-27.
2. C. S. Lewis, *The Complete C. S. Lewis Signature Classics* (New York: HarperCollins, 2002), 640.
3. Lewis, 114.
4. C. S. Lewis, *The Business of Heaven: Daily Readings from C. S. Lewis*, edited by Walter Hopper (San Diego: Harcourt, 1984), 228.
5. Dave Mason, vocal performance of "We Just Disagree," by Jim Krueger, recorded 1977, Columbia.
6. Peter Collier and David Horowitz, *Destructive Generation: Second Thoughts About the Sixties* (San Francisco: Encounter Books, 1989), 304.
7. As quoted by Peter B. Levy in *America in the Sixties — Right, Left, and Center: A Documentary History* (Westport, CT: Greenwood Press, 1998), 267.
8. *Encyclopaedia Brittanica Online*, s.v. "Earth," http://www.britannica.com/EBchecked/topic/175962/Earth (accessed May 6, 2013).

Chapter 2: Who Is God? Part 2

1. Frank Newport, "More Than 9 in 10 Americans Continue to Believe in God," *Gallup.com*, June 3, 2011, http://www.gallup.com/poll/147887/Americans -Continue-Believe-God.aspx.
2. Francesca Chapman and Daily News wire services, "Ricky Martin's Ambition: To Find and Project Peace," *Philly.com*, October 11, 2000, http://articles.philly .com/2000-10-11/news/25588179_1_vocal-cords-videos-hong-kong.
3. See 2 Corinthians 5:21.
4. Psalm 11:7, NIV.
5. Luke 18:19, NIV.
6. Ezekiel 18:20; Romans 6:23.
7. See Matthew 25:41.

Chapter 3: What God Is Like

1. Luke 12:32, KJV.
2. John 10:7,9, NLT.
3. John 13:1.
4. Isaiah 49:15-16, NLT.
5. Jude 1:21.
6. Romans 8:31-32.
7. Read the story in Acts 16.

Chapter 4: Who Is Jesus?

1. See John 14:6.
2. Charles R. Swindoll, *Laugh Again* (Nashville: Thomas Nelson, 1992), 85.
3. See Isaiah 50:7.

Chapter 5: Why Did Jesus Suffer?

1. Mark 10:45, NIV.
2. Isaiah 51:22.
3. R. Kent Hughes, *Mark: Jesus, Servant and Savior*, vol. 2 (Westchester, IL: Crossway, 1989), 168.
4. John 3:16; Ephesians 5:25; Galatians 2:20.

Chapter 6: What Is Faith?

1. *The A. W. Tozer Bible*, King James Version (Peabody, MA: Hendrickson Publishers, 2012), 776.
2. 2 Timothy 3:16-17, TLB.
3. See Mark 10:46-52.
4. Read the whole story in Mark 5:24-34.

Chapter 7: What Is Salvation?

1. Dennis Cauchon, "Millions of Dollars Looking for a Home," USA Today.com, December 6, 2007, http://usatoday30.usatoday.com/news/nation/2007-12-05-lottery_N.htm.
2. John MacArthur, *The MacArthur Daily Bible* (Nashville: Thomas Nelson, 2003), x.

Chapter 8: Can You Lose Your Salvation?

1. Martin H. Manser, ed., *The Westminster Collection of Christian Quotes* (Louisville, KY: Westminster John Knox Press, 2001), 206.

Chapter 10: Leading Others to Christ

1. Psalm 126:5-6, TLB.
2. Hebrews 1:14, NIV.
3. Psalm 34:7.
4. See Hebrews 13:2.
5. John 4:7,9-11, NIV.
6. See Isaiah 55:11.
7. Earnest W. Bacon, *Spurgeon: Heir of the Puritans* (Arlington Heights, IL: Christian Liberty Press, 1996), 114.

Chapter 11: Secrets of the Early Church, Part 1

1. See Matthew 13:24-30.
2. 1 Samuel 16:7.
3. 1 Peter 2:5.
4. Theodore Roosevelt, *The Man in the Arena: Selected Writings of Theodore Roosevelt: A Reader* (New York: Macmillan, 2004), 5.
5. Ephesians 1:12, NIV.
6. John 15:8.
7. Mark 16:15; Matthew 28:20.
8. Dave Tomlinson, *The Post-Evangelical* (Grand Rapids, MI: Zondervan, 1995), 113.
9. Martyn Lloyd-Jones, *Spiritual Depression: Its Causes and Cure* (Grand Rapids, MI: Eerdmans, 1965), 47–48.

Chapter 12: Secrets of the Early Church, Part 2
1. 1 Peter 5:5, TLB.
2. Matthew 18:20.
3. See Psalm 22:3, KJV.

Chapter 13: The Holy Spirit: Power Beyond Ourselves
1. As quoted by Lauren Barlow, *Inspired by Tozer: 59 Artists, Writers and Leaders Share the Insight and Passion They've Gained from A.W. Tozer* (Ventura, CA: Regal, 2011), 189.
2. As quoted by Warren W. Wiersbe, *Be Dynamic: Acts 1–12*, second ed. (Colorado Springs: David C. Cook, 2009), 33.
3. See Matthew 17:1-8; Mark 9:2-8; Luke 9:28-35.

Chapter 14: The Power of Prayer
1. Matthew 7:7.
2. Mark 9:24.

Chapter 16: How to Resist Temptation
1. Matthew Henry and Thomas Scott, *The Holy Bible: With the Text According to the Authorized Version*, volume 3 (London: The Religious Tract Society, 1835), 16.
2. Vance Havner, *All the Days* (Old Tappan, NJ: Fleming H. Revell, 1976), 53.

Chapter 17: Why Does God Allow Suffering? Part 1
1. Randy Alcorn, *Ninety Days of God's Goodness: Daily Reflections That Shine Light on Personal Darkness* (Colorado Springs: Multnomah, 2011), 21.
2. See Isaiah 55:8-9.
3. Charles R. Swindoll, *Job: A Man of Heroic Endurance* (Nashville: The W Publishing Group, 2004), 88–89.
4. See 2 Samuel 18:33.
5. Randy Alcorn, *If God Is Good: Faith in the Midst of Suffering and Evil* (Colorado Springs: Multnomah, 2009), 6.
6. See Philippians 1:23.

Chapter 18: Why Does God Allow Suffering? Part 2
1. Randy Alcorn, *Ninety Days of God's Goodness: Daily Reflections That Shine Light on Personal Darkness* (Colorado Springs: Multnomah, 2011), 95.
2. Randy Alcorn, *If God Is Good: Faith in the Midst of Suffering and Evil* (Colorado Springs: Multnomah, 2009), 289.

Chapter 19: Knowing the Will of God
1. See Genesis 2:18; Proverbs 12:4; 18:22; 1 Corinthians 7:9.
2. See Psalm 46:10.
3. See Acts 8:5-8,26-40.

Conclusion: Immortality
1. "Madonna Reveals Pre-Gig Stress," *BBC News*, July 3, 2001, http://news.bbc.co.uk/2/hi/entertainment/1420364.stm (accessed May 24, 2013).

Other Books by Greg Laurie

Visit: www.kerygmapublishing.com